GUIDE TO MINNESOTA
Outdoors

ACKNOWLEDGMENTS

The author is most grateful to the Minnesota Department of Natural Resources, the National Park Service, the U.S. Forest Service and the U.S. Fish and Wildlife Service for assistance in the preparation of this guide. He is also thankful to Nikki and Ben, who truly know how to enjoy each moment outdoors.

NorthWord Press
5900 Green Oak Drive
Minnetonka, MN 55343
1-800-328-3895

Library of Congress Cataloging-in-Publication Data

Umhoefer, Jim 1953-
  Guide to Minnesota outdoors / by Jim Umhoefer.
        p.   cm.
  Includes index.
  ISBN 1-55971-138-8
    1. Recreation areas—Minnesota—Guidebooks. 2. Recreation areas—Minnesota—Directories. 3. Outdoor recreation—Minnesota—Guidebooks. 4. Minnesota—Guidebooks. I. Title.
GV54.M6U46 1992
790' .06'8776—dc20   92-14037

Printed in the U.S.A.

GUIDE TO MINNESOTA
Outdoors

JIM UMHOEFER

NORTHWORD PRESS
Minnetonka, Minnesota

LAKE BRONSON
ROSEAU
LOST R.
ZIPPEL BAY
INTERNATIONAL FALLS
HAYES LAKE
FRANZ JEVNE
OLD MILL
RED LAKE C.R.
BIG FORK C.R.
LITTLE FORK C.R.
VERMILION R.
TOWER SOUDAN
ELY
DEVIL'S TRACK
KODONCE RIVER
C.R. MAGNEY
JUDGE
OLD CROSSING TREATY
GRAND MARAIS
RAY BERGLUND
CASCADE RIVER
TEMPERANCE RIVER
LAKE BEMIDJI
SCENIC
McCARTHY BEACH
BEAR HEAD LAKE
CROSS RIVER
CARIBOU FALLS
GEORGE H. CROSBY
LITTLE ELBOW LAKE
ITASCA
HEARTLAND
SCHOOLCRAFT
ST. LOUIS C.R.
TETTEGOUCHE
MANITOU
SPLIT ROCK LIGHTHOUSE
GOOSEBERRY FALLS
BUFFALO RIVER
PARK RAPIDS
PINE C.R.
CLOQUET C.R.
FLOOD BAY
TWO HARBORS
DETROIT LAKES
MISSISSIPPI
SAVANNA PORTAGE
DULUTH
JAY COOKE
MAPLEWOOD
CROW WING
BRAINERD
KETTLE R.
MOOSE LAKE
FERGUS FALLS
CROW WING
FATHER HENNEPIN
BANNING
INSPIRATION PEAK
LAKE CARLOS
CHARLES A. LINDBERGH
MILLE LACS KATHIO
HINCKLEY
SNAKE C.R.
ST. CROIX
SAM BROWN
GLENWOOD
ST. CLOUD
WILD RIVER
GLACIAL LAKES
SIBLEY
LAKE MARIA
RUM R.
INTERSTATE
BIG STONE LAKE
MINNESOTA C.R.
MONSON LAKE
N. FORK CROW C.R.
WILLIAM O'BRIEN
ST. CROIX ISLANDS
STILLWATER
LAC QUI PARLE
MONTEVIDEO
HUTCHINSON
LUCE LINE
MINNEAPOLIS
ST. PAUL
AFTON
CLARA CITY
MINNESOTA VALLEY
UPPER SIOUX AGENCY
JOSEPH BROWN
CARVER RAPIDS
LAWRENCE
FT. SNELLING
RICE LAKE
RED WING
FRONTENAC
CAMDEN
FT. RIDGELY
RUSH RIVER
CANNON C.R.
NERSTRAND WOODS
ZUMBRO C.R.
JOHN A. LATSCH
WINONA
LAKE SHETEK
FLANDRAU
MANKATO
STRAIGHT C.R.
FARIBAULT
CARLEY
PIPESTONE
DES MOINES
MINNEOPA
SAKATAH LAKE
RICE LAKE
WHITEWATER
O.L. KIPP
SPLIT ROCK CREEK
ROCHESTER
ROOT RIVER
BEAVER CREEK VALLEY
BLUE MOUNDS
KILEN WOODS
HELMER MYRE
LAKE LOUISE
FORESTVILLE

4

MINNESOTA RECREATION AREAS

Arrowhead Region

Heartland/Vikingland Region

Metroland Region

Southern Region

▲ ....STATE PARKS
△ ....WAYSIDES
□ ....TOWNS/CITIES
〰 ....STATE TRAIL
•••• ....STATE TRAILS / BICYCLE
C.R. ....CANOE ROUTES

Symbol Key

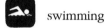 swimming

 boating

 canoeing

 fishing

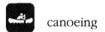 hiking trails

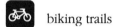 biking trails

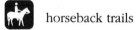 horseback trails

 cross country ski trails

 snowmobile trails

 overlook and scenery

 historical significance

 camping

 handicapped access and facililties

nature hikes

wildlife refuge

6

TABLE OF CONTENTS

INTRODUCTION

"Man's heart away from nature becomes hard. Lack of respect for growing, living things soon leads to a lack of respect for humans, too. Keep your youth close to nature's softening influence."

—Chief Luther Standing Bear

Nature's softening influence is always close at hand in Minnesota. Native people, like the Dakota and Ojibway, have traditionally felt a mental, physical, emotional and spiritual connection to this land that the Dakota called "minisota" ("land of sky-tinted waters"). European settlement has not always reflected that connection.

Now, though, people seem to be thirsty again for the "softening influence" of nature. In Minnesota's state park system, for example, that translates into more than eight million visits per year. State park attendance has jumped nearly 50 percent since 1985.

What can you see outdoors in Minnesota? The land is broad and varied. Three main landforms meet here: the western plains and prairies, the northern coniferous forest and the eastern hardwood forest. Today, over half of the land is crop land and pastures; a third is still forested. Water is everywhere. Minnesota is blessed with 15,391 lakes (10 acres or more in size), 25,000 miles of streams, and more than 90,000 miles of shoreline.

Wildlife thrives here. Timber wolves (the largest population in the lower 48 states), bald eagles (over 160 breeding pairs in the Chippewa National Forest alone), moose, black bears, deer, loons, beavers and scores of other species make their home in the state. Just the chance of sighting them adds a spark of adventure to every outing.

What can you do outdoors in Minnesota? You name it. There are over 12,500 miles of snowmobile trails in the state, 4,200 miles of hiking trails, and over 2,000 miles of cross-country ski trails. From fishing trips to float trips, Minnesota's water sports are legendary. If your outdoor passion includes horseback riding, bicycling, camping or dog sledding, there's a place for you in Minnesota.

Minnesota has a long and impressive record of identifying and preserving its natural beauty. Successes, though, have been neither complete nor easy; the state law that created

Itasca State Park in 1891 passed by one vote, and did nothing to stop the logging that continued there until the early 20th century.

Yet the fact that the best of wild Minnesota is preserved in local, regional, state and national recreation units is testimony to the vision and persistence of those who fought the odds to set aside parcels of land as "every person's country estate." Voices as clear and strong as those of Jacob Brower, Sigurd Olson and Gifford Pinchot helped to rally support for creation of Itasca State Park, the Boundary Waters Canoe Area (BWCA), and the Chippewa National Forest, respectively. The efforts of others, like Mary Gibbs (who stood up to the lumbering interests at Itasca State Park), are equally heroic.

This book, which focuses on 120 state and national recreation units, is a tribute to all who have contributed to outdoor preservation in Minnesota. The Dakota, as well as other cultures, feel that one does not just strive for oneself, but for "mitakuye oyasin" ("all my relations").

• • • • • •

Minnesota's state and national recreation lands consist of many components. The ones featured in this guide are outlined below.

State Parks

Camp Release, a 17-acre site along the Minnesota River, became the first unit in Minnesota's park system in 1889 (the site was eventually turned over to the Minnesota Historical Society). In 1891, Itasca became the first state park (Minnesota was the second state to start a state park system). Since then, the system has evolved into 66 parks, with Grand Portage and Glendalough recently joining the fold.

Itasca is an example of the wide range of facilities visitors will encounter in the state park system. At Itasca, you can plug in your RV, or backpack to an isolated campsite on a quiet lake, or reserve a lakeshore rental cabin. You can eat lunch in beautiful Douglas Lodge and, later in the day, stand under old-growth red and white pines in a designated wilderness area.

The parks reflect Minnesota's diversity. You can observe a buffalo herd on the prairie at Blue Mounds State Park in southwestern Minnesota and spot a moose while hiking at Lake Bronson State Park in the northwestern corner of the state. From the stampeding waterfalls along the rockbound North Shore of Lake Superior to the hawk's-eye vistas atop the Mississippi River bluffs, you'll find a state park that preserves a slice of primal Minnesota.

Many parks are trying to restore glimpses of the pre-settlement landscape. This process involves activities such as controlled burns, planting of native grasses, and the reintroduction of wild turkeys, red-tailed hawks and other native wildlife.

To help visitors discover more about the parks' cultural and natural history, active interpretive programs are scheduled at most state parks throughout the summer. A number of parks feature year-round programs.

Special events abound in the parks. For example, the state Department of Natural Resources (DNR) designates the first Sunday in June as Open House Day. Visitors can enter any state park without a vehicle permit, although other fees and rental charges are in effect. Many parks plan celebrations on Open House Day. Contact individual parks for details (addresses are in the back of this guide).

Fun is the name of the game in Minnesota's State Parks. Several unique clubs add to the spirit of a park visit. The Passport Club charts your park experiences, allowing you to earn patches, free nights of camping, a poster, and an engraved plaque depending on how many of the parks you visit. Visitors who join the Hiking Club also earn patches and free nights of camping by hiking special trails in the state parks. Members receive a fanny pack, hiking booklet, and official Hiking Club shoelaces.

You can get a new line on angling by joining Club Fish. As you catch the different species of fish featured in the members' fishing guidebook, you'll earn cloisonne pins and free nights of camping. The club kit includes the guidebook and a baseball-style cap. There is no deadline for completing the activities suggested by the clubs. Hiking Club and Club Fish members can buy additional products and awards. Ask at any state park contact station or call the DNR Information Center for details.

State Trails and State Canoe and Boating Routes

Minnesota's state trails appeal to a variety of people: bicyclists, cross-country skiers, hikers, snowmobilers and horseback riders. The central and southern Minnesota trails, such as the Root River State Trail, follow abandoned railroad grades that wind through rural scenery. The northern state trails are often longer than their southern counterparts and offer more of a wilderness experience. Many trails have parallel treadways that permit a variety of uses.

The state trail system is one of the best in the country in terms of the amount of developed trail mileage and the quality of treadway. Some trails are designed primarily for bicycling, others for snowmobiling. New routes or improvements to existing corridors are an ongoing process.

A few of the trails included in this guide (Superior Hiking Trail, Cannon Valley Trail and Mesabi Range Trail) are not part of the state trail system. They are included here as examples of a multi-agency approach to recreation trail development.

Canoeing is a great way to explore Minnesota. The state has mapped 19 rivers as Canoe & Boating Routes, including the St. Croix River, which is also a National Scenic Riverway. Rivers and rapids are rated according to the International Scale of River Difficulty. Ratings are estimates based on observation at low or moderate water levels or on secondhand reports. The ratings are as follows:

Class I. Easy rapids with small waves and few obstructions.

Class II. Rapids with waves up to three feet high. Some maneuvering is required.

Class III. Difficult rapids with high, irregular waves capable of swamping an open canoe. Usually considered the limit for an experienced paddler in an open canoe.

Class IV. Long, turbulent rapids with high, irregular waves, constricted passages and blind drops. Decked canoes and kayaks only; open canoes should be portaged.

Class V. Long, violent rapids with complex routes and steep drops or waterfalls. Hazard to life in the event of a mishap. Runnable only by experts in decked boats.

Class VI. Cannot be attempted without great risk to life.

The State Trails and the State Canoe & Boating Routes are administered by the DNR Trails and Waterways Unit. Much of the trail mileage in Minnesota is sponsored by the Grants-in-Aid program, a cooperative cost-sharing effort of the DNR, local governments, landowners and trail groups. The Grant-in-Aid trails link with the state trails and connect many state parks and forests. Cross-country skiers are required to buy a ski pass, and the revenues generated help maintain and develop ski trails. You can purchase them from county auditors, the License Center in St. Paul, or at certain state park offices.

State Forests

Minnesota's 57 state forests (over 3.2 million acres) are managed for timber production, watershed protection, wildlife habitat and recreation. Visitors can hike, camp, horseback ride, ski, snowmobile and enjoy water sports. Camping facilities are primitive (a fee is charged). Maps are available from the DNR. Check the Addresses section in the back of this book.

Only two state forests are included in this guide: the Richard J. Dorer Memorial Hardwood State Forest and the Northwest Angle State Forest. Richard J. Dorer is representative of the facilities found in most state forests; Northwest Angle is unique because of its geographical location and unusual history.

National Parks, Monuments, Forests, Rivers and Wildlife Refuges

Perhaps less well-known than the state park system, some of Minnesota's national recreation lands offer more elbow room and wild country than the typical state park. The federal government (with other public agencies) co-manages a handful of these units, such as the St. Croix National Scenic Riverway, the Mississippi National River and Recreation Area, the lower Minnesota River Valley corridor and the North Country National Scenic Trail.

Senior citizens and disabled visitors are eligible for discounts in Minnesota's national recreation lands. Depending on whether they visit a unit administered by the National Park Service or the National Forest Service, they can obtain Golden Eagle, Golden Age, or Golden Access (for disabled visitors) passports. Check with individual unit offices for details (addresses and phone numbers are listed in the back of this book).

Jim Umhoefer
Sauk Centre, Minnesota

P.S. "If you don't like the weather in Minnesota," the saying goes, "wait until tomorrow." Tomorrow, however, is no guarantee either. Sure, Minnesota's weather is moody: cold snaps in July, rainstorms that can dampen the spirit of even the most enthusiastic outdoors lover, and heat that can make an air-conditioned motel room look better than your tent.

That same unpredictability accounts for those striking lakeshore sunsets that make you wonder why you don't leave the city more often. It also inspires memorable moments, like after a rainstorm when the air smells sweet and fresh and the kids are having a ball splashing in the puddles.

The trick to a truly relaxing Minnesota outdoors trip is to be prepared. Pack the sweatshirt, gloves and hat along with your swimming suit and shorts. Throw in a couple of extra rolls of film and some good mosquito repellent. Leave your watch at home, but bring along a book about birds, wildflowers or trees. To clear your mind, take the back roads instead of the freeway. And if you forget something, be sure it's not your sense of humor!

HOW TO USE
THIS BOOK

This is a comprehensive guide to Minnesota's state and national recreation lands. A commentary describes what you can see and do at each park, forest, trail, waterway and major wildlife refuge of the "land of sky-tinted waters." Historical and geological information is included to give a more complete picture of each unit. Maps and photographs offer a glimpse of what's waiting for you outdoors in Minnesota.

This book is designed for both on-the-road reference and armchair vacation planning. Maybe you'd like to canoe, camp or hike in the Arrowhead Region of northeastern Minnesota. Before your trip, read through that section of the guide to get a feel for the parks, trails and canoe routes in that area. Why is George H. Crosby-Manitou State Park a favorite destination for backpackers? What type of visitor facilities are available in the Superior National Forest? How do expert kayakers get their thrills on the Kettle River each spring? Then, when you leave on your vacation, take the guide with you as a fingertip source of information about side trips and other parks that you might wish to visit.

Most of the recreation lands depicted in this guide include a state highway map index number to help you locate the unit. This will be useful only if you have an Official Minnesota Highway Map. You can get a copy by contacting the Minnesota Travel Information Center (address and phone number are listed in the section on "Planning Your Vacations").

Minnesota's recreation lands are constantly changing: a trail is enlarged, a new visitor center is constructed, or an interpretive program is added. A campground that didn't have showers last year may have them this year. Camping and vehicle permit fees may have gone up since your last visit. To keep abreast of year-to-year changes, you may wish to check with an individual park office before you leave home. You'll find the addresses and phone numbers for all state and national recreation units listed in the back of this book.

You can also use this book in conjunction with the Minnesota State Parks *NATURALLY* brochure, available (free) from the DNR Information Center or from any park office. This brochure can tell you at a glance how many campsites each park has, whether a park has an interpretive program, how many miles of hiking or ski trails you'll find in a park, and other nuts-and-bolts details. The DNR also produces a leaflet containing current camping and vehicle fees. To get your copy of these materials, ask at any park office or refer to the phone numbers and addresses listed in this book.

Just slip the brochure and price leaflet inside the front cover of this book, and you'll be ready to go. If your copy of *Guide to Minnesota Outdoors* comes back from a trip smudged with dirt and smelling of campfire smoke, it will have served its purpose.

PLANNING YOUR MINNESOTA VACATIONS

The bumper sticker says "Explore Minnesota," but for a successful sojourn, you need a plan. It's easy to get information about traveling in Minnesota before you pack your tent and camera. Although this book focuses on state and national parks, forests and trails, you can use the following resources to request other tourism materials or to ask questions about a Minnesota vacation.

Where to Start

MINNESOTA TRAVEL INFORMATION CENTER (Minnesota Office of Tourism) 500 Metro Square, 121 7th Place East, St. Paul, MN 55101. 1-800-657-3700 in the continental United States and Canada; Twin Cities, 651-296-5029; **http://www. exploreminnesota.com**

Contact for travel planning information, including directories of campgrounds, resorts, motels, hotels, and bed and breakfast and historic inns; brochures on biking, canoeing, skiing, snowmobiling, hiking and adventure trips; information on specific towns and regions; and information on things to see and do in Minnesota. You can also get autumn leaf reports and winter snow condition updates for trail users and skiers. The Minnesota Office of Tourism operates 12 Highway Travel Information Centers, located at rest areas along main highways.

MINNESOTA DEPARTMENT OF NATURAL RESOURCES INFORMATION CENTER 500 Lafayette Road, St. Paul, MN 55155-4040. 1-888-MINNDNR in Minnesota; Twin Cities, 651-296-6157; TDD for the hearing impaired, 651-296-5484, or 1-800-657-3929. **http://www.dnr.state.mn.us**

Contact for information on state parks, forests, trails, and canoe & boating routes. You can request maps and get details about horseback riding, hunting, fishing, boating, licenses, water access, and the state park clubs (Passport Club, Hiking Club and Club Fish). Ask about joining the Trail

Explorers Club. Members receive eight newspaper-style issues per year—two each for bicycling and hiking in the summer and cross-country skiing and snowmobiling in the winter in various regions of the state (published by the DNR Trails and Waterways Unit).

MINNESOTA STATE PARKS RESERVATION SYSTEM

With the growing popularity of the state parks, it's harder to enjoy spur-of-the-moment camping trips. Many parks reserve the majority of their campsites, so if you travel to a park without a reservation, you may be out of luck. During peak season in high-traffic areas, it's wise to reserve a campsite in the park that you'd like to visit.

Minnesota State Parks uses Mistix Corporation, a private reservation system, to book family camping and lodging requests. Currently, the following facilities may be reserved through Mistix: family campsites, Itasca State Park lodging, and guest houses at Maplewood, St. Croix and Scenic state parks. Specific sites cannot be reserved. The group centers and group camping areas in the parks are not part of the centralized reservation system. If you wish to reserve one of these areas, contact the individual park office (phone numbers and addresses in the back of this book).

For reservations, the toll-free number is 1-800-246-CAMP or 612-922-9000 in the Twin Cities. The camping reservation fee is $5 (non-refundable and not credited to camping costs). Camping fees are payable upon arrival. Mistix can provide information about the facilities that are reserved. If you need other information about a park, call the park office or the DNR Information Center.

Other Resources

• Minnesota Parks and Trails Council. 26 East Exchange Street, Suite 214, St. Paul, MN 55101-2264. 651-281-0508 or 1-800-944-0707; **http://www.mnptc.org** The Minnesota Parks and Trails Council is a nonprofit citizens group composed of people who share an interest in parks, trails and outdoor recreation in Minnesota. The Council serves as a vehicle to receive gifts of money or land for the preservation and acquisition of key areas that highlight Minnesota's natural heritage. The council was successful recently in helping to acquire the land that now forms Grand Portage State Park.

Members receive regular newsletters, information on current events, and assistance in communicating with the legislature and DNR. Contact the Council if you would like to join its effort to enhance Minnesota's natural resources for future generations.

• Minnesota Recreational Trail Users Association. P.O. Box 27131, Minneapolis, MN 55427-0131. This new group represents a coalition of skiers, bikers and other trail users who hope to guide Minnesota's trails program down a more unified path. Members of this association, the first multi-use trail organization in the country, hope to cultivate contacts in the DNR and the state legislature. The diverse group is trying to find ways to share the land and share the funding by learning how to integrate their own varied values and interests. Contact the DNR Information Center for details about this pioneering organization.

• Minnesota Department of Transportation. Room G-19, Mail Stop 260, Transportation Bldg., St. Paul, MN 55155. 651-296-2216 or 1-800-657-3774 (ask for the D.O.T.). Contact to order Bikeways Maps featuring road analysis, historical and cultural attractions, and public parklands and facilities for bicycle use in Minnesota.

SPECIAL ATTRACTIONS AND ORGANIZATIONS

Great River Road

In a state noted for its scenic drives, the Great River Road should rank near the top of your list. The parkway-like route runs along the Mississippi River from its source at Lake Itasca to Venice, Louisiana (near the Gulf of Mexico). The Minnesota portion, 673 miles long, begins at Lake Itasca and ends at the Iowa border. At Hastings, the Great River Road follows the Mississippi along both sides of the river. To explore Wisconsin's riverbank (with views of Minnesota), cross the river to Prescott, Wisconsin, from Hastings.

River time flows slower than highway time, so stop often to savor life along the Mississippi. You'll discover scores of historical and recreational opportunities to lure you off the road. Camping, fishing, hiking and boating are some of the popular river pastimes. Below Hastings, watch for the river barges that navigate the twisting channels of the Mississippi, and the bald eagles and hawks that soar overhead. For more information about the Great River Road system (which also includes roads in Manitoba and Ontario), call 651-296-5029 or 1-800-657-3700 (Minnesota Travel Information Center).

Lake Superior Circle Tour

Lake Superior is the world's largest freshwater lake. You can drive around the lake on a 1,300-mile route that traverses parts of Minnesota, Wisconsin, Michigan and northern Ontario. The North Shore portion of the tour, between Duluth and Sault Ste. Marie, is famous for its rugged scenery. The South Shore drive features some sandy Lake Superior beaches. For information visit the website at **www.glc.org/projects/circle/circle.html**

Minnesota Historical Society

Minnesota's past is long and colorful. You can relive the days of Indians, explorers, fur traders, lumbermen, soldiers, settlers and entrepreneurs by visiting the state's historic sites. The Minnesota Historical Society was founded in 1849 to preserve the heritage of Minnesota and make it accessible to its citizens. The historic sites across the state bring history to the public through interpretive tours, exhibits, films, craft demonstrations, and living history programs.

The Historical Society owns more than 20 sites, though a handful of these are operated by other organizations. Some sites, like the Oliver H. Kelley Farm and the Forest History Center, enliven the past by featuring costumed guides and special events to make your visit both informative and fun. For general information about the historic sites, call toll-free 1-800-657-3773; Twin Cities, 651-296-6126. To join the Minnesota Historical Society (free site admission, discounts, publications), pick up a membership brochure when you visit one of the historic sites, or call 651-296-0332.

Minnesota Wildlife Lands

State Wildlife Management Areas protect and preserve highly productive wildlife habitat. Hunting, trapping, fishing and wildlife observation are some of the recreational uses of these areas. To get a map of the more than 1,000 Wildlife Management Areas in Minnesota, contact the Minnesota DNR, Section of Wildlife, Box 7, 500 Lafayette Road, St. Paul, MN 55155. Or call 1-800-766-6000; Twin Cities, 651-296-3344.

The Nature Conservancy

The Nature Conservancy is an international membership organization committed to the preservation of natural diversity. Its mission is to find, protect and maintain the best examples of communities, ecosystems and endangered species in the natural world. The Nature Conservancy was incorporated in 1951 for scientific and educational purposes and is a nonprofit, tax-exempt corporation.

The Conservancy has been responsible for protection of more than six million acres in 50 states, Canada, Latin America and the Caribbean. The Conservancy has the largest privately owned nature preserve system in the world.

The Minnesota Chapter of The Nature Conservancy, founded in 1958, is a statewide organization with nearly 14,000 members. To date, the Minnesota Chapter has been involved in protection of over 40,000 acres throughout the state, including the new Glendalough State Park. Preservation strategies include outright purchase, conservation easements, and voluntary agreements. For more information, contact The Nature Conservancy, Minnesota Chapter, 1313 Fifth St. S.E., Suite 320, Minneapolis, MN 55414. Call 612-331-0750 or visit their website at **www.tnc.org/infield/State/Minnesota/**

Scientific and Natural Areas

Minnesota's landscape has changed dramatically since settlement mushroomed in the mid-1800s. Little remains of the natural plant and animal communities that formed following the melting of the last glaciers about 12,000 years ago. The scattered, designated remnants that have escaped exploitation are called Scientific and Natural Areas.

The state's SNA program was started in 1969 to protect and manage the best of Minnesota's natural world. The SNA ensures protection of pristine examples of northern coniferous forests, eastern deciduous woodlands, prairies, and rare plants and animals.

The Scientific and Natural Areas serve as outdoor laboratories for research and teaching. Use of the least fragile sites by environmental education and conservation groups is permitted, but they are not intended for intensive recreational uses like picnicking or camping. Though some natural areas are protected from human disturbance, many others are easily accessible to the public (with parking lots, trails, fences and gates). Examples of sites include an orchid bog, an agate beach, a heron rookery, a prairie remnant, a hardwood cove and an old-growth forest.

To learn more about the SNA program, or to assist in the protection of Minnesota's rarest natural resources, contact Scientific and Natural Areas Program, Minnesota DNR, Section of Wildlife, Box 7, 500 Lafayette Road, St. Paul, MN 55155. Call 1-800-766-6000; Twin Cities, 651-296-3344.

North Country National Scenic Trail

The trail extends for a total of about 4,200 miles, between Lake Champlain in New York and Lake Sakakawea in North Dakota. Currently, over 1,400 miles are available for public use. Trail states are New York, Pennsylvania, Ohio, Michigan, Wisconsin, Minnesota and North Dakota.

At 4,200 miles, the North Country Trail (NCT) will be,

upon completion, the longest foot path in the national scenic trail system. It is in good company. Other national scenic trails (there are eight altogether) include the Appalachian Trail, the Pacific Crest Trail, the Continental Divide Trail and the Ice Age Trail (Wisconsin).

While most of the other national scenic trails have a singular natural feature that distinguishes them, like mountain scenery or glacial topography, the NCT defies any phrase used to describe it. From the grandeur of the Adirondack Mountains in New York, it meanders westward through the hardwood forests of Pennsylvania, through the countryside of Ohio and southern Michigan, along the shores of the Great Lakes and through the glacier-carved forests, lakes and streams of northern Wisconsin and Minnesota. The trail ends on the broad plains of North Dakota, where it meets the Lewis and Clark National Historic Trail at Lake Sakakawea on the Missouri River.

Though the NCT is administered by the National Park Service, its construction and maintenance is a cooperative effort involving a variety of public agencies, private organizations, interested landowners and volunteers. It is a big job. Although it will take many years to complete, trail users are already enjoying more than 1,400 miles open to public use. Completed segments vary in length from 1 mile to over 125 miles.

The North Country Trail began as a U.S. Forest Service proposal in the mid-1960s. When Congress passed legislation creating the National Trails System in 1968, the Appalachian and the Pacific Crest were the first two trails formed. The Department of the Interior (which includes the National Park Service) published a report in 1975 that outlined other trail routes, including the North Country Trail. Congress passed the law that created the North Country National Scenic Trail in 1980.

Because of the maze of public and private interests involved in management of the NCT, development has not been consistent along the proposed 4,200-mile corridor. Trail users should be aware that the type and width of the trail tread, the support facilities available (campsites, access, etc.) and regulations (permits, fees, usage, etc.) will vary from segment to segment.

In Minnesota, NCT development has been enthusiastic but

spotty. Of the 390 miles in the proposed corridor, about 90 miles are usable by the public. Most of these miles traverse existing public lands, such as state parks, state forests and the Chippewa National Forest. This reflects a similar trend in the six other NCT states. Trail development is an ongoing process in Minnesota (and elsewhere): miles are added, campsites are developed, and maps are improved each year.

Rivers, lakes and forests characterize the North Country Trail for much of its route through Minnesota. The NCT enters the state from Wisconsin, near Minnesota's Jay Cooke State Park near Duluth. At Savanna State Forest (west of Duluth), the trail crosses a continental divide that separates the waters flowing into Lake Superior from those flowing into the Mississippi River. Savanna Portage State Park lies just to the south.

The 68-mile segment through the Chippewa National Forest is the longest continuous NCT route in the state. This segment skirts south of Leech Lake and features designated campsites and access points. A small guidebook gives a mile-by-mile portrait of the NCT in the Chippewa National Forest. You can camp in a pine grove where the view stretches to the east. The NCT also intersects a network of cross-country skiing and hiking trails.

West of the Chippewa National Forest, the NCT passes through the Paul Bunyan State Forest and enters Itasca State Park, where you can cross the headwaters of the Mississippi River. Then the trail joins with the Bad Medicine Lake Trail system. Together, the completed trail in Itasca State Park and the adjoining Bad Medicine Lake segment are about 16 miles.

The NCT turns southward as it passes through the White Earth State Forest, the Tamarac National Wildlife Refuge, and Maplewood State Park. The trail soon heads west again, passing Fergus Falls and entering North Dakota past Breckenridge.

A major NCT addition through Minnesota's Arrowhead Region is currently in the planning phase. This would add a new dimension to the system, linking the Superior Hiking Trail, the Border Route and Kekekabic trails in the Boundary Waters Canoe Area, and a future corridor from Ely to Grand Rapids. This potential route would intersect the current NCT near Remer in the Chippewa National Forest. Though this is just a proposal for now, it points out some exciting possibilities for this already horizon-stretching trail.

RESOURCES:

• North Country National Scenic Trail, Bill Menke, National Park Service, 700 Rayovac Dr., Suite 100, Madison, WI 53711. 608-264-5610.

• North Country Trail Association, 49 Monroe Center, Suite 200B, Grand Rapids, MI 49503. 616-454-5506; **www. northcountrytrail.org**

• North Country Trail Association, West End Trail Council, John Leinen, Jr., 111 Quandt Ct. South, Lakeland, MN 55043.

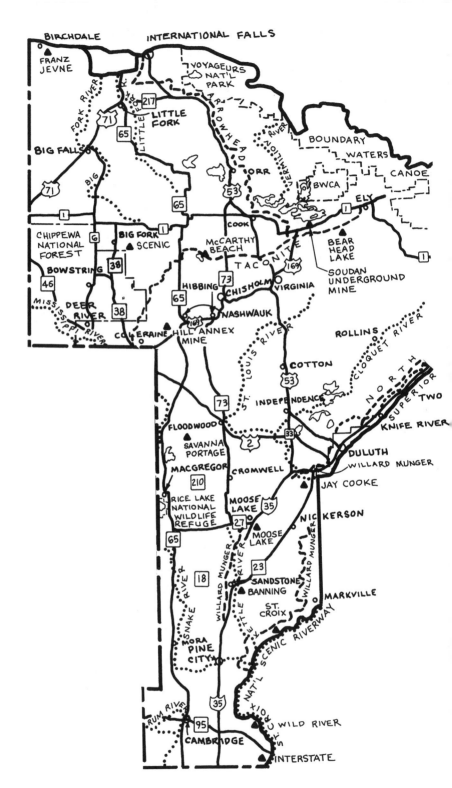

ARROWHEAD REGION

Arrowhead State Trail
Banning State Park
Bear Head Lake State Park
Big Fork River Canoe and Boating Route
Boundary Waters Canoe Area (BWCA)
Cascade River State Park
Cloquet River Canoe and Boating Route
Franz Jevne State Park
George H. Crosby-Manitou State Park
Gooseberry Falls State Park
Grand Portage National Monument
Grand Portage State Park
Hill Annex Mine State Park
Interstate State Park
Jay Cooke State Park
Judge C.R. Magney State Park
Kettle River Canoe and Boating Route
Little Fork River Canoe and Boating Route
McCarthy Beach State Park
Moose Lake State Park
North Shore State Trail
Rice Lake National Wildlife Refuge
St. Croix National Scenic Riverway
St. Croix State Park
St. Louis River Canoe and Boating Route
Savanna Portage State Park
Scenic State Park
Snake River Canoe and Boating Route
Soudan Underground Mine State Park
Split Rock Lighthouse State Park
Superior Hiking Trail
Superior National Forest
Taconite State Trail
Temperance River State Park
Tettegouche State Park
Vermilion River Canoe and Boating Route
Voyageurs National Park
Wild River State Park
Willard Munger State Trail

▲ ....STATE PARKS & RECREATION AREAS
△ ....WAYSIDES
■ ....NATIONAL MONUMENTS
— — — — ....STATE TRAIL
•••• ....CANOE & RIVER ROUTES

ARROWHEAD STATE TRAIL

St. Louis and Koochiching counties. 140 miles (128 miles developed), from the junction of the Taconite Trail (10 miles west of Tower) to Ericsburg, about 10 miles south of International Falls.

"The woods are lovely, dark and deep . . ." wrote Robert Frost in his poem, "Stopping by Woods on a Snowy Evening." Though he was referring to a New England forest, he may have felt the same had he hiked through the forest along the Arrowhead State Trail.

The trail rambles for about 140 miles through the "lovely, dark and deep" woods of northeastern Minnesota. The remote forest setting and easy access to connecting trails and nearby public lands lure trail users to this region year-round.

The trail has three "personalities." The first 25 miles, from the junction of the Taconite Trail north, is almost entirely ash and spruce swamps (winter use only). This section is wide and predominantly straight. The towns of Tower, Peyla and Cook are the closest communities for services at the southern end of the trail.

The middle segment of the Arrowhead Trail (about 75 miles) winds through a rolling region of heavy timber laced with streams and lakes. Many of the hills have large areas of exposed ledge rock and enormous boulders. The forest is a mixture of hardwoods and conifers. You might crest a ridge of white pine, descend into a stand of mixed hardwoods, and then climb another ridge of oaks and maple. The variety of trees makes for spectacular fall hikes.

This section is open all year for hiking, horseback riding, mountain biking, cross-country skiing or snowmobiling. The trail is isolated, so prepared visitors carry a map and compass, bring extra food, water and clothing, and tell someone about their route and estimated time of arrival. Clothing that covers exposed skin and insect repellent are good ideas during the summer.

Hunters and fishermen use the trail as walk-in access to public lands and the trout streams and remote lakes of the

The Temperance River tumbles on a restless path to Lake Superior.

31

area. Camping is permitted only at the trail shelters, which are spaced about 7 to 10 miles apart. Since the public lands are managed for multiple use, you may come upon areas of timber harvesting. Supplies and services are available in Cook, Orr and Buyck.

The northern 40 miles of the Arrowhead Trail to International Falls is similar to the first segment. The terrain varies from aspen-covered uplands to lowlands of ash and spruce. This section is open only for winter use. The entire Arrowhead Trail is groomed for snowmobiling at least once per week (usually from December until late March or early April). You can find services in Ericsburg and International Falls.

The Arrowhead Trail connects with many national and state forest trails, as well as local Grant-in-Aid trails. Most of this trail mileage is for winter use only. The Arrowhead Trail and the connecting routes provide access to the Boundary Waters Canoe Area, Voyageurs National Park, Superior National Forest and the Kabetogama State Forest. Bear Head Lake and Soudan Underground Mine state parks and the Vermilion River Canoe & Boating Route are short drives away from the southern end of the Arrowhead Trail. Wildlife is plentiful throughout the region. Observant (and lucky) visitors may spot moose, deer, coyotes or timber wolves.

BANNING STATE PARK

*Pine County. Four miles north of Sandstone. Park entrance is
off I-35 and Highway 23. Highway map index: K-12.*

It's common to see experienced kayakers practice for
hours in the challenging Kettle River rapids. The river flows
for 10 miles through the long, slender park, but it's the two
miles of powerful, churning rapids that make a kayaker's
pulse quicken at the mention of Banning. Even the names of
the individual pitches are a call to white-water adventure:
Blueberry Slide, Mother's Delight, Dragon's Tooth and Hell's
Gate.

No matter how experienced you are in a kayak or decked
canoe, always respect the river. More than one life has been
claimed here when people have overestimated their skills or
underestimated the hazardous rapids (especially in high
water). When in doubt, scout ahead or portage. Be
especially wary of the high, cold water of April and May.
After the snow melts, the swollen Kettle rises to levels that
only experts should attempt.

As a general rule, the largest waves in the rapids are as
high as the gauge reading on the Highway 23 bridge (east of
the park entrance). The rapids will be too low to run if the
gauge reads a foot or less. The water level fluctuates
repeatedly, however, so that what is runnable today might
not be a few days hence. As summer progresses, the rapids
calm down enough so that less experienced kayakers (or
paddlers in canoes with flotation devices) can give it a try.
Autumn rains raise the river level again, but not as high as
during spring. Depending on water level and temperature,
the Banning Rapids vary in difficulty from Class II to Class V.
Check the introduction to this book for descriptions of
difficulty ratings.

The rest of the Kettle River in Banning State Park, above
and below the rapids, is easier to canoe. The Kettle is a state
canoe route as well as a state-designated wild and scenic
river. There are two canoe landings and two drive-in boat
landings in Banning: the Highway 23 bridge and below the
Sandstone Dam for canoeists, above the rapids and near
Robinson Park (in Sandstone) for boats.

Canoeists and boaters like to try for bass, northern and walleye in the slower waters of the Kettle River and below the Sandstone Dam. Below the Banning Rapids, canoeists can paddle the brief distance up Wolf Creek to see a pretty waterfall. The park provides three primitive canoe-camping areas: at Rustler Bend (above 1-35), near Highway 23 (on the park's eastern edge) and at Blueberry Slide (just above the rapids).

The semi-modern campground at Banning has 34 sites (11 electric) that give campers a sense of privacy. On peak weekends and during fall color season, you'll have to get here early or make a reservation to get a site. Camping is also available at Moose Lake and St. Croix state parks.

Banning State Park is less than 100 miles from the Twin Cities, attracting visitors who want to use the river, watch the kayakers, hike or picnic. The park's shaded picnic area is a short walk from the Kettle River and the trails that flank it. There is another picnic area in Sandstone's Robinson Park. This is the site of an old sandstone quarry, and picnickers sometimes watch rock climbers scaling the quarry walls. A summertime naturalist program features a variety of guided activities on the weekends at Banning.

Today, the park's forests consist mostly of aspen and birch with occasional stands of pine. The woods and wild river form a wilderness-like setting, though the land was not always so untouched. The original white- and red-pine forest was cut down, and the logs were floated down the Kettle River to sawmills. The land surrounding the river was mined for copper and quarried for sandstone, and the river itself was dammed to generate electricity. The sandstone, quarried along the river near Hell's Gate, was valued for its strength and warm pink color. When structural steel became common in buildings, sandstone use declined and the town of Banning, once a bustling village near the quarries, faded. All that remains today are weathered concrete ruins along the riverbank and some remnants of the quarry processing buildings. The scars of development are slowly disappearing in a second-growth forest that shelters deer, bear, and, along the riverbanks, smaller animals like beaver, muskrat and otter.

The park's hiking trails begin at the picnic area and hug the riverbank on both sides to Hell's Gate rapids. These paths are also used as portage trails. There is another trailhead in the campground where hikers can walk north to the picnic area, down to the river, or south to Wolf Creek Falls and the town of Sandstone.

At the northern end of the park are some sandstone formations called the Log Creek Arches. There is no direct park access to the arches, but the manager can give you directions. The arches and Wolf Creek Falls are better viewed during autumn through the thinning foliage.

As you hike downhill to reach the river trails, you'll hear the increasing roar of the rapids. The quarry walls here are usually moist, and the gentle drip, drip, drip joins the constant chorus of river sounds. The riverbank trail passes by several groupings of "kettles" eroded into the sandstone. The kettles, some 10 feet deep, were formed by water and swirling stones that gouged the ovals in the rock over thousands of years.

The closer you get to Hell's Gate rapids, the tougher the trail becomes as it climbs and drops below rocky cliffs (wear good-grip tennis shoes). In places where the cliffs overhang the trail, moisture drips on hikers as they duck underneath. The Kettle River is calm above Hell's Gate, which is typical of the Banning Rapids: quiet pools followed by sudden pitches.

Rocky ledges jut out over the river above Hell's Gate, affording a chance to peek downriver in the direction of the thundering rapids. When you first stand above Hell's Gate, you can understand how it came by its name. Rock walls squeeze the cascading river. The loud, boisterous rapids resemble boiling root beer with lots of foam. If you're lucky, some kayakers will be practicing their white-water skills and you'll have a front-row seat for the show.

Winter

Banning's snowmobile trails are not extensive, but connect with local trails for a longer ride. Snowmobiling is popular on the nearby Willard Munger State Trail, which crosses public land along the St. Croix River, including the Nemadji, St. Croix and Chengwatana state forests and St. Croix State Park. Regional Grant-in-Aid trails provide additional snowmobile mileage in the St. Croix Valley.

Some of the park's winter trails are used by snowmobilers

and cross-country skiers. Separate cross-country ski trails, designed for intermediate skiers, loop north along the river from the winter parking lot or head up to the campground and then south to the Wolf Creek Falls area.

BEAR HEAD LAKE STATE PARK

St. Louis County. 18 miles east of Tower. Take Highway 169 east to County 128, then turn south on 128 to the park entrance. Highway map index: M-7.

For many visitors, Bear Head Lake Park is intended as a stopover on the way to the Boundary Waters Canoe Area (BWCA) wilderness or the millions of acres of lakeland woods and streams in northeastern Minnesota. But you may discover, as others have, that this park has just the recreational elements you're looking for.

Bear Head Lake (690 acres) is mostly known for bass, panfish and walleye fishing. Eagles Nest Lake No. 3, touching on the northwestern corner of the park, is larger than Bear Head Lake and also has a boat landing. You can rent boats or canoes for use on Bear Head Lake at the park contact station. The lake has a large body with two bays that look like antlers. The "antlers," North Bay and East Bay, are fun to explore by canoe because of the many small islands, inlets and coves.

Most of the park's development is on the peninsula that separates North and East bays. An inviting sandy beach lies on the tip of the peninsula. The picnic area, just behind the beach, is graced by cross-breezes that discourage mosquitoes during the summer.

The fishing on other park lakes is also good, but requires a hike. The longest hike is down to Blueberry Lake to try for northerns and panfish. You can also try the action on Grassy Lake by taking the shorter portage trail from County 128 (the entrance road). Cub Lake, nestled in a forested bowl just a short hike from the road, is fished for brook trout, while rainbow trout are taken in Norberg Lake. Follow the trail from the roadside parking lot to this lake, which is also protected by a ring of hills. Some anglers like to stream-fish for brook trout near Grassy Lake.

The park's 17-mile-long trail system weaves among the lakes and connects with the Taconite State Trail. Horseback riding and hiking are the main summer uses for this trail.

Some adirondacks (three-sided shelters) are placed along the more distant trails in the 4,400-acre park, with others being considered. The trail system may be enlarged in the future.

Most of the forest cover consists of aspen and birch, but there are also stands of white pines, tamaracks and cedars. Moose may be seen in the marshes and ponds of the park, where they like to feed on aquatic plants during summer. I saw several deer while hiking down to Becky Lake. Black bears and timber wolves live in the region, but aren't commonly spotted. Canoeing along the secluded shores of Bear Head Lake or hiking on the park's isolated trails offers the best chances to observe wildlife. Look overhead, too, for eagles, hawks and ospreys.

Backpackers who hike into the site on Becky Lake or one of the three on Blueberry Lake often report sightings of deer and occasionally moose or bear. If you want to backpack in the park, you'll have to boil or treat your drinking water. Bring plenty of insect repellent if you plan to camp during the height of midsummer fly and mosquito season.

The 73 semi-modern sites at Bear Head Lake are well separated from each other, preserving the quiet atmosphere of the campground (reservations are recommended). The 100-person primitive group camp, at the head of East Bay, can be reserved through the park office. There is a boat access for use by the groups in the primitive camp.

The rolling hills here are actually accumulations of glacial debris. Volcanoes and ancient seas produced the bedrock of the area, which the glaciers later sculpted into today's landscape. Before European settlement, the forests were mostly white and red pine, but extensive lumbering and forest fires destroyed the tall trees.

Winter

Bear Head Lake State Park's hiking trails are transformed into ski touring trails to satisfy everyone's taste. Beginners like to practice their stride on the campground and lakeshore trails, while intermediate skiers can tour from the picnic area to Norberg Lake and back on a loop route. Advanced skiers will find the new trails scenic as well as challenging.

Snowmobilers and skiers can start from the picnic area

parking lot. From here, you can snowmobile up to the Taconite State Trail which links with the Bear Island State Forest trail system. The Superior National Forest also has an extensive snowmobile trail network.

The park lakes attract scores of winter ice fishermen, especially to Cub Lake, one of the busier fishing spots. Kids like to inner-tube down the hills that surround Cub Lake. If you're planning to winter camp here, water is available from hand pumps. Snowshoeing and hiking are permitted throughout the park.

BIG FORK RIVER CANOE & BOATING ROUTE

Itasca and Koochiching counties. 165 miles from Dora Lake to the Rainy River, on the Canadian border.

The Big Fork River would still be familiar to the Indians and fur traders if they were to canoe it today. Scattered farms, towns and bridges remind modern explorers of the 20th century, but the rest of the route remains primitive.

The rapids and white-water stretches are for experienced canoeists only, although novices can enjoy this wilderness river if they portage the obstacles. Some of the portages are rough and brushy.

Planning is vital for all canoeists on an isolated river like the Big Fork. Drinking water, for example, is hard to come by along the way. You have to disinfect and filter the river water, or pack your own. Potable water is available at the Highway 6 campsite (River Mile 74), at Johnson's Landing (RM 65) and at the few river towns that you'll paddle through. Outfitters in Bigfork and Grand Rapids can assist with your preparations.

The upper channel of the Big Fork is wide, shallow, and bordered with wild-rice beds. Frank L. Vance tried to harvest the rice by building one of Minnesota's first wild-rice processing mills near here in the early 1890s. He also invented a reaper to increase production, but he went out of business shortly after a ban was placed on mechanized harvesting. The wild rice is still harvested, during a regulated season, using the ancient methods of the Indians.

The scenery changes below Bigfork as the hardwood-softwood forest envelops the river like a green cloak. The banks become steeper, and the current picks up velocity in the deeper channel. From here to the Rainy River you'll encounter rapids of varying difficulty.

During high water, some of the rapids become challenging Class II, although most are rated Class I. (Some are impassable in low water.) There are two notable exceptions, however. The rapids and small waterfalls at both Little American Falls (RM 103) and the town of Big Falls (RM 51) should be portaged. The former is rated Class IV in low water and Class III in high water, though with its 6-foot ledge and large souse holes, it's best to portage. The Big Falls rapids is a dangerous series of four falls that drop 35 feet in a quarter-mile. This rapids rates Class IV in low water and Class VI in high water, when it's filled with 6-foot backrollers and big souse holes.

The river quiets down into a meandering stream below Big Falls. The current is still steady and you'll navigate through some Class I rapids, though they may wash out in high water. This stretch of the Big Fork is popular with less experienced canoeists because of the easy paddling.

This route has a colorful history. Klondike Landing, 9 miles below Bigfork, is the site of an old logging camp. Busties Landing (RM 119) is named for an Ojibway chief, Busticogan, who was rewarded by the government for caring for surveyors stricken with smallpox. An early Hudson's Bay Company post stood at the confluence of the Sturgeon and Big Fork rivers, where some campers have found Indian artifacts.

Grand Mound, at the junction of the Big Fork and Rainy rivers, is the largest prehistoric burial mound in Minnesota, measuring 40 feet high and more than 100 feet across at the base. The Laurel Indians, who lived around the upper Great Lakes some 2,000 years ago, probably constructed this monument. Stop at the visitor center to find out more about how these people lived in the northern lake-forest wilderness. This site is administered by the Minnesota Historical Society.

A trip down the Big Fork is like a journey into the past. It still is possible to see most of the same species of wildlife that lived in the forest 200 years ago. The caribou are gone, but timber wolves, lynx, moose and bear wander the woods while bald eagles and ospreys soar overhead. Walleyes, northerns, smallmouth bass and muskies inhabit the river.

BOUNDARY WATERS CANOE AREA (BWCA)

St. Louis, Lake and Cook counties, 1.2 million acres, Ranger district offices located in Grand Marais, Tofte, Ely, and Cook. See also: Superior National Forest.

The BWCA is the crown jewel of the Superior National Forest. It is the country's only lakeland wilderness. Over 1 million acres in size, the BWCA stretches for 150 miles along the Canadian border between Lake Superior and Voyageurs National Park. The BWCA boasts over 1,000 lakes that are 10 acres or larger (motors are permitted on only a few of these). Its trails are water routes: 1,500 miles of lakes, rivers and portages first traveled by Indians and explored by French-Canadian voyageurs more than two centuries ago.

Some days you won't see another human. This is especially true if you choose a route that requires frequent and/or long portages. On those days, you'll hear only natural sounds: fish jumping, the wind in the pines, the mournful calls of the loons. At other times (on the easier and more frequently used routes), you'll meet canoeists at the portage trails.

Even though the BWCA is a wilderness (in fact, it's officially known as the Boundary Waters Canoe Area Wilderness, part of the National Wilderness Preservation System), about 180,000 people paddle its waters each year. To protect the wilderness ecosystem and to allow each person to experience the quiet beauty and solitude of the BWCA, a visitor distribution system is used. A limited number of free permits are available each day for just under 100 separate entry points. Each overnight party (up to 10 people) must have a permit. Day-use hikers and paddlers do not need one, though motor permits are required. You can get a BWCA permit from any Superior National Forest Ranger District Office or cooperating business. Reserving a permit as early in the year as possible makes sense. Weekends and holidays, especially in late July and August, are most in demand. It is possible to get a walk-in permit if one is still available.

You don't have to be an expert to experience the Boundary Waters. Canoe outfitters offer as much or as little help as you need for a successful trip, including food, camping and cooking equipment, and your entry permit. They can also assist in designing your route, selecting campsites, and pointing out the best fishing spots.

Although the Boundary Waters region is served by several resort areas, the BWCA itself is preserved in a natural state. There are no roads, shelters, electricity or other amenities. Camping is permitted only at designated sites. Cans and bottles are not allowed in the BWCA; what you pack in, you must pack out. Campers are asked to leave behind no trace of their visit.

The Border Route Trail offers hikers a chance to see wildlife.

The key to enjoying a visit to the BWCA is to plan a trip that matches your experience and expectations. If you're interested in a full wilderness experience, design a canoe trip of several days to a week or more. Circular routes can be planned through a number of lakes and rivers, with campsites moved every day or two. This type of trip provides canoeists with a great deal of variety and offers an intense outdoors adventure.

Another option is to canoe to a site that can be used as a base camp. Then you are free to relax at camp, or explore during the days without portaging all of your camping gear.

While the BWCA is a wilderness, it is ringed by dozens of resorts, campgrounds, and other accommodations. Visitors can stay at one of these and make easy day trips into the Boundary Waters. Accommodations can be found near Ely, Crane Lake and Lake Vermilion to the west, and along the Gunflint Trail out of Grand Marais to the east.

The deep pine forests and rugged outcroppings of billion-year-old volcanic rock in the BWCA contain some visual surprises. Indian pictographs, or rock paintings, are the most striking of these. One of the finest examples of original Indian pictographs is found on the shore of North Hegman Lake, a short canoe jaunt off of the Echo Trail

Boundary Waters Canoe Area map

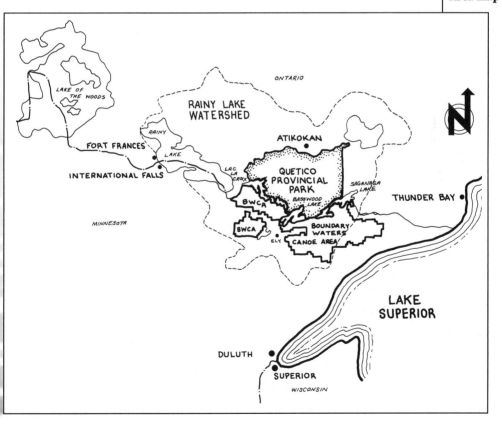

(County 116, northwest of Ely). Similar pictographs are found throughout the area of the Laurentian watershed. Indian occupation of the Hegman Lake area dates back at least 9,000 years, and a succession of cultures have since flourished and disappeared. These particular rock paintings probably were painted within the last 500 to 1,000 years. Watch carefully, or you may miss them.

The BWCA, though famous for its canoe routes, is also a haven for hikers. Most of the area trails feature scenic hiking with vistas of forests and lakes. Two trails deserve mention because of their length and wild nature. The 40-mile Kekekabic Trail cuts off near Alworth Lake and continues northeast toward the Gunflint Trail. This former firefighting trail is minimally maintained, unsigned, and requires wilderness skills.

The other footpath, the 38-mile Border Route Trail, parallels the water routes along the Canadian border. The western trailhead is 30 miles north of Grand Marais off the Gunflint Trail, at the end of the road to Loon Lake; the eastern trailhead is at Little John Lake at the end of the Arrowhead Trail (County 16), about 20 miles north of Hovland. The Border Route Trail runs along high cliffs with spectacular views of wilderness forests and lakes. Hikers pass through ancient stands of cedar and pine. On both the Kekekabic and Border Route trails, you'll have the chance to see moose, bears and wolves. Wilderness skills (map reading, compass use, first-aid knowledge, etc.) are necessary on this trail, too. BWCA permits are required for overnight use on both trails.

Quetico Provincial Park, the Canadian counterpart to the BWCA, is also an unparalleled lakeland wilderness famous for its canoe water routes. The provincial park lies just across the border from the BWCA and is governed by similar regulations.

Canoeists can plan trips that begin in the BWCA and loop into Quetico. However, visitors entering Quetico by water from the United States must report to a Canada Customs officer at Saganaga, Basswood or Sandpoint Lakes before paddling to a Quetico park station. Entry permits are limited and may be reserved. For information concerning permit reservations and Quetico Provincial Park rules, contact: District Manager, Ministry of Natural Resources; Atikokan, Ontario P0T 1C0 (807-597-2735).

CASCADE RIVER STATE PARK

*Cook County. 9 miles southwest of Grand Marais on Highway
61. Highway map index: Q-7.*

The 2,800-acre park and surrounding forests are home to
timber wolves and black bears, in addition to moose, but
Cascade River is best known for its winter deer herd. Deer
gather in the Jonvik deer yard, the largest in Minnesota, to
find protection from wind and cold and to browse in the
North Shore forests of aspen, birch and white cedar. Hiking
along the 18-mile trail system, you'll pass through upland
forests of spruce, fir and maples. You can get a bird's-eye
view of the myriad shades of green that sweep over the
surrounding land from the overlooks.

The busiest park trails straddle the Cascade River canyon,
leading up to the many waterfalls that tumble toward Lake
Superior. The paths are the handiwork of the Civilian
Conservation Corps (CCC) of the 1930s. A park sign
describes the Cascade River as flowing "through a twisting,
rocky gorge in a series of rapids that descends 225 feet in a
distance of one mile." The mist that sprays the gorge walls
fosters moist colonies of mosses and lichens. Great cedar
and fir trees rise like pillars from the rock formations above
the river.

The North Shore area has an almost endless variety of
wildflower habitats (bogs, marshes, coniferous forests,
deciduous woods, rocky ledges). In the park, springtime
wildflowers include bird's-eye primrose and starflowers.
Others, like moccasin flowers, orchids and touch-me-nots,
also show off their brightly colored blossoms, a product of
long days and cool nights. You might enjoy the self-guided
wildflower tour of Oberg Mountain, about 15 miles
southwest of the park on Highway 61 in the Superior
National Forest. Early June is usually the peak of bloom on
Oberg Mountain.

Some park trails climb into the Sawtooth Mountains,
entering the Superior National Forest. By arrangement with
the U.S. Forest Service, these trails lead up to adirondacks
(three-sided shelters) on top of Lookout Mountain, Moose

47

Mountain and another bluff-top overlook. Take a picnic lunch with you; each shelter has a table, fire ring and pit toilet. Along some of the trails, you'll be treated to broad vistas of Lake Superior. Other paths afford views of the inland bluffs.

Backpackers can hike up to the adirondacks and use them as walk-in campsites. One of the five backpack campsites in the park and the surrounding forest is along the shore of Lake Superior on the park's north end. The main campground has 40 semi-modern campsites and an enclosed shelter. Cascade River also maintains two year-round group camps (25 people each) which can be reserved through the park office.

The fishing action at Cascade River State Park revolves around stream angling or shore casting. The nearest boat landings for deepwater fishing are in Grand Marais and Tofte. Anglers like to try for pink (humpback) and chinook salmon, or lake trout in the fall. Stream steelhead fishing can be good in spring and fall. Brook trout and resident rainbows are taken above the first falls in the Cascade River. Besides the Cascade, nine other streams empty into Lake Superior in the park.

The Superior Hiking Trail, a footpath that follows the ridgeline of the North Shore of Lake Superior, cuts through Cascade River State Park. When completed, the trail will stretch from Duluth to the Canadian border (about 250 miles).

Besides hiking, mountain biking awaits adventuresome visitors near the park. With over 2,000 miles of county and national forest backwoods roads, mountain biking attracts more enthusiasts each year to the North Shore. You can rent mountain bikes locally in Lutsen and Grand Marais. Stop at the Tofte Ranger Station to pick up area maps and get information. It's easier than you think to get lost in the forest up here; experienced bikers carry accurate maps, compass, tool kit, tire patch kit, water, food and rain gear. Always tell someone where you are going and when you expect to return.

Sea kayaking is another unusual way to experience the wild beauty of the North Shore. No matter how familiar you are with the North Shore by land, you'll gain a new perspective from the water. Kayaks are not difficult to handle on Lake Superior. If you'd like to give it a try, stop at Lutsen Resort for information about full- and half-day kayak tours during the summer and the fall color season.

Good fishing, boating, and canoeing abound in the lakes and streams of northeastern Minnesota. Nearby main road accesses into the Superior National Forest and Boundary Waters Canoe Area (BWCA) are the Caribou, Sawbill and Gunflint trails. Many U.S. Forest Service roads branch off these routes. If you're visiting up here in autumn, take a drive through the Sawtooth Mountains to photograph the intense reds, yellows and oranges of the hardwood forests. Drive to nearby Lutsen Mountain to enjoy the scenery on the gondola ride or the alpine slide.

Other attractions await you in Grand Marais, northeast of Cascade River on Highway 61. This attractive lakeshore community features the Grand Marais Art Colony and hosts the annual five-day Fishermen's Picnic during the first week in August.

Winter

It's easy to keep warm during the winter around Cascade River State Park. The park's 17 miles of cross-country ski trails are designed for all abilities and link with neighboring Cascade Lodge's trail system and others in the area. Adirondacks are available for ski or walk-in camping, but check with the park manager before starting out. You can get water for camping or day use in the park office. Cross-country skiers can rent equipment at Cascade Lodge. Lutsen Mountain also has cross-country ski trails as well as downhill skiing.

The two miles of snowmobile trails in the park provide access to more extensive routes in the Superior National Forest. They also connect with the North Shore State Trail and various Grant-in Aid trails. The Cook County Ridge Riders and the Lutsen Trailbreakers snowmobile clubs sponsor snowmobile rides, social gatherings and area grooming projects.

Snowshoeing and hiking are the best ways to see the wintry lower Cascade River gorge. The gorge's beauty is particularly striking when the tenacious ice stills the falls in a severe winter.

49

The Sawtooth Mountains are blessed with miles of scenic, thrilling, ski-touring trails for all skill levels. The North Shore Mountain Ski Trail is a cooperative project of Cascade River and Temperance River state parks, the DNR, the Lutsen-Tofte Tourism Association, Superior National Forest and private landowners. This group connected existing trails and added new loops to form a 215-kilometer (135-mile) network that offers both quiet paths and difficult routes. Private lodges along the way cooperate to offer a ski-through program, allowing skiers to ski from one establishment to the other while lodge employees transfer the luggage. A similar program has been developed along the Gunflint Trail.

CLOQUET RIVER CANOE & BOATING ROUTE

The Cloquet River is one of the state's most primitive canoe routes. Most of the river flows through the wild lands of the Cloquet Valley State Forest, inspiring a sense of isolation that explorers may have felt. You'll discover its remoteness before pushing off downstream. Few highways cross the river, and you may have to drive 100 miles or more (partially on rough back roads) to pick up canoes. Outfitters are located in Duluth and Virginia.

The Cloquet has two distinct personalities. The upper section, from Indian Lake to Island Lake Reservoir, is for experienced canoeists only. Rapids are usually short and are separated by long sections of quiet water. Except for a couple of high-water Class IIIs above Island Lake, the rest of the upper rapids are rated Class II. Each rapids has a portage trail. You could canoe above Indian Lake, though the long boulder-bed rapids (Class I and Class II) are runnable only in high water. The riverbanks above Island Lake are covered with dense stands of red and white pine, fir, spruce, aspen and birch trees.

White Sides Rapids, above Island Lake, is probably the river's most difficult pitch. Rocky outcrops and thick boulder beds make this rapids too much of a challenge for most canoeists. Just below White Sides is an 8- to 12-foot waterfall that develops as water is drawn out of Island Lake. When the reservoir is high the ledge is covered and the majority of canoeists don't notice it. If you wish to end your trip on Island Lake, the Minnesota Power picnic area and boat launch on the north shore (just east of County 4) is a handy takeout. The reservoir is big, though, and it's best to keep an eye on the weather before canoeing into open water.

Because the upper river is characterized by so many steep, rocky stretches, medium to heavy stream flow is necessary for an enjoyable run. During summer, the rapids may be runnable only after heavy rains. Stream flow usually peaks in late April, decreases during summer, and rises again during fall rains. When the bridge gauge south of Brimson reads

51

below 3.5, many of the upper Cloquet's rapids will be too rocky to run.

The lower Cloquet, from Island Lake Reservoir to the St. Louis River, is easier to canoe. Although there are many rocky Class I rapids, waves are small and navigation is not too difficult, the only exception being a steep Class II drop near the confluence with the St. Louis River. Stream flow is controlled by discharges from Minnesota Power's dam on Island Lake Reservoir. When the river is extremely high, the rapids become more difficult. To get more information about releases, call Minnesota Power's System Dispatch at 218-722-2641 (ext. 2602). You can also get water level information from the DNR in St. Paul or at the DNR's Grand Rapids office at 218-327-1709.

The lower Cloquet River is not quite as wild as the upper. The forests are similar, but you'll pass under more bridges and notice some buildings and farmland. In spite of these signs of civilization, the route is mostly primitive and requires careful preparation. When on a relatively inaccessible river like the Cloquet, experienced canoeists let someone know their itinerary.

Because of its isolated nature, the river valley supports an abundance of wildlife. Great blue herons are common sights, but you might also hear the drumming of a ruffed grouse, or spot a moose browsing in a backwater or a bear along the bank. There are timber wolves, bald eagles and otters here too, though they aren't common. Northerns and walleyes are the primary game fish on the Cloquet, though some canoeists like to try for smallmouth bass. Brook trout lurk in the colder headwaters and tributaries of the upper Cloquet; brown trout (also near cold-water tributaries) and channel catfish inhabit the lower Cloquet.

Besides the Cloquet Valley State Forest, regional side trips could include Jay Cooke and Savanna Portage state parks, plus the parks and attractions of the North Shore. You can continue your canoe trip on the St. Louis River Canoe Route as far as Cloquet. The river is too shallow and rocky below that point.

Before European exploration, the Cloquet River valley was the home of the Dakota tribe. As the Ojibway Indians were pushed westward by the whites, they in turn pushed the Dakota out of the forests to the prairies. After the Ojibway

Indians ceded their land in 1854, railroads and lumber inspired rapid settlement. Logging camps sprouted on the riverbanks, and dams and sawmills were built. The names of some of the Cloquet River rapids, such as Dry Foot Brown's, McCabe's, and Camp G, recall the lumber days in this valley. One of the rapids is named for J. C. "Buzz" Ryan, district ranger of the Cloquet Valley State Forest for more than 40 years.

FRANZ JEVNE
STATE PARK

Koochiching County. Just east of Birchdale on Highway 11. Highway map index: H-4.

Perched along the Canadian border, little Franz Jevne State Park offers a picture-window view of Ontario across the Rainy River. Fishing and canoeing attract most visitors to the park, and you can hike for a mile along the river. Franz Jevne has 10 rustic campsites, interspersed among the trees that cloak the riverbank.

GEORGE H. CROSBY-MANITOU STATE PARK

Lake County. On County 7, 8 miles northeast of Finland. Highway map index: O-8.

Trails are arduous and camping is for backpackers only at George H. Crosby-Manitou State Park. Minnesota's most primitive park flanks the untamed Manitou River in one of the deepest gorges on the North Shore.

Of the park's 21 backpack sites, 16 are stretched along the length of the Manitou River, while the rest are spaced around Bensen Lake. Not all of the sites are on the water; two at Bensen Lake are a short distance into the forest, and several are uphill from the Manitou River. One of the latter has a hilltop view of Lake Superior and the Wisconsin shore (on clear days). Campers work harder at these sites, however, having to tote water from the river or lake. Drinking water is available only at the park office, so campers must boil or treat the water they draw from Bensen Lake or the river.

The sites are popular among backpackers. The only sounds are wind and water and the occasional howl of a timber wolf. Most of the sites are separated enough that you probably won't notice other campers. Some sites have several tent pads that can accommodate up to 14 campers, and primitive toilets are provided at each camping area. Garbage cans are located only at the trailhead parking lot and at the park office. The smell of garbage and food attracts bears. To discourage unwanted guests, hang your food on the poles provided and pack out all trash. The nights can get cold at Crosby-Manitou when cool breezes off Lake Superior whistle up the river valley.

If you'd like to just hike or picnic here, several private and public campgrounds are located within 10 to 20 miles of the park. Day visitors can fill their canteens at the park office. There is a small walk-in picnic area on Bensen Lake next to the boat/canoe landing. If you like to fish, there are brook trout and splake in the lake, and brown, rainbow and brook trout in the Manitou River. No motors are permitted on the lake. There is no direct access to Lake Superior in the park, but boat landings are located in Silver Bay and Schroeder.

The 23 miles of foot trails at Crosby-Manitou pass through hilly, rocky terrain covered by forests of maple, birch and evergreens. The paths are steep in many places and the loops are designed for long walks by experienced hikers. The hiking is difficult in spots, so plan to set a leisurely pace. The trail around Bensen Lake is the shortest, easiest path in the park.

The busiest trail follows the Manitou River, linking most of the backpack sites. Watch for thick-trunked white cedars on this route. Within the park, the river falls 100 feet in a series of cascades. Take the Humpback Trail toward campsite No. 2 for the best view of the waterfalls. Between Highway 61 and Lake Superior, the Manitou River cuts through a steep gorge before dropping into the lake. There is no public access to the lower river.

A few side spurs lead up to hilltops where you can see the energetic river as it tumbles down to Lake Superior. From atop Crosby Hill, I watched a squall blow inland from Lake Superior, streaking the gray-black sky with rain. Afterward, a lone sea gull drifted up the valley, darting and diving in the wind currents. The brief shower left a fresh smell in the air and added a luster to the thick, green foliage of the valley.

The uplands of the North Shore were partially formed by thick layers of lava that poured from ancient volcanoes. These flows are visible today in the rock outcrops that line the waterfall gorges along the Lake Superior coast. Arctic glaciers later crept over the land, gouging and dislodging the rock. As the last glacier melted, it formed an ancestor of Lake Superior. The Manitou River flows through a valley that glacier meltwater helped to form.

When the Indians lived here, woodland caribou were plentiful, but the animals later disappeared as heavy logging destroyed their habitat. Ironically, logging and fires have resulted in an abundance of wildlife in the park. The new growth that has sprouted since the logging era provides excellent food and shelter for deer herds. As the number of deer increased, so did the population of their main predator, the timber wolf. Hikers occasionally find deer kills in the park. Moose are also common in the forests of northeastern Minnesota. They are strong and can be dangerous, but they seldom attack.

The region surrounding George H. Crosby-Manitou State Park is loaded with public trails, campgrounds and trout streams. Tettegouche and Temperance River, nearby state parks, both have trout streams. Caribou Falls State Wayside also has a popular trout stream and a waterfall a mile upstream from Highway 61, but there are no developed facilities. You'll find primitive campgrounds and a network of trails in the Superior National Forest and Finland State Forest.

Because many people are lured by the backcountry experience that Crosby-Manitou offers, it's a good idea to reserve a site on the weekends. Call the state parks reservation number to reserve a site, then call the Tettegouche State Park manager (who also manages Crosby-Manitou) within 10 days of your arrival. Tell the manager how far into the park you wish to hike and an appropriate site will be designated for you. Midweek visitors may not need reservations.

Winter

The 11 miles of narrow, rugged cross-country ski trails at Crosby-Manitou State Park are designed primarily for intermediate and advanced skiers. All other trails can be snowshoed or hiked. Water is available at the office for winter campers and trail users. Ice fishing is permitted on Bensen Lake.

If you're lucky (depending on your perspective), you might experience the hushed beauty of a North Shore snowfall from a valley overlook. This is a feast of the senses: a tingling as big flakes bombard your face, a white wall of wind-driven snow, wet snow spattering against tree trunks and, after a snowfall, the piney scent of the northwoods and the icy blue of Lake Superior against the white/gray/green winter forest. This is a good time to scout for wildlife or identify their tracks. Deer, for example, gather in a winter yard along the lower Manitou River.

There are no snowmobile trails in the park, but several routes nearby include the Sawtooth Trail, Tolands Red Dot Trail and North Shore State Trail. The Finland State Forest and Superior National Forest both have snowmobile and ski-touring paths.

GOOSEBERRY FALLS STATE PARK

Lake County. About 12 miles northeast of Two Harbors on Highway 61. Highway map index: N-9.

There are five waterfalls in Gooseberry Falls State Park. The most dramatic ones are the Upper and Lower Falls near the Highway 61 bridge. The river tumbles 30 feet over the Upper Falls, glides to the two-tiered Lower Falls and plunges 60 feet into the last pool before spilling into Lake Superior. The Fifth Falls, though scenic, is not as spectacular as the ones near the highway bridge, but because it's about a 1.5-mile one-way hike, it's not as crowded, either. A footbridge near the Fifth Falls allows hikers to return to the parking lot on the other side of the river.

Because the big waterfalls are so close to the road, sightseeing crowds can be as thick as the riverbank trees. Even so, the falls are a "must see" before heading upriver or into the conifer, aspen and birch forests on the 18-mile trail network. You can hike the length of the park along the Gooseberry River or explore the uplands on trails dotted with overlooks. Small trail shelters are scattered along the main paths.

The Gitchi Gummi Trail is a good place to observe the Lower Falls, and it offers ridgetop vistas of Lake Superior as well. On the other side of the gorge, the Lower Rim Trail leads to Agate Beach, at the mouth of the river. Early summer seems to be the prime time to search for agates along the beach. Agates are a type of quartz stone distinguished by bands of color.

Besides beachcombing, shore fishing for trout and salmon is a popular pastime in the park. Brook, brown and rainbow trout are taken farther upstream, but check with the manager about special trout regulations on the North Shore before wetting your line. If you'd like to try some deepwater sport fishing, charter service and boat landings are located in Two Harbors. Swimming is not permitted in the park. Although the Gooseberry is not always the furious, thundering river that it becomes following heavy rains, it deserves respect at all times. More than one swimmer has drowned after underestimating its powerful currents.

The inhospitable shoreline of Lake Superior in Minnesota was born from volcanoes 700 million years ago. Lava flowed over older formations and formed bedrock. You can see hardened lava along the lakeshore (south of the river) and at the Upper and Lower Falls. After the volcanic activity, glaciers advanced and retreated over Minnesota, sculpting Lake Superior's basin and most of the landforms that we see today.

Scuba divers sometimes use Gooseberry Falls State Park as a base of operations for underwater explorations of the lake. Many ships have sunk along the Lake Superior shoreline, though none are in park waters. Some divers just like to snoop around, looking for lost fishing lures and other submerged treasure. Split Rock Lighthouse, a state park and historic site just northeast of the park, was constructed to help ships safely sail along the dangerous coast. Exhibits at the lighthouse give further details about local shipwrecks and how the lighthouse was built.

The 72-site semi-modern campground is close enough to both the lake and river that the water sounds might lull you to sleep. The group camp, along the river above the Upper Falls, is also blessed with a constant chorus of rushing water. The campground is usually full on summer weekends, and it may even be packed on week nights. Highway 61 (North Shore Drive) is a nationally famous scenic route and Gooseberry is the first state park along the way, so if you don't have camping reservations, plan to arrive early. Bicyclists and backpackers sometimes like to set up in one of the walk-in sites near the main campground. Fall camping is less crowded here, but the weather is unpredictable.

The interpretive center, on the east side of the river just across the Highway 61 bridge, is the starting point for some naturalist programs. The center also houses a bookstore and several exhibits. The outdoor amphitheater is next to one of the picnic area shelters, behind the campground. Programs range from guided hikes that focus on birds or plants to rock and mineral identification at Agate Beach. One program recalls the lasting work of the Civilian Conservation Corps (CCC) at Gooseberry State Park in the 1930s. The Corps built the park's stone buildings and laid out the campground, picnic areas, and trails.

Winter

About 14 miles of cross-country ski trails to suit all tastes
help to make Gooseberry State Park busy year round. The
Two Harbors City Trail provides an additional 9 miles of
beginner to intermediate ski trails within a short distance of
the park.

Snowshoeing and hiking are permitted throughout the
park. Campers have a specially designated winter camping
area with drinking water available. A warming house is open
for everybody.

Snowmobiling at Gooseberry is limited to a relatively short
trail that starts at the interpretive center. This trail connects to
the North Shore State Trail, which stretches for 150 miles
from Duluth to Grand Marais and links with many local
Grant-in-Aid trails.

GRAND PORTAGE NATIONAL MONUMENT

Cook County. 36 miles northeast of Grand Marais on Highway 61. Highway map index: S-6.

No county or state fair could compare to the color, smells and sounds of celebration at the late-18th-century fur trade rendezvous at Grand Portage. Its collection of characters, including Ojibway Indians, voyageurs, and North West Company partners, would gather yearly in mid-July for an intense two-week marathon of business and pleasure along the shore of Lake Superior.

From 1784 to 1803, Grand Portage was the largest post within hundreds of miles. With 16 wooden buildings clustered inside a palisade, the station served as business office, marketplace, fur depot, and living quarters. This was the site of the rendezvous, eagerly awaited during the dreary winter months by everyone connected with the company.

Grand Portage was the linchpin in a 3,000-mile water trade route that stretched from Montreal, capital city of the Great Lakes fur trade, to Lake Athabaska in northwestern Canada. Beaver and other fur-bearing animals were the currency that fueled this vast trade network. The demand for fur stemmed from European fashion at the time, particularly for elegant hats.

Where streams were unnavigable, canoemen carried boats and cargo over a "portage," or trail. Christened by French explorers and missionaries sometime after 1722, Grand Portage was "the Great Carrying Place," an 8.5-mile forest path that bypassed rapids, gorges and waterfalls on the lower Pigeon River and was the main throughway to Canada's prime fur country.

In 1784, it became the inland headquarters of the North West Company, an association of Highland Scots and other independent traders headed by Simon McTavish and his partners. After the Great Lakes region passed into British domain following the French and Indian War, the route over the Grand Portage was inherited by the company, which hired a backwoods navy of voyageurs to transport furs.

Grand Portage, at the mouth of the Pigeon River on Lake

Superior, was a convenient meeting place for the voyageurs. Because of the vast continental distances involved, the voyageurs evolved into two groups: the north men, or "winterers," and the Montreal men, also called "pork-eaters."

Following the rendezvous, the north men set out from Grand Portage for the isolated trading posts in the northern Canadian wilderness. The trade goods they carried, including wool blankets, kettles, axes, firearms, traps, and liquor, were bartered for the furs that Indian trappers had gathered. With the breakup of the ice in mid-May, the north men began the two-month journey back to the Grand Portage rendezvous with their bounty of furs. The north canoes ("canots du nord"), designed to navigate on narrow, rapid water, were about 26 feet long and carried from four to six voyageurs.

The Indians that the north men dealt with were expert canoeists and hunters. Tribesmen taught the voyageurs to fashion canoes from birch bark and guided them along the age-old water routes into the wilderness. Many north men, who spent most of the year living with the native people, married Indian women.

As the north men began their trek eastward to Grand Portage in the spring, the Montrealers propelled their craft up the Ottawa River, then westward across the Great Lakes to meet their counterparts for the rendezvous at Grand Portage. The "pork-eaters" paddled 36-foot birchbark canoes that could carry 4 tons of freight and 8 to 16 men. These large lake canoes were called "canots du maitre" (master canoes), perhaps referring to the company partners who were also canoemen and often accompanied the voyageurs. Washington Irving described these partners as "lords of the lakes and forests." At Grand Portage, the Montrealers unloaded their trade goods, exchanging them for the furs they would haul back to Montreal after the rendezvous for shipment to European markets.

Hundreds of voyageurs spent the better part of July camped outside the stockade at Grand Portage. "The North men live under tents," wrote explorer Alexander Mackenzie, himself a North West Company partner, "but the more frugal pork-eater lodges beneath his canoe." Food was plentiful and liquor flowed freely. Many voyageurs spent the wages they had just earned for the past year's work on the spot. Friends were reunited. Fistfights and brawls exploded as longstanding rivalries flared.

On the final night of the rendezvous, the partners and their invited guests feasted and danced in the Great Hall. Outside, the voyageurs and Indians staged a celebration of their own, the local Ojibway in their ceremonial dress and the canoemen sporting their trademark plumed caps, bright wool jackets, and fringed sashes. Festivities continued until daybreak. Soon the north men and pork-eaters parted ways and paddled off into another season, hoping to finish their journey before freeze-up.

This cycle continued until 1803, when the company, trying to avoid American taxation, licensing, and citizenship, moved north and established a new post at Fort William (near present-day Thunder Bay, Ontario). The buildings at Grand Portage and Fort Charlotte, the western station of the portage trail, were abandoned and foot traffic disappeared.

Today, Grand Portage is a national monument with a reconstructed stockade and buildings (open from mid-May to mid-October; small entrance fee). Visitors can tour the Great Hall and nearby kitchen. Ask to see the 12-minute "Northwest Passage" film shown in the Great Hall. In the stockade yard, you can see a fur press that converted the bulky furs into easily handled cargo. Sixty beaver pelts, wrapped in burlap or cotton, were compacted and tied into a neat 90-pound bale. Climb the lookout tower for a view of the grounds and Lake Superior. Outside the stockade is the warehouse, which now houses historic items including two authentic birchbark canoes.

You can still experience the excitement of the rendezvous at Grand Portage National Monument. During the second weekend in August each summer, Grand Portage slips back to the late 18th century, as Indians, voyageurs, North West Company partners, and other guests re-create the fur-trade era for a modern-day rendezvous.

Mount Rose, the knoll rising behind the stockade, offers a bird's-eye overview of Lake Superior and the stockade. You can pick up a self-guiding trail leaflet for this half-mile hike at the trailhead (across the road from the parking lot). There is a picnic area near the parking lot. Food and overnight lodging are nearby at the Grand Portage Lodge.

From the dock at Grand Portage National Monument, a boat leaves daily during summer for Isle Royale National Park (Michigan). The park, 22 miles offshore, is visible beyond Hat Point on clear days. Isle Royale is a rocky, forested wilderness that is a favorite of backpackers and hikers. There are more than 200 islands in the Isle Royale archipelago, which stretches for about 50 miles from northeast to southwest and is 9 miles wide at its widest point. Rugged hiking trails, scattered backcountry sites, and a lodge are the only developed areas in the park. For information, contact Isle Royale National Park, 87 N. Ripley St., Houghton, MI 49931.

The Witch Tree, a spiritual symbol and place of reverence for the Ojibway Indians for centuries, stands on Hat Point about 2.5 miles east of the Grand Portage National Monument. Ma-Ni-Do-Gee-Zhi-Gance, or Spirit Little Cedar Tree, rises a few feet above Lake Superior, twisting mysteriously from shoreline rocks. Tobacco and other gifts were placed near the base of the 300- to 400-year-old tree to ensure safe travel around the point.

The life of the voyageurs, though much romanticized, was never easy. In return for adventure and camaraderie, they sacrificed comfort, health and permanent homes. Some drowned in cold, swollen river rapids. Others were disabled after years of shouldering two 90-pound packs at a time over the portages.

The Grand Portage trail was a tough one. It took the voyageurs about 2 1/2 hours to carry their backbreaking packs along the 9-mile portage between the stockade and the company's smaller storage depot at Fort Charlotte on the Pigeon River. Even without packs, that is a challenging pace. Hikers today will experience some of the same conditions that the voyageurs faced 200 years ago—mud, rocks, mosquitoes and flies. A few earthen mounds and depressions mark the site of Fort Charlotte. There's a primitive campsite near the river (campers must register in advance).

The trail bisects the reservation of the Grand Portage Band of Ojibway Indians, who in 1958 donated the land that became the national monument. The Band also cooperated with state, county and local agencies and private individuals in the recent formation of Grand Portage State Park, which highlights Pigeon Falls on the lower Pigeon River. Another nearby North Shore attraction is Judge C.R. Magney State Park, southwest of Grand Portage on Highway 61.

GRAND PORTAGE STATE PARK

Cook County. 42 miles northeast of Grand Marais on Highway 61. Highway map index: S-6.

Ernest Hemingway nicknamed it "the Big Wild." The undeveloped tip of Minnesota's Arrowhead is noted for its thundering waterfalls, wilderness lakes, and deep forests. Moose, bear, timber wolves and deer have plenty of elbow room. Hemingway, who wandered these woods frequently, also loved the region for its spaciousness.

Dakota, Cree, Ojibway and other native people knew that they could traverse this forest wilderness of lakes and streams by following a maze of water routes. When the explorers, missionaries and voyageurs came into this country in the mid-17th century, they asked the Indians to show them the way. During the fur trade era, voyageurs navigated a 3,000-mile water route that stretched from Montreal to Lake Athabasca in northwestern Canada.

When they reached unnavigable streams, canoemen carried boats and cargo over a "portage," or trail. Grand Portage, the "Great Carrying Place," bypassed rapids on a 21-mile section of the lower Pigeon River and was the acknowledged throughway to Canada's prime fur country. The Indians, and later the voyageurs, had worn an 8.5-mile path from the settlement at present-day Grand Portage on Lake Superior to a spot upriver on the Pigeon where they could continue northwest by canoe. Grand Portage, including the stockade settlement and the portage trail, is now a national monument (6 miles southwest of Grand Portage State Park on Highway 61).

Today, the lower Pigeon River attracts travelers because of the very gorges, rapids and waterfalls that the voyageurs struggled to avoid. Up until the early 1990s, the highest, most dramatic waterfall in the state (on the Pigeon River, which forms the U.S.-Canadian border) was inaccessible to the general public. Now, the 120-foot Pigeon Falls, known locally as High Falls, is the focal point of the new 307-acre Grand Portage State Park.

Pigeon Falls commands your attention. From the park

overlooks, you can watch the racing river split into two torrents behind a rock wall on the edge of the precipice. As the water hurtles to the bottom of the rocky gorge, its formidable voice overpowers the other sounds of the aspen/birch forest along the Pigeon River.

In keeping with the untamed nature of the falls and the river, Grand Portage State Park will remain as undeveloped as possible. Currently, the park includes about a mile of frontage on the Pigeon River. You can view the falls and river gorge from several rustic overlooks. Near the beginning of the half-mile trail leading from the parking lot off Highway 61 to the lookout over Pigeon Falls stands the Wolf Birch, Minnesota's largest paper birch. The 67-foot-tall tree is 109 inches around and its crown spans 80 feet. The park is designed for day use only; the nearest public campground is at Judge C.R. Magney State Park, southwest of Grand Portage along Highway 61.

Grand Portage became a state park through an alliance of agencies and individuals. Mark and Joan Strobel were not the first people to envision Pigeon Falls as a state park, but they were the most recent and perhaps the most persistent. Mark first saw the spectacular falls from Middle Falls Provincial Park, which protects the falls on the Canadian side of the river. Using the provincial park as a model of minimal development and preservation of uncluttered beauty, the Strobels got to work advocating a state park on the Minnesota side of the Pigeon River.

The Strobels joined the Minnesota Parks and Trails Council and Foundation in 1985. The council is a non-profit volunteer organization concerned with the establishment, development and protection of parks throughout Minnesota. The group brings parks and trails issues before the DNR and the legislature.

The council approached Lloyd K. Johnson, who owned the land along the U.S. side of the falls, about buying his land for use as a state park. The Grand Portage Band of Minnesota Chippewa, whose reservation surrounded Johnson's land, also was interested in buying it to preserve the falls. In addition, a developer wanted to buy the land for use as a large resort.

Finally, a unique agreement was reached. The council would buy Johnson's land and then sell it to the state for development of a state park. The park planning committee included Cook County citizens, the DNR, the park council and the Band. It was agreed that the Grand Portage Band would officially own the land, and the state DNR would develop and maintain the park.

Grand Portage State Park was dedicated in September of 1990. The persistence of the Strobels and the cooperation of the agencies involved combined to preserve Pigeon Falls forever as part of "the Big Wild."

In 1958, the Grand Portage Band donated the land that is now the Grand Portage National Monument. For an unusual experience, visit the state park around the second weekend in August and plan to attend the annual Rendezvous Days at the national monument. This lively, colorful festival is a re-enactment of the yearly fur-trade-era celebrations that were held at Grand Portage.

HILL ANNEX MINE STATE PARK

Itasca County. Just off Highway 169 in Calumet. Follow the signs to the Hill Annex Mine Clubhouse. Highway map index: J-8.

One of Minnesota's newest parks is a 500-foot-deep hole in the ground. The Hill Annex Mine, listed on the National Register of Historic Places, was one of the nation's largest open-pit mines, generating over 64 million tons of iron ore during its 66-year existence.

Today visitors can experience the immensity of the mine by taking a 90-minute trolley bus tour, which travels over 300 feet down into the pit. The tour is given at regular hours on a daily basis, and there is an admission charge. There are no campsites available in the park.

INTERSTATE STATE PARK

*Chisago County. Park entrance is off Highway 8 at the
southern edge of Taylors Falls along the St. Croix River.
Highway map index: L-15.*

At the point where the smooth-flowing St. Croix River
suddenly plunges over rocks and twists through a narrow,
cliff-lined gorge are two unusual state parks. Both are called
Interstate State Park, formed as a joint venture between
Minnesota and Wisconsin in 1895 to preserve the wild
scenery of the St. Croix Dalles. These were the first interstate
state parks in the United States.

Each state operates its own park but cooperates with the
other by offering complementary services. The Wisconsin
side, for example, has a large campground, while the
Minnesota segment has a small but busy 37-site (22 electric)
semi-modern campground. Wild River and William O'Brien,
two Minnesota state parks that are upriver and downriver
neighbors to Interstate, also feature spacious semi-modern
campgrounds. The Wisconsin park has a guarded swimming
beach, but there is no swimming on the Minnesota side.
Both parks have boat landings (fishing is good for most
game fish, including northern, walleye and smallmouth
bass). Canoes can be rented in Minnesota's park or you can
tour the dalles (the steep precipices that form the walls of
the river valley) on excursion boats that dock at the park's
northern end in Taylors Falls. The St. Croix River is a state-
designated canoe route.

Each park sponsors naturalist-led interpretive programs
designed to help visitors understand the complex forces that
shaped the dalles and the St. Croix River Valley. The
Minnesota park has a visitor center and a small museum. On
the Wisconsin side, the Ice Age Interpretive Center details
the role of glaciers in the park, one of nine units in
Wisconsin's Ice Age Natural Scientific Reserve.

It's not surprising that Minnesota and Wisconsin joined
forces to preserve the craggy dalles. Both states share
backgrounds that are partially reflected in the names that the
Indians gave them: Minnesota, "sky-tinted waters" (from the
Dakota), and Wisconsin, "gathering of the waters" (from the
Ojibway). The states share another distinction. The St. Croix,

which originates in northwestern Wisconsin, in 1968 became one of the first rivers to be designated a National Wild and Scenic River. Headquarters for the St. Croix National Wild and Scenic Riverway (including the Namekagon River in Wisconsin) is located in St. Croix Falls.

The wonders of the dalles and the forces that shaped them have long attracted international study by geologists. They come to see the basalt rock formations formed from the fiery violence of ancient volcanoes and earthquakes. Following the lava flows, great seas washed over the area, depositing sediments that hardened into rock on top of the basalt. More recently, meltwater from receding glaciers roared south, carving out the broad St. Croix River Valley. Only the basalt formations were partially able to withstand the torrent of eroding water, resulting in the beautiful dalles, potholes, and cliffs that we see today.

You can see scores of potholes (one is 60 feet deep) from the short Pothole Trail, which starts from the park's northern parking lot. The 1.25-mile-long River Trail also starts from this parking lot, passing several overlooks on its way to the campground. Curtain Falls Trail begins at the south-side contact station, climbs to the bluff tops where you'll get good views of the river valley, then loops back down to the tunnel under the highway to return to the contact station. The variety of terrain in the park supports a mixture of bottomland forest, hardwood groves, and pine woods. Bald eagles, ospreys and hawks are among the 150 species of birds that have been observed in the park.

The 290-acre park attracts heavy day use from travelers on scenic Highway 8. Most of the crowds concentrate around the southern end of the park, where shore fishing and picnicking are popular. Some naturalist programs are conducted in the enclosed shelter in this area.

Two unusual park activities are rock climbing and kayaking. Climbers scale the basalt cliffs that tower above the river in the narrow dalles. Kayakers run the rapids in the dalles below the highway bridge, practicing rolls and other maneuvers. Only experienced climbers and kayakers should attempt these dangerous sports.

The St. Croix River Valley was home to both Dakota and Ojibway Indians at various times. Daniel Greysolon, Sieur du

Luth, was the first European explorer to travel from Lake Superior down the St. Croix to the Mississippi River. Fur traders later turned this passage into a major transportation route.

Following a century and a half of fur trade, logging became the new economic base for this region. Boom towns grew swiftly throughout the white-pine country, and the new industry attracted lumbermen like W.H.C. Folsom. Folsom, a civic leader and historian, built a Greek Revival-style house overlooking the river valley. This 19th-century house in Taylors Falls (run by the Minnesota Historical Society) is open to the public.

To get the logs to distant sawmills, lumber companies floated them down the St. Croix River each spring from the northern pineries. Occasionally, the churning mass of logs would jam, choked in the narrow, rocky throat of the dalles. The granddaddy of all jams occurred in 1886 when 150 million board feet of logs were stacked like toothpicks for three miles upstream. Two hundred men worked for six weeks to clear the jam, while thousands of tourists lined the riverbanks to witness nature's revenge on the lumbermen.

Winter

Although there is no cross-country skiing at Interstate State Park (Minnesota), you can ski on the Wisconsin side, and at William O'Brien and Wild River state parks in Minnesota. Interstate doesn't have snowmobile trails either, but you can snowmobile on the eastern segment of the Willard Munger State Trail and on various nearby Grant-in- Aid trails.

Camping is permitted in the park during winter, but you'll have to carry your own water. Hiking is allowed throughout the park (trails are not maintained). Interstate's naturalist programs end after Labor Day, but both Wild River and William O'Brien state parks continue their interpretive programs during the winter. Privately owned downhill ski areas are located nearby on both sides of the river.

JAY COOKE STATE PARK

Carlton County. 3 miles east of Carlton on Highway 210.
Highway map index: L-10.

The St. Louis River, which flows through Jay Cooke State Park, has been the connecting link between the upper Mississippi River and Lake Superior for centuries. Like other rivers that spill into Lake Superior, it plunges for several hundred feet down rocky canyons in the space of a few miles, creating impassable falls and rapids. To reach calmer water above these obstacles, the Indians, explorers and fur traders had to portage around them.

The 7-mile-long trail that bypassed the spectacular rocky gorge of the lower St. Louis River was called the Grand Portage. It was a rough trail of steep hills and swamps that began at the foot of the rapids above Fond du Lac and ended near Maple Island. It was divided into 19 pauses (rest stops) spaced one-third to one-half mile apart. To portage the freight, each voyageur carried two or three packs weighing up to 90 pounds each. These were supported by a portage strap, which passed around the voyageur's forehead and reached to the small of his back. Once he reached a pause with his load, the voyageur would jog back to the last stop for more packs. It took an average of three to five days for a crew to complete the Grand Portage, sometimes longer under bad conditions. It was backbreaking labor, and the voyageurs would be plastered with mud and covered with mosquito and fly bites.

Once past the portage, the fur traders paddled up the St. Louis River to the Savanna Portage, another grueling trail (6 miles long) that provided access to the Mississippi River. Or they continued on the St. Louis to Lake Vermilion and the Rainy River. These routes were used for thousands of years by the Indians before explorers and fur traders came from Europe. The Grand Portage was still in use as late as 1870, but a new railroad meant the end of the old passage.

If you want a firsthand look at the portage trail, a portion of it has been renovated for hiking in Jay Cooke State Park. Over 50 miles of foot trails and 10 miles of horseback trails await visitors who want to explore the country that the voyageurs saw. Some trails follow the river while others head into the wooded hills and valleys of the park.

At Jay Cooke, you'll see ash, maple and basswood forests as well as white pine and spruce woods. These forests support a large population of deer as well as black bears, timber wolves and coyotes. Eagles nest along the river; marsh hawks and pileated woodpeckers also inhabit the park.

A swinging bridge is the only access to the trails across the river and is a good spot to see the tangled mass of jagged rock in the St. Louis River bed. The craggy outcrops have been folded and fractured. Heat, pressure and other natural forces have tortured the rock beds so much that the river gorge is a geological curiosity studied by groups from around the country.

The mood of the St. Louis River changes from season to season. At times, the water thunders over the ancient slabs of bedrock; at other times it trickles and splits around rocky outcrops. Oldenburg Point, a popular picnic area with an open shelter, offers good views of the snarled mass of rock.

The other picnic spot is along the St. Louis by the River Inn, an enclosed shelter and visitor center. The River Inn is the gathering place for ecumenical worship services and many of the naturalist programs. The seasonal naturalist is a good source of park background information. On various outings, you might search for wild orchids or learn about the Thomson Pioneer Cemetery (a park historic site). Kids like the displays and "touch boxes" in the River Inn.

The river is not safe for swimming or boating (although it is a state-designated canoe route above Cloquet), but the fishing is good. Brown trout are taken in the St. Louis River (some walleye and northern in slower stretches) and in Otter Creek. Brook trout are found in Silver and Otter creeks. There are two dams on the St. Louis River near the park: the Thomson Dam (near the northwest boundary) and the Fond du Lac Dam (near the northeast boundary).

The park's 80-site (21 electric) semi-modern campground is located across the road from the River Inn. The group camp has two tenting sites with space for 30 people in each. Across the river in the backcountry of the 8,800-acre park are several backpack campsites that require a hike of 2 to 3 miles. Boil your drinking water at these sites to be safe. The main campground is usually busy on summer weekends and can fill quickly. The walk-in sites are becoming more popular with people who discovered the wilder side of the park while hiking and decided to backpack on their next visit.

The park road (Highway 210) is a pretty route for cars and bicycles, but heavy traffic makes biking hazardous at times. Bicyclists will enjoy the paved Willard Munger State Trail that runs from Carlton to West Duluth. The trail provides a scenic and safe biking experience for people of all ages. Maps are available along the trail and at the park office. You can also mountain bike on designated trails in the north part of the park.

Jay Cooke State Park features two unique attractions. One is the North Country National Scenic Trail. This is a 3,200-mile foot path (not yet completed) that stretches from Lake Champlain in New York to Lake Sakakawea in North Dakota, crossing seven northern states along the way. Part of the trail passes through the park.

The other attraction is the National Whitewater Center, on the St. Louis River below the Thomson Dam. The Center sponsors the Champion International Whitewater Series Race in early August each year. This exciting five-race series features top-ranked international slalom racers as well as experienced local paddlers looking to compete against the best. In 1991, more than 160 paddlers from 12 countries gathered in Carlton for the event. To find out more about local white-water races, future volunteer positions, or kayak and canoe courses, contact the University of Minnesota-Duluth Outdoor Program (218-726-7170).

Winter

Jay Cooke State Park has space for long winter hikes or ski outings, and trails to challenge all abilities. The park has 35 miles of designated ski loops and several side spurs that lead to overlooks of the snowy hills and valleys. You'll have to cross the swinging bridge to ski on the trails across the river. Considering the variety of cross-country trails and the distances they cover, you might want to come back again before season's end.

Jay Cooke's 12 miles of snowmobile trails join the Willard Munger State Trail at the north end of the park. There are additional area snowmobile trails in the Fond du Lac and Nemadji state forests. The manager can give further details about local Grant-in-Aid trails.

JUDGE C.R. MAGNEY STATE PARK

Cook County. About 14 miles northeast of Grand Marais on Highway 61. Highway map index: R-6.

As the turbulent Brule River races toward a jutting rock mass on the brink of a waterfall, more than half the stream disappears into a huge pothole. The channel on the east side of the rock drops 50 feet, in two steps, into the gorge below. The western channel pours into the unknown depths of Devil's Kettle. The Kettle, in Judge C. R. Magney State Park, is still a mystery because no one knows where the water re-enters the river.

The 1.25-mile hiking trail that follows the frothy white water of the Brule upstream to Devil's Kettle passes the Lower and Upper Falls along the way. Two picnic areas straddle the lower Brule, connected by a footbridge that is next to the trailhead parking lot.

You'll hear the thunder of tumbling water through the conifer forest before the trail splits. To the left, the trail leads to Lower Falls. Veer right to continue to Upper Falls, a 15-foot drop. A continuous cloud of mist keeps the gorge walls moist. Morning hikers may see a rainbow through the vapor. About a quarter-mile farther upstream is the Devil's Kettle. You can look into the Kettle from a platform that juts into the river below the falls. On the hike back downriver, Lake Superior beckons like a blue jewel through the trees.

The Brule River, originating in Brule Lake, flows for about 6 miles through the park before spilling peacefully into Lake Superior. Trout anglers often hike upstream above the falls on unmaintained trails to try for brook or rainbow trout. The steelhead trout spawning run in the spring and the salmon run in the fall provide excellent fishing opportunities. The nearest Lake Superior accesses are in Hovland and Grand Marais. In May, the swollen Brule lures expert white-water kayakers to the park. The water is high and dangerous, though, with several portages required. Check with the manager beforehand for current conditions.

The aspen, birch, maple and conifer forests that flank the Brule River provide good cover for timber wolves, moose, black bear, deer and porcupine. Bobcat and lynx also inhabit northeastern Minnesota, but are rarely seen. During summer, be prepared for the mosquitoes: Cover exposed skin and use repellent. Watch out for the bandit chipmunks that blatantly steal from picnic tables and won't take no for an answer.

Each of the 36 rustic sites in the campground is surrounded by trees. The peaceful, wooded setting appeals to a variety of campers. The campground fills often during the summer and into the fall color season, attracting travelers headed to and from Canada.

You might come across some old foundations in the campground. These were part of the Grover Conzet Work Camp of the 1930s, a project that began during the Great Depression. The men who lived here worked on many forest projects.

When the land was designated a park in 1957, it was called Bois Brule State Park. In 1963, the state legislature changed the park's name to Judge C.R. Magney State Park as a memorial to the former state supreme court justice and conservationist who helped establish many of the state parks and waysides along the North Shore. Magney realized that much of the North Shore would be privately developed one day, but visualized the parks as becoming "every man's country estate."

Winter

Judge C. R. Magney State Park is relatively quiet during the winter. Cross-country skiers can explore the forest on 5 miles of trails. Hiking and snowshoeing are other ways to experience Magney during the winter (there are no snowmobile trails in the park). Campers should check with the manager when they arrive to find out about getting water. A hike upriver to the waterfalls and Devil's Kettle will be rewarded with the sight of fanciful, surrealistic ice sculptures.

KETTLE RIVER CANOE & BOATING ROUTE

Carlton and Pine counties. 55 miles, from Highway 27 near Moose Lake to the St. Croix River.

Mention the Kettle River to white-water canoeists and their eyes light up at the thought of the Banning Rapids, a collection of challenging, frothy drops with picturesque names like Blueberry Slide, Mother's Delight, Dragon's Tooth, and Hell's Gate. This river is known for its wild scenery, hundred-foot bluffs, rugged sandstone cliffs and dense woods.

The Kettle is classed as one of Minnesota's wild and scenic rivers, but there was a time when it was not so pristine. In the late 1800s the mature forests of white and red pine along its route were cut down. The land was mined for sandstone and copper, and the river was dammed for electricity and sawmills.

Today, the Kettle River has regained some of its wilderness character, even though it is within 100 miles of the Twin Cities. You'll pass towns, farms and bridges on the upper stretches, but most of the river is bounded by hardwoods mixed with small stands of conifers.

Deer are commonly spotted from the river, although black bear, bobcat and other forest mammals share the tree cover. Beaver, muskrat and otter are occasionally sighted along the Kettle's course. Several species of duck and some Canada geese nest near the river.

The Kettle River reacts swiftly to heavy rain. The fluctuating water level means that rapids that are runnable today might be dangerous following a storm. If the Highway 48 bridge gauge reads above 4.5 feet and the Highway 23 gauge reads above 1 foot, then most of the Kettle rapids are canoeable. Except for a few quiet stretches, most of the river is usually too shallow to canoe by late summer.

The Highway 23 gauge is the one to read before running the Banning Rapids. Don't overestimate your white-water ability—these rapids are forceful and perilous, with waves that can rear up as high as the gauge reading. If you'd like to bypass the rapids or scout them before running, take the 1.5-mile portage trail on the left bank.

Most of the pitches in the Banning Rapids vary in difficulty from Class II to Class IV, depending on low, moderate or high water. Experienced white-water lovers prefer the maneuverability of kayaks on these rapids, although some use open canoes stuffed with flotation devices when the water level is lower. April is usually the peak month for high water flow in the Banning Rapids. Consult the DNR's canoe route map or *A Gathering of Waters,* a guide to Minnesota's rivers, for tips about the specific rapids.

Just after Hell's Gate rapids, Wolf Creek joins the Kettle River on the right bank. Follow the creek into the woods about 100 yards to see a pretty 10-foot waterfall. A mile below Wolf Creek is the town of Sandstone and an access in Robinson Park. This city campground and picnic area also features remnants of some sandstone quarries.

The last 6.5 miles of the route is known as the Lower Kettle River Rapids, a series of long boulder-bed pitches. They are impassable in low water (below 4.5 feet on the Highway 48 bridge gauge) and are rated Class I or II in high water. As the water level rises, some boulders are covered, making navigation a bit easier. This holds true for up to about 10 feet on the gauge. Above that level, water plunging over rocks forms 3-foot backrollers that can swamp a canoe. When the river is this high, the lower rapids are rated Class III.

The Kettle River flows through or near many public land units. Moose Lake State Recreation Area and General C. C. Andrews State Forest are both near the upper Kettle. Banning State Park (straddling the famous rapids), Sandstone National Wildlife Refuge and the Kettle River Scientific and Natural Area border the middle stretch of the river.

The Lower Kettle River Rapids drop through St. Croix State Park and the Chengwatana State Forest, crossing the Willard Munger State Trail. You can switch from white-water to quiet-water canoeing by continuing downstream from the Kettle onto the St. Croix River, which is both a state canoe route and a National Scenic Riverway.

LITTLE FORK RIVER CANOE & BOATING ROUTE

St. Louis and Koochiching counties. 140 miles, from the town of Cook to the Rainy River on the Canadian border.

The wilderness canoeing on the Little Fork River enhances Minnesota's reputation as a canoeist's dream. Though the upper and lower thirds of the route are punctuated by bridges, homes and farmland, the middle stretch (more than 40 miles long) is true wild country. Because of its primitive character and numerous rapids, the Little Fork is best suited for experienced canoeists.

Most of the Little Fork's rapids are encountered on the upper river. With the exception of Hannine Falls (Class VI), these rapids vary in difficulty from Class I to Class II. Hannine Falls (River Mile 121) is a jagged, sloping 15-foot drop followed by 150 yards of Class II rapids. Portage the falls.

The first middle-river rapids drops into the Nett Lake Indian Reservation. You'll need a permit from the Reservation Conservation Office to fish, hunt or camp on reservation land. Below the reservation are Seller's (RM 72.8) and Deadman's (RM 65) rapids. Seller's Rapids is a quarter-mile of Class II boulder bed; Deadman's (much easier than it sounds) is also rated Class II. Both of these rapids are easier to run in high water. The largest lower-river rapids, called Flat Rock, is a Class II pitch about 9 miles above the town of Little Fork.

The Little Fork River can rise swiftly following heavy rains. It is canoeable for most of the summer, but some rapids are unrunnable during low water periods. Stream flow peaks in April and decreases all summer, but rises again during late season rains. It's best to check current conditions before pushing off downstream. High water washes out some Class I rapids, but can form large standing waves in others. Scout each rapids ahead of time and portage when necessary. Unfortunately, many rapids have undeveloped portages.

The pocket DNR river map is a handy in-canoe guide for

the Little Fork. The guidebook *A Gathering of Waters* also has good background information about this route and all of the state's designated canoe trails. Although these sources are carefully prepared, some hazards may have been omitted. Check with local DNR personnel or the outfitters in Cook and International Falls for details.

The banks of the Little Fork support dense growths of pine, spruce, fir, aspen and birch. Thick cedar trees tower overhead as you paddle near the Valley River confluence. The high clay banks in this stretch sometimes break free because of erosion, sliding into the river with trees still upright. Farther downriver, the pine forest turns into hardwoods and then gradually (around Littlefork) into farm country.

Wildlife thrives in the Little Fork River Valley. Moose like the marshes and swamps, while deer browse around farm fields. Black bears and timber wolves roam the forests, though it's unlikely that you'll see any. You might spot beaver and muskrat in the tributaries and backwaters, plus several kinds of ducks.

Bring along your fishing gear and you may land a muskie, northern, walleye or smallmouth bass. Trout have been caught in some stretches of the river and in its tributaries. The water has a cloudy appearance in sections because of suspended clay and other solids. You'll have to carry your own water or disinfect and filter the river water.

Dakota and Ojibway Indians are the most recent native people to live in this region. A Middle Woodland people, the Laurel Indians, built a huge burial mound near where the Big Fork River meets the Rainy River. Grand Mound, the largest prehistoric burial mound in Minnesota, is operated as a historic site (with an informative visitor center) by the Minnesota Historical Society. The site is 17 miles west of International Falls on State Highway 11.

State parks near the upper Little Fork River include Bear Head Lake, McCarthy Beach and Soudan Underground Mine. Nearby state trails are the Big Fork and Vermilion River canoe routes and the Taconite State Trail.

McCARTHY BEACH STATE PARK

St. Louis County. On County 5, about 20 miles northwest of Hibbing. Highway map index: K-7.

McCarthy Beach State Park covers 2,500 acres, but most visitors get only as far as the shoreline, picnic area and campground on the narrow isthmus between Sturgeon and Side lakes. About 18 miles of trails wind through the forested ridgetops and valleys of the park, terrain well worth exploring for its abundant wildlife. More than 175 species of birds and three dozen species of mammals live in or near the park.

The campground here can fill daily from mid-June to mid-August with visitors who come for fishing and sunny afternoons on the beach. The main campground, on Side Lake, offers 45 semi-modern sites and one loop with 14 rustic sites.

MOOSE LAKE STATE PARK

Carlton County. One mile east of I-35 at the Moose Lake exit. Park entrance is off County 137. Highway map index: L-11.

The 1,200-acre Moose Lake Park attracts both vacationers passing through and those who return for the intimate atmosphere. All the park's development is wrapped around one section of three-armed Echo Lake. Though the campground is small and lacks a shower building, plans call for new sanitation facilities that will upgrade its classification from rustic to semi-modern. A trail swings from the campground down to the lake and around one of the arms to the day-use area. Visitors can enjoy a shoreline picnic on Echo Lake or a leisurely afternoon on the swimming beach.

Canoes and boats launch onto Echo Lake from the park's

landing. Northern, sunfish and largemouth bass are the most common catches. The T-shaped lake is ideal for canoeists, who can enjoy a lazy afternoon paddling along the shoreline. If you don't have a boat or canoe for fishing or exploring, you can rent one in the park. Dawn and dusk are good times to scout for wildlife along the shore. Deer and even black bear are occasionally spotted. Birds that have been observed at Moose Lake include bobolinks, bluebirds, swallows and eastern kingbirds.

The community of Moose Lake is a popular year-round vacation destination. Water-skiers and anglers can launch onto Moosehead Lake from a landing in town. Moose Lake State Park borders this lake, but there is no developed access from the park.

Winter

Moose Lake State Park maintains over six miles of beginning to intermediate cross-country ski trails. The park's four miles of snowmobile trails connect to several local trail systems. One of the park's snowmobile routes heads east toward Nemadji State Forest. Park routes also link with the Moose Lake Trail, a network of more than 100 miles of groomed trails with accesses in Moose Lake, Barnum, Iverson and Mahtowa. This system, in turn, links with the Willard Munger State Trail and the Aitkin County trails.

You can camp year-round at Moose Lake (water is available). Ice fishing attracts cold-weather anglers, who try for panfish and northern.

NORTH SHORE STATE TRAIL

St. Louis, Lake and Cook counties. 153 miles, from Duluth to Grand Marais (with expansion plans up to the Canadian border).

If being "away from it all" means the absence of crowds, towns and routine, then the North Shore State Trail is worth a trip. Ninety-five percent of the trail traverses public land. And much of that land is remote enough that it's wise to carry a compass, map, food and water, and extra clothing.

Other precautions on this multi-use trail include common-sense ideas, like telling someone where you are going and when you plan to get back. Or packing along repellent and covering exposed skin during insect season. Snowmobilers already know the importance of planning ahead and of staying warm. Staying on-trail is important, too, because landmarks are few and the forest is great along the corridor (the trail is marked by orange blazes, directional arrows and State Trail signs).

Keep these cautions in perspective, though; they are the same no matter where you wander in wild country. If you are prepared for an outback experience, then your trek on the North Shore Trail will be enjoyable and safe.

For most of the trail, you'll be in the Arrowhead's backcountry. The surrounding area includes some development and logging activity, but the great majority of the route is "natural." The North Shore Trail twists through the forests beyond the bluffs that overlook Lake Superior, and provides access to some of the most rugged and beautiful scenery in Minnesota. Trail parking lots are spaced along the corridor, where forest roads cross the route. Trail-side shelters and campsites (14 of them) make it easier to plan backpack trips or to pause for a picnic break.

Though you can hike or horseback ride anywhere on the trail during summer or fall, some sections are wet, which makes for hard travel. The 70-mile segment from the town of Finland to Cook County Road 6 (north of Grand Marais) is usually in good shape for hiking or riding. The trail is also hikeable from the Martin Road parking lot in Duluth to the parking lot on the French River, about a 14-mile stretch. In addition to the shelter/campsites, you can camp on adjacent public land except where posted.

Wildlife sightings are frequent. You never know what will cross the trail through the woods or in the air. You might spot moose, deer, bear, fox, raptors, waterfowl, song birds and possibly timber wolves. Overviews of rivers, lakes and valleys are common. During fall, the maple-covered ridges catch fire in red, orange and yellow.

The North Shore State Trail is a favorite of anglers who walk in to remote, lightly used trout streams. Hunters also take advantage of the access to the backwoods. Snowmobiles are the only off-road vehicles allowed on the trail. The corridor is groomed weekly along its entire length.

If you'd like to find out more about the past and present of the North Shore, stop at the state park or forest offices, or at local information centers along your route. The North Shore State Trail is too long to appreciate in a fast trip, so be flexible enough to change plans if you'd like to try a side jaunt. Always check ahead for trail conditions before snowmobiling or hiking.

RICE LAKE NATIONAL WILDLIFE REFUGE

Aitkin County. Includes 3 units: Rice Lake NWR (18,104 acres), Mille Lacs NWR (.5 acres), and Sandstone NWR (2,045 acres in Pine County). Refuge entrance is about 5 miles south of McGregor off Highway 65.

As the leaves begin to change color in early September, the old ways meet modern times at Rice Lake National Wildlife Refuge. Local Ojibway Indians harvest a portion of the wild rice crop from Rice Lake, using the traditional methods of those who came before them.

There is a rhythm and respect to this method, as two harvesters push off in a canoe or boat to gather the rice. A standing boatman, or poler, maneuvers the ricing craft. A ricer sits in the front, middle or rear and alternately works each side of the boat. Rice stalks are bent over the boat with a 30-inch ricing stick and gently stroked or tapped with another stick to dislodge ripe grains. Machines are prohibited. This ensures that adequate rice will remain to reseed the lakes and that wildlife can also share in the harvest.

The main area for wild rice on this refuge is the 4,500-acre Rice Lake. About half of the lake has ideal water depth (one to four feet) for wild rice growth. Water levels are controlled by dikes and gates to prevent floodwaters from entering the lake, to provide for water intake during dry summer months, and to release water in autumn. This helps ensure waterfowl food and cover as well.

The wildlife refuge was established in 1935 to preserve its valuable habitat for waterfowl. The Civilian Conservation Corps (CCC) completed many projects on the refuge during the 1930s and 1940s. Rice Lake covers 25 percent of the 18,000-acre refuge. Water is the key to the refuge's productivity. Rainfall and snowmelt, held behind glacial moraines (ridges) on a flat glacial plain, trap sediment and rotting vegetation. Year after year, the muck gets deeper and vegetation grows more abundant. The refuge is an energy collector: the sun's energy, in the form of decaying plants and animals, accumulates and is stored in the bogs and marshes.

The land's natural water drainage toward the south has been blocked by the glacial ridges. This wet area is slowly filling in with sediment and vegetation, becoming a floating or muskeg bog—a natural haven for wildlife. The bog lands are flat expanses of poorly drained organic soils, known as peat. They support a dense, spongy mixture of flowering plants, grasses, low shrubs and small stands of black spruce, balsam fir and tamarack. The peat makes bog soil acidic and tints bog waters a clear amber color.

Shallow lakes with marshy shorelines dot this landscape. The lakes are slowly being taken over by the encroaching bog. Scattered islands and glacial ridges rise above the surrounding bog and are covered with timber and other upland plants. The refuge lies in a transition zone between the coniferous forests of northern Minnesota and the hardwood forests to the south. Quaking aspen is the most plentiful tree species, but you'll also see stands of hard maple, red oak and other mixed hardwoods on the higher ground. Balsam fir, white pine, white cedar, American elm and soft maple are also common.

The Rice River bisects and drains the refuge, flowing from the southeast corner to the northwest, finally emptying into the Mississippi River about 20 miles west of the refuge. Fishing is popular along the Rice River (especially from the river bridge), with northerns providing most of the action. Mandy Lake and Twin Lakes are also open to fishing, but you'll probably have better luck on the river. Boats (no motors) are allowed on refuge fishing areas.

Small game hunting is permitted in a specially designated area on the refuge. You can pick up hunting and fishing leaflets, as well as information about birds, mammals, and wild rice, at the refuge office and entrance kiosk.

Rice Lake NWR is especially noted for its concentrations of ring-necked ducks, which often number over 70,0000 birds during fall migration. The refuge's main nesting species of ducks are mallard, bluewinged teal and wood duck. Canada geese also remain to nest during the summer months.

The mixture of lakes, marshes, forestlands, grasslands and croplands attract a wide variety of other migrant and resident wildlife. Observant visitors might spot deer, black bear, otter, beaver, sandhill crane, bald eagle, grouse (ruffed and sharptail), numerous wading and diving birds, raptors and an occasional moose or gray wolf.

Old logging roads double as hiking trails during summer and cross-country skiing and snowshoeing paths in winter. Snowmobiles, horses and off-road vehicles are not permitted on the refuge. A woodland hiking trail, about three-quarters of a mile long, is adjacent to the Twin Lakes Picnic Area. You can also hike on a 2-mile trail near Mandy Lake. The trails and old logging roads cross nearly every habitat type found on the refuge.

The refuge is open during daylight hours. Restrooms are provided, but no drinking water is available. Swimming and camping are not allowed. You'll find motel lodging in McGregor and public campgrounds at Savanna Portage State Park and near Big Sandy Lake Dam.

Rice Lake NWR hosts a week-long fall open house in mid-October each year. In addition to a 9.5-mile, self-guided auto tour route, several service roads are open to the public. Stop at the office for hiking trail maps and other information.

The refuge administers two proposed National Wilderness Areas. A 1,400-acre unit, located in the southwestern part of the refuge, preserves a typical northern bog area and includes the 6-acre island in Rice Lake. The second area, Mille Lacs National Wildlife Refuge, is composed of Spirit and Hennepin islands. These two small boulder islands, totaling only about half an acre, are protected for their nesting colonies of gulls and terns. Public use on the Sandstone NWR, also administered by Rice Lake NWR, is currently limited to boat fishing on the Kettle River.

ST. CROIX NATIONAL SCENIC RIVERWAY

*Pine, Chisago and Washington counties (Minnesota);
Bayfield, Sawyer, Washburn and Burnett counties
(Wisconsin). 252 miles, from the Namekagon dam (northeast
of Cable, Wisconsin) to the Mississippi River.*

In addition to being a state canoe and boating route (the
Minnesota segment), the St. Croix River is one of the eight
original streams included in the National Wild and Scenic
Rivers System. The St. Croix National Scenic Riverway,
including the Namekagon River of northwestern Wisconsin,
flows through some of the most scenic and undeveloped
country in the upper Midwest. The good news is that even
beginning canoeists can handle most of the river, and it's all
within easy reach of the Twin Cities metropolitan area.

Many St. Croix River trips start on the Namekagon River at
the County K landing (below the Trego dam) in
northwestern Wisconsin. Various outfitters in Minnesota and
Wisconsin will shuttle canoeists and gear to this access or
farther upriver. Canoeists get a backcountry experience on
the Namekagon because there is little development visible
from the river. The Namekagon flows for about 100 miles
before meeting the St. Croix River 6.5 miles upstream from
the Minnesota-Wisconsin border.

The St. Croix rises at Solon Springs, Wisconsin, becomes
the border river above Danbury, and then flows for 140
miles until it merges with the Mississippi River. It is narrow
and shallow until joined by its major tributary, the
Namekagon River. From Danbury to the mouth of the Snake
River, you'll see few signs of civilization as you paddle
through dense second-growth forests and past pine-covered
islands. The majestic red and white pine all but disappeared
during the logging frenzy of the late 19th century.

The Upper St. Croix, from the Namekagon to the St. Croix
Falls dam, is punctuated by several Class I-II rapids. Most of
these are rated Class I and are not difficult. As you canoe to
the lower end of St. Croix State Park (which extends for
more than 20 miles along the Minnesota riverbank), you'll
encounter a 5-mile stretch of rapids above the confluence of

St. Croix
National
Scenic
Riverway
map

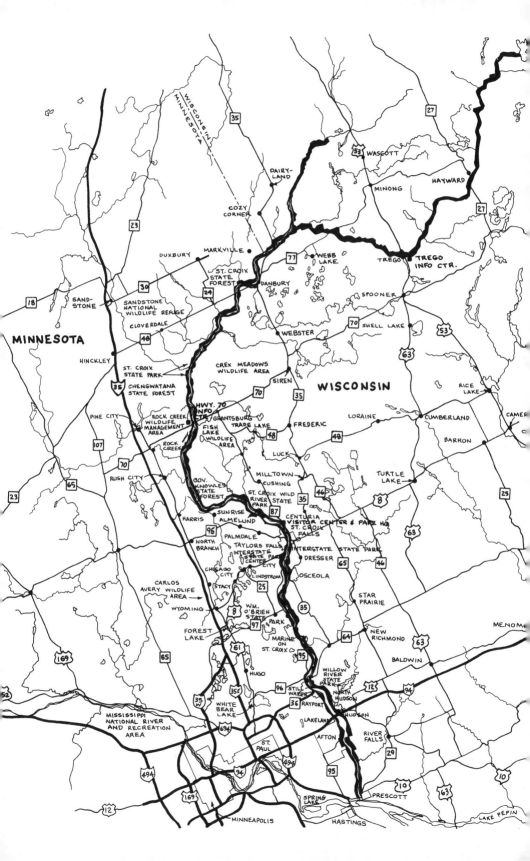

the St. Croix and Kettle rivers. The Kettle River Rapids (RM 110-105) are a series of Class I and II drops interrupted by some wooded islands. The high, cold water of spring makes these pitches even more difficult, though some canoeists avoid the worst sections by keeping close to shore on the wide channel.

The St. Croix quiets down below the mouth of the Kettle River, wrapping around a series of rocky islets. The going is easy from here to the St. Croix Falls dam, which must be portaged. This is the dividing point between the Upper and Lower St. Croix National Scenic Riverway. National Park Service Headquarters is located just above the dam in St. Croix Falls, Wisconsin.

The upper river, formed by draining water from Glacial Lake Duluth, cut a deep, narrow gorge through bedrock to join the lower river at present-day Taylors Falls. This ravine, called the St. Croix Dalles, towers 200 feet above the deep river (average depth here is 70 feet). Pine trees perch on rocky toeholds, and hikers can see 60-foot-deep potholes formed by swirling rocks and gravel. A strong rapids at the start of the dalles rates Class II in low water and a challenging Class IV in high water. Though there are few obstacles here, standing waves from 3 to 5 feet high can swamp an open canoe.

South of the dalles, the St. Croix is a relaxed river with lots of side channels and backwaters. The valley hillsides are heavily wooded, with occasional rocky bluffs poking through. Below the mouth of the Apple River to just above Stillwater is a 7-mile stretch that is full of long, narrow islands where the National Park Service allows camping. Some of these islands, which compose Boomsite Park, were used as sorting stations by lumbermen before sending logs downstream to sawmills.

Near Stillwater, the largest town on the route, the St. Croix widens and deepens into Lake St. Croix. Steep wooded bluffs still border the channel, but many hillside homes contrast with the less settled upper St. Croix. You may see powerboats of all sizes (some towing water-skiers), sailboats, and houseboats. Houseboats reflect the river's easy pace, especially on Lake St. Croix. Fishing is popular along the whole route. The Namekagon is noted for its brown trout, and trout fishing can also be good in some tributaries. The upper reaches of the St. Croix River are frequented by muskie fishermen. Other parts of the river harbor walleye, sauger, northern and crappie, with channel catfish in the lower section.

The riverway retains its wild and scenic character partially because of the public lands that bound it on both sides. On the Minnesota side of the upper river, canoeists pass by the St. Croix and Chengwatana state forests, and St. Croix and Wild River state parks. Interstate State Park, on the lower river at Taylors Falls (and St. Croix Falls in Wisconsin), opened in 1895 as the first interstate park venture in the country. Also on the lower river, on the Minnesota side, are William O'Brien and Afton state parks.

Water-use regulations apply on the lower St. Croix to alleviate conflicts between canoeists, powerboaters and swimmers. There are special no-wake zones, for example, and some rules govern water-skiing and motorboating. Contact the Minnesota DNR or the St. Croix National Scenic Riverway Headquarters for details.

There are many landings and primitive campsites along the riverway. You can also camp in designated sites in the state parks and forests on both sides of the river. Riverway communities offer accommodations and supplies, including commercial canoe outfitters. The St. Croix National Scenic Riverway maintains four visitor centers along the route: Stillwater, Minnesota; Highway 70 on the Minnesota side of the river (5 miles west of Grantsburg, Wisconsin); Trego, Wisconsin; and the headquarters in St. Croix Falls, Wisconsin. Contact one of the visitor centers to get riverway maps and other information.

ST. CROIX STATE PARK

Pine County. 16 miles east of Hinckley on Highway 48. Park headquarters is on County 22, five miles south of the park entrance. Highway map index: L-13.

This is Minnesota's largest state park, so there are many quiet spots in St. Croix's 34,000 acres of elbow room. Yet other spots, like the campground and interpretive center, are bustling. Visitors can hike into the backcountry or stick to developed portions. Though most of the roads are not paved, it's possible to see much of the park from your car. There's vehicle access to the fire tower, landings, campsites and overlooks.

Perhaps the most scenic of the park's 127 miles of hiking trails is in the southwest corner, along the Kettle River. This area is characterized by tree-covered banks that flank the Kettle. St. Croix State Park has 75 miles of bridle paths.

The park's longest trail is the Willard Munger State Trail. Horseback riders and hikers use it during summer, though it is spongy in many sections. North of the park, the Willard Munger forms part of the North Country National Scenic Trail (according to the master plan). This 3,200-mile foot path, not yet completed, will stretch from Lake Champlain in New York to Lake Sakakawea in North Dakota, crossing seven northern states along the way.

Horseback riders can park their rigs overnight in the camping area next to the trail center. Some riders also drive north into the St. Croix State Forest, where the trails are hillier and there is another campground for riders. Primitive camping for riders is also available in the St. Croix and Chengwatana state forests. The flat terrain of St. Croix State Park can be marshy in early summer and after heavy rains, so riders should check with the park manager for current conditions.

A hard-surfaced 6.5-mile trail from Lake Clayton to the campground is designed for bicycle and wheelchair use. I saw a deer while bicycling here, but deer are plentiful everywhere in the park. Overhead, you might see marsh hawks or ospreys, which have good hunting in the St. Croix River valley. Bears are occasionally spotted, but are not common.

The St. Croix River, which forms the park's 21-mile eastern boundary, attracts anglers and canoeists. Fishing can be good for muskies, northern, bass and sauger. Walleyes are taken in the lower Kettle River as well as in the St. Croix. Hay Creek is popular for trout fishing.

Canoeists can choose from three nearby routes. The St. Croix is both a state canoe route and a National Scenic Riverway. The Kettle River (on the park's western edge) and the Snake River (in the Chengwatana Forest, just south of the park) are also state canoe routes. You can rent canoes in the park and make arrangements for shuttle service in the park concession building. There are two canoe landings on the Kettle River and three on the St. Croix. In addition, there's a drive-in boat landing just downhill from the campground.

Lake Clayton, at the south end of Hay Creek, has a guarded swimming beach. A picnic area spreads out through the trees behind the beach, and another picnic area is located above the river near the campground. Bicycle rentals, snacks, gifts and some groceries are available in the concession building near the campground picnic area.

Watch park bulletin boards for schedules of summertime naturalist programs. These include canoe caravans, Indian rope-making lessons, stargazing, and night hikes.

The park has camping facilities befitting its size. There are more than 213 semi-modern sites (42 with electrical hookups) split into numerous loops along the St. Croix River. Even so, the campsites can fill up on weekends. Small playgrounds and game areas are located between the three main campgrounds.

There are a handful of walk-in campsites along the trail at the far end of the campground. Backpackers can hike into sites along Bear Creek and Crooked Creek (register for backpack sites at the park office). Four sites for canoe camping are marked along the Kettle River and eight are located on the St. Croix River.

Group camping at St. Croix State Park is more elaborate than at other state parks because St. Croix has the space to develop large complexes. Three separate group centers in the park feature dining halls, kitchens, cabins, showers, lodges and craft buildings. Swimming is possible at two of them. The centers (St. John's Landing, Norway Point and Head of the Rapids) have a combined capacity of 395. Each is like a little village, complete with administration buildings, staff quarters and infirmaries. Ask the manager about rates, reservations and winter use.

St. Croix State Park also maintains a primitive group camp for up to 200 campers. The modern Guest House, located at Norway Point, can accommodate up to 15 people and is available year-round (reservations are suggested).

Winter

St. Croix State Park's size translates into miles of trails for cross-country skiers and snowmobilers. Eighty miles of snowmobile trails are marked and groomed, including the Willard Munger State Trail, which extends north through the Nemadji State Forest and south to Wild River State Park. Combined with the network of Grant-in-Aid trails, it's possible to snowmobile from Anoka County to Duluth.

Although some skiers also use the Willard Munger State Trail, the park grooms more than 20 miles of cross-country ski loops. These trails are designed for beginning and intermediate skiers. Primitive camping, hiking and snowshoeing are also available at St. Croix. When you need a break, warm up by the fireplace in the chalet, located near the trail center parking lot.

ST. LOUIS RIVER CANOE & BOATING ROUTE

St. Louis and Carlton counties. 90 miles, from Highway 53 (near Forbes) south to Cloquet.

The St. Louis River is diverse enough that experienced and beginning canoeists will enjoy a trip on this route. Although there are frequent boulder-field rapids throughout the river, they are all rated Class I or Class II at normal water levels.

You can put in below the Highway 53 bridge on the upper river and will encounter only a handful of Class I rapids and a dam that must be portaged (RM 84.3). The steep banks on the northern river section support heavy woods of maple, aspen and birch mixed with small stands of conifers.

The middle river from Toivola to Floodwood is slower-paced and wider. You'll notice some farmland interspersed with hardwood forest. There are a couple of campsites about 12 miles apart on this stretch that make it easy to plan a weekend canoe outing with the kids. If you need gear, outfitters are located in Duluth and Virginia.

The rapids between Floodwood and Cloquet are for experienced canoeists only. About two miles below Floodwood there's a long stretch of Class I to Class II rapids that extends to Gowan. The river channel widens again and you'll pass by some 75-foot bluffs covered with hardwoods. The pace is lazy from Gowan to the confluence with the Cloquet River, and there are four campsites spaced along the left bank. Most inexperienced canoeists end their trip at the U.S. Highway 2 access about a mile below the confluence.

About four miles downstream from the Highway 2 access are two stretches of boulder-bed rapids: one is rated Class II-III and the other is Class I-II. These ratings depend on low or high water, but consider them more dangerous during the cold, peak levels of spring runoff.

Once past these drops, the river again calms down as you paddle into the deep pools formed by the dam at Cloquet. The last takeout before the Knife Falls dam is on Dunlap

Island in Cloquet (road access is from Highway 33 or Main Street). The route ends here. Below Cloquet, the river becomes hazardous because of dams and the St. Louis gorge. The gorge, in Jay Cooke State Park, is worth seeing, but not by boat. The best views of the jagged riverbed rock formations and the tumbling stream are from the swinging bridge over the gorge.

Chances are good for spotting some of the wildlife that northeastern Minnesota is noted for while on the St. Louis River: moose, deer, beavers, bald eagles and ospreys. Black bears and timber wolves are occasionally sighted. Walleye and northern are the main game fish caught on the river, though smallmouth bass are common from the mouth of the Whiteface River to Cloquet, and channel catfish are landed from Floodwood to Brookston.

Savanna Portage, McCarthy Beach and Hill Annex Mine are other state parks in the St. Louis River area. Nearby forests include the Superior National Forest and the Cloquet Valley and Savanna state forests. The Cloquet River Canoe Route (a family river in the southern section) empties into the St. Louis River below Brookston.

SAVANNA PORTAGE STATE PARK

Aitkin County. 17 miles northeast of McGregor. Take Highway 65 north of McGregor to County 14 and 36; then follow this road for 10 miles to the park entrance. Highway map index: J-10.

Savanna Portage State Park (Minnesota's third largest) is named for a centuries-old footpath used by Dakota and Ojibway Indians, and later by explorers, missionaries and voyageurs. This trail is a 6-mile-long portage between the East Savanna and the West Savanna River. The Savanna Portage was a vital link between the St. Louis River watershed and that of the Mississippi River on the canoe/fur trade route from Lake Superior to the Upper Mississippi. "Savanna" (open grassland) refers to the marsh grass on the eastern segments of the trail.

Modern voyageurs can still follow this route. The eastern end of the 6-mile trail is best hiked during fall and winter. You can canoe from the West Savanna River (below Little Savanna Lake) to Big Sandy Lake and the expanses of the upper Mississippi River. Ask the manager about the water level on the West Savanna River before attempting this trip.

Canoeing is popular on Loon Lake and Lake Shumway, both of which have drive-in boat landings. You can rent boats or canoes at Loon, Shumway or Savanna lakes. Fishing on the lakes is mostly for northern, bass and panfish (especially crappies). Loon Lake is a stocked trout lake which requires a trout stamp (available locally). Only electric motors are allowed on the park lakes, and speeds are limited to 10 mph. Water-skiers will have to drive to Big Sandy Lake (boat landing is 5 miles from the park).

Loon Lake has an enticing picnic and beach area set among the pine trees that surround the shoreline. Children like to linger on the play equipment on the shady grounds. The changing rooms are located in a beautiful half-timbered building that resembles the other European-style structures in the park.

The 60-site semi-modern campground (16 electric sites) is

located on Lake Shumway. The campground can fill quickly on weekends, so plan to arrive early or call ahead for a reservation. Many campers enjoy fishing from the pier near the campground loops. Some people bring their bikes to Savanna Portage to pedal through the campground and on the park roads. You can also mountain bike on 10 miles of park trails. The primitive group camp is on Savanna Lake.

Backpackers can hike to six primitive campsites within the 15,818-acre park (register at the park office). Some prefer to pack into these sites during autumn, when the hardwoods change color among the conifers.

The Remote Lake Solitude Area of the Savanna State Forest adjoins the park to the west. Interested visitors will find a network of backcountry trails with six shelters spaced along the loops. The trailhead parking lot for the Solitude Area is on the state park entrance road. The Savanna State Forest, which almost surrounds the park, also contains the Floodwood Game Refuge (on the park's northern boundary). As you drive toward the park entrance on County 14-36, you'll pass the state forest Ranger Station and a lookout tower near Big Sandy Lake.

Chances of spotting wildlife are good on the park's 22 miles of trails. Savanna Portage is a combination of rolling hills, lakes and bogs that support a rich variety of animals and birds. Bear, moose, deer and timber wolves are the largest forest residents in the park, but deer are most commonly sighted. Otter, muskrat and beaver live in the wetlands of the park.

Most of the park's trails weave through the hilly country between Loon Lake and Lake Shumway. The Continental Divide Trail starts at Lake Shumway, following the divide up to the park road between Savanna and Wolf lakes. Water to the east of this divide flows into Lake Superior and the Atlantic Ocean. Water on the west side flows into the Mississippi River and the Gulf of Mexico.

Winter

Experienced winter campers can ski-pack into the primitive camping areas. Whether camping or not, you can keep warm by hiking, snowshoeing, or cross-country skiing. Savanna Portage State Park grooms 16 miles of trails for beginner and intermediate skiers. The Remote Lake Solitude

Area also has intermediate ski-touring trail loops.

Snowmobilers have the run of over 60 miles of groomed trails in the park. These paths tie in with Grant-in-Aid trails in Carlton and Aitkin counties. The neighboring Savanna State Forest has about 33 miles of groomed snowmobile trails that link with those in the state park.

SCENIC STATE PARK

*Itasca County. About 7 miles east of Bigfork on County 7.
State highway map index: I-7.*

At Scenic, the indoor interpretive programs (films, discussions, etc.) are held in a beautiful, sturdy lodge on the shores of Coon Lake. The lodge was built during the Great Depression by the Civilian Conservation Corps (CCC). The forest murals were painted by a CCC artist. Outdoor activities include hikes under the park's tall pines, campfire programs and wildflower walks.

There are about 14 types of orchids in the wilds of Scenic State Park. Hikers might see several varieties of lady's slipper, Minnesota's state flower. Some wildflowers, like moccasin flowers, flourish in conifer bogs. The round-leafed sundew, also common in small marshes, works for its food by trapping insects on a drop of adhesive at the ends of its hairs.

Scenic has 14 miles of foot trails that pass through stands of virgin red and white pines. Some trails circle the pine-covered shorelines of Coon and Sandwick lakes and also lead to Pine Lake and Lake of the Isles. Cedar and Tell lakes have no road or foot access. The park also features 5 miles of mountain-bike trails.

The Chase Point Trail, which follows the crest of a narrow, serpentine ridge, is the park's most impressive trail. The skinny, steep ridge marks the position of a former subglacial river. Water flowing in an ice tunnel deposited sand and gravel on its floor, leaving the long ridge, or esker, when the surrounding ice melted. Many of the lakes in the area were also engendered by glaciers. Called kettle lakes, they are water-filled depressions formed by melting ice masses left behind by retreating glaciers.

Besides loons, watch and listen for pileated woodpeckers and songbirds while hiking. Bald eagles, ospreys and hawks can often be seen soaring overhead. Deer are plentiful in the park and can be easily observed by quiet hikers. In the northern section of the park along the backpack trails, campers occasionally report spotting a moose or black bear. On rare nights, the howl of a timber wolf pierces the stillness of the forest.

**Scenic
State
Park's
foot trails
pass
through
stands of
virgin red
and white
pines.**

Scenic State Park caters to most camping tastes. The two main campgrounds have about 120 semi-modern sites (with 20 electrical hookups). The 150-person primitive group camp, with hand pumps and a canoe access, is on Lake of the Isles in the southern end of the park. Ask the park manager how to reserve the Sandwick Chalet, a four-bedroom rental unit overlooking Sandwick Lake.

The 2,900-acre park has 12 backpacking sites. The northern ones, along Pine Lake, have a couple of adirondacks (three-sided shelters) and a nearby hand pump. If you're backpacking or hiking up to Pine Lake from the lodge parking lot, you'll pass a forestry tower, recently reopened.

Canoeists may use six of the lakeshore walk-in sites (some with adirondacks) on Coon and Sandwick lakes for overnight trips. Water must be hauled in or treated; there is no hand pump at these sites. Canoe or backpack groups can reserve a site by contacting the manager ahead of time.

Boat accesses for Coon Lake, which connects with Sandwick Lake, are located near each of the park's two campgrounds. You can rent boats and canoes in the park. Water-skiing is not permitted on either lake and speeds are limited to 10 mph. Fishing is mostly for walleye, northern, bass and panfish. The swimming beach is on Coon Lake near the lodge and northern campground.

Canoeists like the park because they can either "rough it" at the primitive shoreline campsites or enjoy the amenities of a semi-modern site in one of the main campgrounds. Scenic State Park has miles of quiet lakeshore to explore. The lakes are small enough that it's easy to paddle to shore in case a storm brews.

Winter

Campsites with electrical hookups are available for fall sportsmen and winter campers by prior arrangement with the manager. (The campground is not usually plowed unless there is a special request for a site.) You can get water from the hand pumps. Ski-in camping is possible at the park's backpack sites, most of which have adirondacks.

The parking lot by the lodge is used as a winter trailhead. Scenic has over 12 miles of snowmobile trails that connect with local trails to Bigfork and to extensive routes in the

George Washington State Forest. There are other snowmobile trails in McCarthy Beach State Park, the Chippewa National Forest and nearby Big Fork and Koochiching state forests. The towns of Marcell, Bigfork and Effie provide access to miles of Grant-in-Aid trails.

Scenic State Park's 10 miles of cross-country trails are designed for beginner and intermediate skiers. You can circle Coon and Sandwick lakes on skis, using the adirondacks for rest stops. A hand pump is available near the forestry tower north of Coon Lake. The Chase Point Trail is perhaps the most scenic ski path in the park. You can also cross-country ski in George Washington State Forest and McCarthy State Park.

Ice fishing on Scenic's lakes is mostly for northerns (spearing) and crappies. The lodge (with fireplace) stays open all year.

SNAKE RIVER CANOE & BOATING ROUTE

Aitkin, Kanabec and Pine Counties. 85 miles, from Aitkin County 26 to the St. Croix River.

The Snake River has a split personality. From McGrath to Mora, it rumbles and rolls through long stretches of difficult rapids. But between Mora and Pine City, there are few rapids and the pace is gentle enough for beginners.

The upper Snake offers a challenge for experienced white-water enthusiasts as it surges through the Upper Snake River Falls (Class II-III), dropping three feet in 50 yards. About a mile downstream, the river tumbles 20 feet in three-quarters of a mile at the Lower Snake River Falls (Class III-IV). Scout the rapids from the marked portages before running them if you're not familiar with the river. During high water, paddlers will be safer in a kayak or decked canoe.

You'll canoe through thick forest for most of the route. The riverbanks are lined with an assortment of hardwoods, sprinkled with small stands of black spruce and white pine. Three state forests border on the Snake: the Solana State Forest (just north of McGrath), the Snake River State Forest (below the Upper and Lower Falls) and the Chengwatana State Forest (near the mouth of the river). Below Grasston to Cross Lake, the banks open into a wide farming valley. But then the river runs for 12 miles below forested sandstone bluffs before spilling into the St. Croix River.

The river level varies widely during the year. The upper and lower sections can be adventuresome during high water in early season, but are usually too shallow for canoeing during the summer. The easy stretch of the Snake, between Mora and Pine City, is canoeable for most of the season.

Deer, black bears and other forest wildlife may be spotted along the way. Fishing can be good for walleye, northern, smallmouth bass and catfish. Try some of the lakes on the route for panfish.

SOUDAN UNDERGROUND MINE STATE PARK

St. Louis County. Near Soudan on Highway 169. Highway map index: L-6.

Soudan offers the world's only undergound iron mine tour. Here you'll tour Minnesota's oldest and deepest underground mine, first riding an elevator, then boarding an electric train. From the train, it's a short walk to a 32-step spiral staircase that leads up to the Montana slope, where guides explain the mining process. The year-round temperature in the mine is about 52 degrees Fahrenheit, so dress warmly (sturdy shoes are advised also). A nominal fee is charged for the hour-long tour.

SPLIT ROCK LIGHTHOUSE STATE PARK

Lake County. About 20 miles northeast of Two Harbors on Highway 61. Highway map index: O-9.

The November gale raged for two days on Lake Superior. By the time it abated, 29 vessels were damaged, two of them foundering on the rocky shoals and sharp reefs of the coastline near present-day Split Rock Lighthouse State Park.

After this infamous storm in 1905, pressure for a lighthouse on the isolated rocky headland of Split Rock prompted Congress to authorize money for its construction. The U.S. Lighthouse Service completed the facility in 1910 and operated it until 1939, when the U.S. Coast Guard took over. The station closed in 1969, made obsolete by modern navigation equipment. The lighthouse prevented many tragedies, however. Storms brew quickly and can strike with a vengeance on Lake Superior. Her choppy waves and cold water (40-45 degrees Fahrenheit) are the enemies of sailors in distress. The lighthouse keepers kept watch on the weather and warned vessels of danger with a two-toned fog siren and an oil vapor beacon (electric after 1940).

Some of the wreckage from the 1905 gale is still evident. The steamer Edenborn and her barge, Madiera, were stranded near the mouth of Split Rock River. The barge eventually drifted away and sank several miles to the east. You can see the outline of the submerged barge from the cliff when the lake is calm. The Lafayette and her barge, Manila, were smashed against the rocks near Encampment Island, 12 miles to the southwest. Lake Superior has claimed many other ships from different storms. Besides those along the North Shore, divers will find numerous wrecks around the Apostle Islands of Wisconsin.

The compact station includes the recently renovated brick light tower, a fog-signal building, a trio of identical keepers' dwellings, plus several outbuildings and the ruins of a tramway. Disabled visitors are able to tour the site by way of a paved path.

The Minnesota Historical Society, which administers the site, offers tours of the buildings and grounds at the light station between May 15 and October 15. A modern History Center houses interpretive displays, a gift shop and a theater, where a 20-minute film on the construction of the lighthouse and the life of a lighthouse keeper is shown. The History Center is open daily during the peak season and weekends the rest of the year.

Recent park development has made it easier for more people to get a shoreline perspective of the lighthouse. The lonely landmark on the sheer-walled promontory is one of the most photographed scenes in Minnesota, and is visible from the picnic area just downshore.

The park's trail system has also been expanded. It's now possible to walk near the lakeshore from the lighthouse to the Split Rock River (for which the lighthouse is named), about 2.5 miles to the southwest. Several overlooks throughout the park offer vistas of the shoreline rock formations, Lake Superior and the lighthouse. An all-season trail center serves as a picnic shelter and interpretive display area, cross-country ski trailhead, and access point to the Superior Hiking Trail.

The park features a cart-in campground, a pleasant twist

on the usual drive-in sites. Visitors park their vehicles in a central lot, then load their camping gear in a large cart provided by the park. Campsites range from 120 feet to a half mile away from the parking lot. About half of the 20 cart-in campsites are spaced along Lake Superior, while the rest are only a short distance from the lake. For those who want a more isolated camping experience, four backpack sites are spread along the lakeshore up to 2.2 miles from the parking lot.

Currently, the closest boat access to Lake Superior is in Beaver Bay, northeast of the park, but a future access could be built near the mouth of the Split Rock River. Lake fishing is good for lake trout, salmon and steelhead. Rainbow, brook and brown trout are taken in Split Rock River.

Little Two Harbors, a small fishing village in the shadow of the lighthouse, was once the home of 12 commercial fishermen. As trout and herring populations declined during the 1950s, the village became deserted and today is marked only by concrete foundations and submerged footings. The trail between the picnic area and the campground follows along the shoreline of Little Two Harbors Bay.

The rocky bluffs along the park's shoreline are formations of anorthosite. At the turn of the century, speculators mistakenly identified this mineral as corundum, one of the hardest substances in the world. Corundum could be sold profitably to eastern manufacturers of grinding wheels.

Three companies started to mine the abrasive along the North Shore: Minnesota Abrasive Company, Minnesota Mining and Manufacturing (3M), and North Shore Abrasives. The latter company located its mine at Corundum Point, just northeast of the Split Rock River. The only company to survive the mistaken identification was 3M.

Winter

Eight miles of cross-country ski trails are marked for intermediate and advanced skiers. Hiking and snowshoeing are allowed throughout the park. Snowmobiling is not permitted at Split Rock Lighthouse State Park, but there are extensive snowmobile trails in the area.

The all-season trail center in the picnic area serves as a warming house for all park visitors. Winter campers can get water in this building and find refuge if the weather becomes too rough.

SUPERIOR HIKING TRAIL

St. Louis, Lake and Cook counties. 250 miles, between Duluth and the Canadian border (over 220 miles will be open to the public by 1993—from Knife River to the Canadian border).

This young trail has already inspired praise from afar. The U.S. Forest Service and *Prevention Magazine* have selected the Superior Hiking Trail as "one of the 12 best trails in the National Forests."

The already-famous footpath's formula for success is simple. It represents the union of the world's largest freshwater lake and the vast forest lakeland of northeastern Minnesota along a stretch of rugged, dramatic coastline.

The shoreline between Duluth and the Canadian border is legendary for its natural beauty, highlighted by eight state parks, a handful of waysides, and a cluster of coastal communities. The parks and small towns are linked by Highway 61, recognized as one of the most scenic drives on the continent.

Though the drive is beautiful, it is not the essence of the North Shore. You have to get out of the car and take to the trails to discover the magic of the streams, waterfalls, mountains, inland lakes, forests and Lake Superior. You can pick from scores of trails that offer intimate glimpses of parts of the North Shore. Until the Superior Hiking Trail, though, there was no footpath that linked all of the natural attractions of the North Shore as Highway 61 does for asphalt vagabonds.

When completed, the Superior Hiking Trail will challenge backpackers who wish to hike the 250-mile route from end to end. The trail, accessible from marked entry points off of Highway 61, is also ideal for day hikers who may wish to explore the North Shore at a more leisurely pace.

Pace is not important on the Superior Hiking Trail. It is a rustic route that doesn't pretend to accommodate all tastes. Its narrow, hilly, rough-edged nature excludes all motorized traffic and makes it tough on joggers and skiers. Because of potential trail damage, mountain biking and horseback riding are discouraged. It is a classic footpath, patterned in the tradition of the Appalachian Trail. In fact, it's not what you accomplish but what you experience on the Superior Hiking Trail that makes it a unique resource in the state.

The North Shore is noted for its rocky headlands, sheer cliffs, cobble beaches, and secluded coves ringed with a varied mantle of pine, basswood, birch, maple and aspen. The Sawtooth Mountains (glacier-worn, tipped beds formed from an ancient mountain range) add to the region's distinctive character. The northwest faces of these hills are bare, rocky bluffs overlooking valleys with lakes and streams. Rivers have cut rocky gorges through the Sawtooth Mountains on their way to Lake Superior. These streams fall 130 to 320 feet in a mile, creating continuous cascades, waterfalls, rapids and pools.

The Superior Hiking Trail shows off the best of the North Shore. For the most part, the trail follows the ridgeline overlooking Lake Superior, dipping down only to reach parks or towns. Smaller loops branch off from the trail, forming links to resort areas or providing access to other

Superior Hiking Trail map

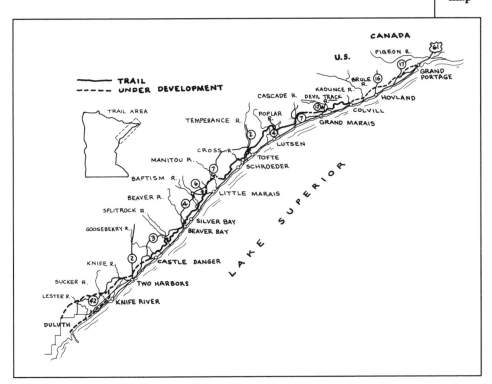

scenic attractions. Some of the branch loops climb to the peaks of the Sawtooth Mountains (Carlton, Britton, Leveaux, Oberg, Lookout or Moose mountains).

Surprises are everywhere. You may come upon a blueberry patch or watch a hawk circling in the updraft near a cliff. Just as you get used to the closeness of the forest, you may round a bend to witness the blue majesty of Lake Superior spread out before you. Sometimes you'll stand above inland lakes, tucked in a valley carpeted by conifers and hardwoods.

Fall is the most spectacular season for many hikers who know the North Shore. The slopes of the Sawtooths are painted with the blazing orange and red of the sugar maples, the yellow of the birch and aspen, and the rich shades of green of the conifers. Overhead, flocks of migrating birds follow the shore as they fly southward.

If you'd like to camp along the trail, primitive sites are located about every 5 to 6 miles. More civilized camping is available in the state parks or in nearby private campgrounds. Resorts, motels and other visitor services are located near the towns along the shore.

You don't have to be a seasoned backpacker to enjoy the Superior Hiking Trail. Day hikers can take advantage of the lodge-to-lodge package, where you can stay at one resort and hike on to another. Your luggage will be waiting for you each evening.

All of the participating lodges (in the Silver Bay to Grand Marais area) have easy access to the trail via spur paths or shuttles. Hikers plan their days based on ability and interests, though common outings range from 5 to 10 miles. The packages are flexible and can be adapted to include additional people or additional days. For information or reservations, contact the Lutsen-Tofte Tourism Association, P.O. Box 2248, Tofte, MN 55612 (218-663-7804; ask for the lodge-to-lodge reservation coordinator).

The Superior Hiking Trail has also been discovered by endurance runners. In 1991, the first Superior Trail 100 was run on the twisting, roller-coaster route of the trail. This 100-mile race, which lasts a day or longer, is held on the Silver Bay to Grand Marais segment. Contact the Superior Hiking Trail Association for more details.

Winter use on the Superior Hiking Trail depends partly on

snow depth. With little snow cover, the trail is relatively easy to hike. Since the route is not groomed, deeper snow means that interested hikers (or snowshoers) will have to work harder to have their fun.

Although cross-country skiing is not prohibited, it is not practical on some sections of the trail. Sharp turns, moderately steep grades and a narrow treadway add up to difficult skiing in spots. There are numerous groomed cross-country skiing opportunities around the North Shore communities and also in the state parks, state forests and the Superior National Forest.

The Superior Hiking Trail Association (SHTA) publishes a bimonthly newsletter and sells clothing, mugs, patches and fanny packs. The SHTA also has compiled a trail guide that includes maps, trip planning details, and natural and cultural information on the North Shore region. A schedule of organized hikes, including a winter snowshoe outing, is available. If you would like to join the Superior Hiking Trail Association, volunteer to work on trail projects, or want to get current maps and information, consult the address and phone number listed in the back of this guide.

SUPERIOR NATIONAL FOREST

St. Louis, Lake and Cook counties. 3 million acres, including more than 1 million acres in the BWCA. Forest headquarters is in Duluth; Ranger District offices are in Aurora, Cook, Ely, Grand Marais, Tofte. See also: Boundary Waters Canoe Area.

The Superior National Forest is one of the last remaining wilderness areas in the Midwest. It stretches in a pie-shaped wedge across Minnesota's northeastern Arrowhead, from the Canadian border on the north, to the North Shore of Lake Superior on the southeast. The vastness of the region is legendary; over 3 million acres of lakes, rivers and forests (comprised mostly of pine, aspen, maple and birch). Like other national forests, the Superior is managed for timber production and resource management, as well as for recreation.

You don't have to know how to portage a canoe or wear fishing lures in your hat to explore the forest. Several well-maintained roads, called "trails," lead into the heart of the region. The Echo Trail (County 116) winds for about 50 miles northwest of Ely on a gravel road through the forest to Crane Lake Road. Though the Echo Trail is largely undeveloped, there are many resorts, private campgrounds and canoe outfitters near Ely and Crane Lake, which is also an entry point to Voyageurs National Park.

In the eastern half of the forest, the Sawbill (County 2), Caribou (County 4), Gunflint (County 12) and Arrowhead (County 16) trails lead into the forest from the North Shore of Lake Superior. The Tofte Ranger District office is near the start of the Sawbill Trail. You can also drive from Illgen City, on the North Shore, to Ely on Highway 1 (the Isabella Ranger District office is along this road).

The Gunflint Trail is the most famous of these forest roads. This 60-mile paved route connects Grand Marais (on the North Shore) to Sea Gull Lake. The gateway at the beginning of the Gunflint Trail features a bear and a voyageur, recalling the French fur trappers who knew the water routes almost as well as the Indians, and the wildlife that still roams the forest today. The Gunflint is more developed than the other "trails," with over a dozen resort lodges, several canoe outfitters, bed and breakfast inns, and a couple of private campgrounds.

During winter, many of the Gunflint Trail resorts offer a lodge-to-lodge ski program. While you ski during the day, your gear is transported to the next lodge. A unique twist on this idea is yurt-to-yurt skiing. You can also find dog sledding and snowshoeing adventures along the Gunflint. For more information about the eastern part of the Superior National Forest, stop in Grand Marais at the Gunflint Ranger District office or at the Tip of the Arrowhead Visitor Center (1-800-622-4014).

The Sawtooth Mountain Range, along the North Shore, is one of the most rugged and scenic sections of the forest. In addition to the roads already mentioned, you can explore the area on a number of designated forest drives.

This is a popular destination for fall color viewing. The hiking, skiing and snowmobiling are always spectacular. Moderately steep but beautiful trails climb to the summits of Carlton Peak, Moose Mountain and others. Oberg and Leveaux Mountain national recreation trails (about 2 miles north of Highway 61 on Forest Road 336 between Lutsen and Tofte) offer some of the most picturesque hiking in the state. Minnesota's highest point, Eagle Mountain (2,301 feet), is northwest of Grand Marais in the BWCA.

Two North Shore trails are noteworthy. The North Shore State Trail currently runs from Duluth to Grand Marais on the inland side of the forested hills that overlook Lake Superior. This snowmobile trail (large segments are dry enough for hiking and horseback riding) will eventually extend up to the Canadian border.

The Superior Hiking Trail, when completed, will stretch for 250 miles from Duluth to Canada. This trail, already usable from Two Harbors to Grand Marais, will link eight state parks along Highway 61. Hikers can camp in designated sites along the trail or step out of the wilderness momentarily to spend the night at a lodge or resort along the way.

Mountain biking attracts more enthusiasts to the forest each year. Over 2,000 miles of country and forest roads offer challenging, scenic bike travel. Many of these roads lead to resorts and forest campgrounds. Getting lost is a possibility. Tell someone where you are going and when you expect to be back. Carry a compass, tool kit, tire patch kit, water, food, rain gear and a reliable map.

Camping facilities in the Superior National Forest range from fully developed campgrounds to secluded primitive sites. Many of the forest's 27 campgrounds have swimming beaches, boat landings and interpretive trails. Echo Lake and Crescent Lake campgrounds have group camping sites. The forest maintains over 200 primitive campsites outside the BWCA. While many are accessible by water only, others can be reached by foot or vehicle. Contact the nearest ranger district office for help in locating these sites. Most campgrounds are open from spring through late fall. At least one campground in each area is open during the winter, but roads are often unplowed, limiting access.

With over 2,000 lakes and a network of streams and rivers, the Superior National Forest lures visitors with a menu of water sports. The lakes and rivers of the forest offer good fishing, while kayaking, sailing, water-skiing and canoeing are other popular activities. You can also jump into the water at one of a dozen swimming areas.

The Forest Service maintains over 30 boat launch sites in addition to those providing access to the BWCA. The launch sites range from paved lots and ramp access to those where boats and canoes must be carried down to the water. There are 12 primitive canoe routes outside the BWCA. Often, these little-known areas offer a sense of solitude similar to that found in a remote corner of the Boundary Waters. Consult the forest map for locations of launches and canoe routes.

For those who prefer forest day trips, nearby towns offer services such as campgrounds, stores, restaurants and lodging. Although a number of communities surround the Superior National Forest from the Iron Range to the North Shore, the main entry points into the forest are Cook (west), Ely and Isabella (central), and Grand Marais (east).

Your first stop in Ely, if you're interested in heading into the forest or the BWCA, should be the Voyageur Visitor Center. The Center, headquarters for the U.S. Forest Service, features displays, pamphlets, and film and slide shows about the Superior National Forest. You can also get BWCA permit information. Daily and weekly interpretive programs cover such topics as wild edible foods, map reading and outdoor cooking. Guided hikes are scheduled to local lakes and bogs to learn about plant and animal life.

Ely is home to the International Wolf Center (IWC). Minnesota has the largest wolf population, 1500-1700 animals, in the lower 48 states. The IWC is a nonprofit organization dedicated to providing information about the wolf and its relationship to other species, including humans. IWC education programs include seasonal "wolf weekends," research expeditions, traveling exhibits, a speakers bureau and observations of a live wolf pack at the nearby Voyageur Visitor Center. For details about the IWC, call 1-800-475-6666.

For another perspective on the region, visit the Vermilion Interpretive Center on the Vermilion Community College campus. Contact the Ely Chamber of Commerce (1-800-777-7281) for information about special events, like the All-American Sled Dog Championships, and attractions, like the Hidden Valley Recreation Area (downhill skiing and ski jumping).

TACONITE STATE TRAIL

Itasca and St. Louis counties. 165 miles, from Grand Rapids to Ely.

The most difficult part of using the Taconite State Trail is choosing which distraction or side trail to investigate. The 165-mile route from Grand Rapids to Ely winds through lake-studded countryside, with access to four state parks and a handful of state and national forest recreation areas.

The multiple-use trail's growing popularity is due to the variety of terrain along its corridor as well as to the 1,000-mile network of connecting loops and spurs through the forests of northeastern Minnesota. You could snowmobile, cross-country ski, hike, backpack or horseback ride here year after year and discover a new route each time. Because of wet segments during snow-free months, many of the connecting trails (and parts of the Taconite) are best suited for winter use.

The southeastern half of the Taconite State Trail is dominated by birch forests, gentle hills and spruce and tamarack bogs. The northeastern reaches of the trail are characterized by towering pine-covered ridges and massive slabs of granite. The trail winds past points of interest such as the Luna Lake CCC logging camp, Star Lake logging camp and several old log trapper's cabins.

The route is dotted with accommodations and convenient pit stops, either just off the trail or a short scoot down a connecting trail. Lakeside overlooks are frequent. During winter, snowmobiles provide easy ice fishing access to many of the backwoods lakes. The trail is groomed on a regular basis and highway crossings and turnoffs for towns and connecting trails are noted well ahead of time. Shelters with fire pits and toilets are spaced about 15 miles apart.

The three state parks along the route (McCarthy Beach, Soudan Underground Mine and Bear Head Lake) each have their own trail systems. You'll also pass through or near the Superior and Chippewa national forests, and Bear Island, Sturgeon River and George Washington state forests. Scenic State Park is accessible by a connecting trail that leads through the George Washington State Forest. The Arrowhead State Trail (140 miles) turns off of the Taconite about 10

miles west of Tower and heads up to International Falls
through heavy forest. The 86-mile Tomahawk Trail links Ely
to the North Shore of Lake Superior.

"Taconite" refers to northeast Minnesota's mining industry,
which is concentrated in several iron ranges that roughly
parallel the trail. Several vantage points along the
southwestern portion of the trail overlook open-pit mines,
man-made canyons from an era when Minnesota was the
country's greatest producer of iron ore.

TEMPERANCE RIVER STATE PARK

Cook County. 1 mile northeast of Schroeder on Highway 61. Highway map index: P-7.

The Temperance River got its name because it has no "bar" at its mouth. The lower river, preserved in Temperance River State Park, tumbles past some curious rock formations on its restless path to Lake Superior. Over the centuries, swirling sands and pebbles in the churning water have carved potholes into the lava rock formations. The potholes vary in size and some are still being enlarged.

Large parking areas by Highway 61 make it easy for visitors to stop and observe the tumultuous river as it tumbles toward Lake Superior. A short trail leads down to a footbridge across the rocky gorge that hems in the cascading river. After heavy rains, the water churns violently through the narrow gorge, as if gathering strength for its fruitless struggle against the mass of Lake Superior. You can see the river's outline far out into the lake before it fades into the great water.

Across Highway 61, a trail winds upstream toward Hidden Falls. When you come to a long, quiet pool in the river, stop and listen for the sound of falling water. As you follow the sound, you'll come to a deep, narrow chasm that is wider on the bottom than it is on top. The wild water (especially after storms) that spills through here is still cutting and shaping the gorge.

Temperance River State Park, though small (about 200 acres), has more than 8 eight miles of hiking trails. The most scenic ones follow the ravine through a dense coniferous forest. While hiking on these paths, you'll be able to see some old potholes, marking the route of the river during a time when it was much broader than it is now. From the park's boundary, you can continue on federal trails through the neighboring Superior National Forest.

TETTEGOUCHE STATE PARK

Lake County. 4.5 miles northeast of Silver Bay on Highway 61. Highway map index: O-8.

Plummeting 80 feet over a rocky ledge, sheer High Falls in Tettegouche State Park is Minnesota's highest waterfall (120-foot Pigeon Falls, in Grand Portage State Park, is shared with Ontario). Tettegouche showcases the best of North Shore scenery: rocky palisades along Lake Superior, steep inland bluffs and cliffs, a productive fishing river and isolated forest lakes.

The highlight of Tettegouche is an extensive, challenging trail system that twists and rolls with the terrain. There are two trailheads in the park. One is near the park entrance at the Baptism River Highway Rest Area. The other is at the end of the road that leads to the campground.

The park office and rest area are in an all-season facility that also features interpretive displays. The nearby picnic area and hiking trails take advantage of Lake Superior shoreline vistas. The Tettegouche Lake Trail provides frequent views of the expansive lake. A self-guided interpretive trail leads to the precipitous cliffs of Shovel Point, the most prominent feature of the park's mile-plus stretch of shoreline. Looking downshore from Shovel Point, you'll see Palisade Head, another prominent formation. The park manages this area for day use, including hiking, rock climbing and rappelling.

High Falls is about a 1-mile hike through the forest from the Highway 61 parking lot. It's a shorter jaunt from the second trailhead parking lot. You can also hike to Two Steps Falls (on the Baptism River) and farther upriver to High Falls from two campground trail spurs.

The suspension bridge across the Baptism River above High Falls is part of the Superior Hiking Trail, which traverses the park.

The hiking trails in the eastern part of the park climb through a birch/aspen forest. Farther inland, the terrain changes to high forested ridges overlooking secluded lakes and streams that are typical of northeastern Minnesota's Sawtooth Mountains. The lakes (Mic Mac, Tettegouche, Nipisiquit and Nicado) all require a 3- to 4-mile hike from the trailhead parking lot. The forest is a mixture of sugar maple and basswood on the bluff tops, with scattered stands of white pine and oak.

More than a dozen side spurs lead up to ridgetop overlooks or down into valleys. One trail climbs to the top of Mount Baldy (1,000 feet above Lake Superior), where you can see the Apostle Islands of Wisconsin on a clear day. The Sawtooth Mountains are so brilliant in autumn that the U. S. Forest Service has designated a handful of roads in the Superior National Forest for a special Fall Color Tour. These roads climb into the Sawtooths from Schroeder, Tofte and Lutsen (northeast of the park on Highway 61).

If you hike around Mic Mac Lake, you'll come upon Tettegouche Camp, a former logging camp. After the red and white pine were logged off, the Alger-Smith Company sold the camp and surrounding acreage in 1910 to the "Tettegouche Club," a group of businessmen from Duluth who used the area as a fishing camp and retreat.

Three rustic cabins in Tettegouche Camp will be renovated and available for rent singly or as a group by the mid-1990s, according to long-range plans. The cabins will be open during winter for cross-country skiers (sanitation facilities and water will be available). The camp lodge will be renovated for a trail center. You can contact the park office for details about the cabins and how to reserve them when they are finished.

You can fish for northerns, walleyes and panfish on the park's inland lakes, but access is only by foot. Motors are not allowed, and boats and canoes and ice shanties must be taken out of the park at the end of each day. Fishing in the Baptism River can be good for chinook salmon (especially in October) and for brown, brook, rainbow and steelhead trout. The closest boat landing for Lake Superior deep-sea fishing is in Silver Bay. The boat access to Lax Lake, which touches the southwest corner of the park, is on County 4, north of Beaver Bay.

Tettegouche's 34-site semi-modern campground is frequently full during the summer (reservations are recommended). You can also camp at many public and private campgrounds in the area surrounding the park. Finland State Forest and Superior National Forest have primitive campgrounds.

Visitors may also be able to backpack camp in a major new 4,000-acre addition to the 4,700-acre Tettegouche State Park. Though plans for development of this large parcel of land to the south and west of the old park boundaries are not firm yet, chances are that it will remain as pristine as possible.

Winter

When the new trail center is completed, it will be open for winter visitors. This will also be the trailhead for snowmobilers, cross-country skiers and hikers. The park's 7 miles of snowmobile trails connect to other paths in the Finland State Forest and Superior National Forest. Snowmobilers also have access to additional trails, such as the North Shore State Trail, Tolands Red Dot Trail and the Sawtooth Trail.

Tettegouche State Park grooms 12 miles of cross-country ski loops designed for intermediate and advanced skiers. Some of these trails lead to overlooks of the inland lakes and Lake Superior. It's possible to ski or hike to the interior park lakes to ice fish. Snowshoeing, hiking and winter camping are other ways to experience the park during the winter.

VERMILION RIVER CANOE & BOATING ROUTE

St. Louis County. 39 miles, from Vermilion Dam to Crane Lake.

The scenic Vermilion River alternates from slow-moving water to some rapids with steep drops guaranteed to quicken pulses. Experienced and expert paddlers will need decked canoes or kayaks for some of the pitches; High Falls, 4 miles upstream from Crane Lake, must be portaged by all. The river is a good route for expert canoeists as well as novices who are careful to portage around rapids.

Because much of its flow comes from Vermilion Lake, the river rises and falls slowly and can usually be canoed into October. When the U. S. Geological Survey gauge below the Vermilion Dam reads above 4 feet, then most of the rapids are runnable. Heavy rains swell the tributaries enough that the middle and lower rapids can be attempted even when the gauge reading is low.

Starting just below the dam, there are four rapids within the first 3 miles. Each of these rapids has a developed portage trail. The river then enters the Chain of Lakes, 7 miles of wide, peaceful water. Access points for this section are on Twomile Creek and Eightmile Creek, which both empty into the river. Take County 422 to reach Twomile Creek, and County 24 to reach Eightmile Creek (this road then parallels the river up to Buyck).

Once below the Chain of Lakes, the river tumbles over a dangerous 20-foot cascade, with several vertical ledges, called Table Rock Falls (Class IV-VI). Portage this one on the right side. The next three-quarters of a mile is continuous rapids (Class III-IV) that spill through a steep, narrow canyon. The nearby mile-long portage that bypasses all of this is the longest one of the route.

The next couple of rapids are both Class I-II rocky runs above Buyck. The Vermilion quiets down again for some 6 miles until it drops through the Class II Chipmunk Falls (River Mile 18.2). Just above Chipmunk Falls, you can take a half-mile side trip up the Pelican River (RM 19.7) to see a rapids and waterfall. About 2 to 3 miles below Chipmunk Falls, the river squeezes under 100-foot pine-covered cliffs in the Snowshoe Narrows. Wild-rice beds flank the river as the hills recede.

This section of the Vermilion calmly winds toward Crane Lake, as if saving strength for its energetic rush through High Falls, the Chute and the Gorge. High Falls, also known as Vermilion Falls or Upper Gorge, is a 25-foot-high, narrow, twisting ravine (Class VI) that must be portaged at any water level. The portage begins on the left bank where the river wraps around a rocky island above the falls.

The Chute is a winding 10-foot drop (Class III-V) over a ledge and some big boulders. The powerful current crashes into undercut formations on both sides of the channel as the rapids smooth out. Then, about a mile and a half above Crane Lake, you'll run into a Class II-III rocky rapids. Suddenly, the river lurches left and roars down two steep ledges before entering a rugged canyon, with sheer 50-foot walls, called the Gorge (Class III-V). The rocky isolation of the Gorge makes the rapids even more hazardous in case of a mishap. The long portage starts above the rapids on the left bank and ends where the river widens just above Crane Lake.

The Vermilion River is a popular, but unusual, state canoe route. Because it is bounded mostly by public lands in the Kabetogama State Forest and the Superior National Forest, the U.S. Forest Service maintains the nine primitive campsites, and the Minnesota DNR publishes a map of the river.

VOYAGEURS NATIONAL PARK

Koochiching and St. Louis counties. 218,000 acres (including 84,000 acres of water) along the Canadian border. 12 miles east of International Falls off Highway 11.

Watercraft are the main mode of transportation in present-day Voyageurs National Park. The park is named for the French-Canadian voyageurs ("travelers") who navigated the 3,000-mile water route from Montreal to Lake Athabasca in northwestern Canada during the fur-trade era of 150 to 300 years ago.

Voyageurs National Park lies on the "Voyageurs Highway," a water route that extended from Lake Superior into the interior of the continent. The voyageurs transported trade goods inland to barter with Indians for the furs that they then carried back to Montreal for export abroad. Today, the Boundary Waters Canoe Area (BWCA) of Minnesota's Superior National Forest, Quetico Provincial Park in Ontario, and Voyageurs National Park combine to form a vast network of public land in an unparalleled lakeland wilderness.

The voyageurs would recognize this region today. If you want to experience Voyageurs National Park, you must do so by water. Even the hiking trailheads are accessible only by water. Though the voyageurs and Ojibway Indians used birchbark canoes, park visitors use any form of boat, including canoes, kayaks, sailboats, motorboats, cabin cruisers and houseboats.

While the BWCA Wilderness (east of the park) is primarily canoe country, Voyageurs National Park, for the time being, is mainly for motorboats. The park, about 40 miles long from east to west and varying in width from 3 to 15 miles, is centered around the Kabetogama Peninsula. The park lies in the southern portion of the Canadian Shield. Like in the BWCA, the exposed rocks at Voyageurs are among the oldest formations in the world.

The 26-mile-long peninsula (75,000 acres) is heavily forested and dotted with small lakes. Hiking trails on the peninsula offer the chance to explore the park's interior and to fish and camp. Winter travel on the peninsula is by cross-country skis, snowmobiles or snowshoes. The 7-mile Rainy Lake Ice Road, from the Rainy Lake Visitor Center around the northwestern tip of the peninsula, provides automobile access into the park.

A handful of big lakes dominate the park area. Rainy Lake (the largest at 350 square miles), Namakan Lake, Sand Point Lake and Crane Lake are border waters. Kabetogama Lake, which means "lake that lies beside the big lake" (Rainy Lake) in the Ojibway language, forms the southern shore of the Kabetogama Peninsula. The park boasts over 30 lakes in all. Anglers can try for northern, smallmouth bass, walleye and crappies on park waters. Ice fishing is popular in winter. Area fishing guides can show you where and how to fish Voyageurs. You'll need an Ontario fishing license when fishing the Canadian side of the border lakes.

There are four entry points to the park, all off of Highway 53. County 23 (from Orr) leads to Crane Lake at the park's east end. The Ash River Trail (County 129) takes you to Ash River, and just up Highway 53 from this turnoff is County 122, which heads north to Kabetogama. In International Falls, turn onto Highway 11 and drive 12 miles east to Island View on Rainy Lake.

The four entry points are also resort areas where you can find lodging, campgrounds, restaurants, grocery stores, boat rentals and other services. Sixty resorts lie near the park. They offer everything from cabins, hotel rooms and houseboat rentals to guide service and charter trips by boat or floatplane.

Voyageurs National Park operates visitor centers in each of these areas except Crane Lake. For information, films, exhibits, navigational charts and other visitor services, stop by one of these centers. Rainy Lake Visitor Center is open year-round, while Kabetogama Lake Visitor Center and Ash River Visitor Center are open seasonally. Check at the visitor centers for schedules of naturalist activities, such as guided trips on concession-run tour boats, canoe trips, children's programs and campfire talks.

As you might expect in a water-based park, many of the interpretive activities are on the water. You can join costumed interpreters and a naturalist as you help paddle a

VOYAGEURS NATIONAL PARK

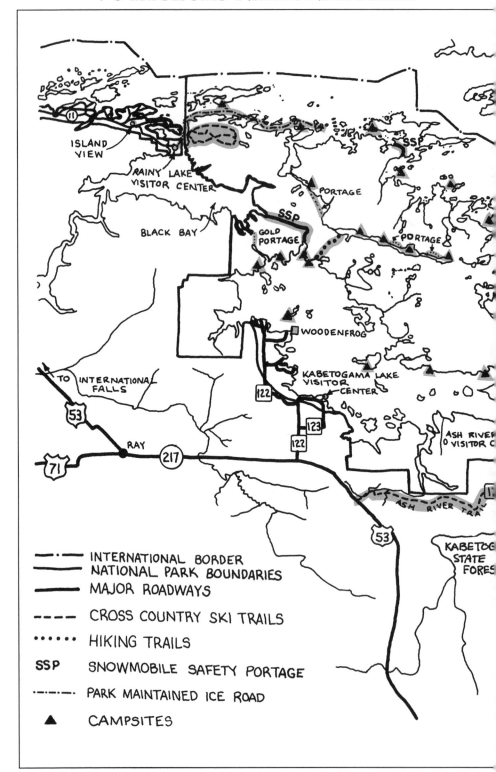

Legend:

- — · — · — INTERNATIONAL BORDER
- ———— NATIONAL PARK BOUNDARIES
- ———— MAJOR ROADWAYS
- - - - - CROSS COUNTRY SKI TRAILS
- · · · · · HIKING TRAILS
- SSP   SNOWMOBILE SAFETY PORTAGE
- — ·· — ·· — PARK MAINTAINED ICE ROAD
- ▲   CAMPSITES

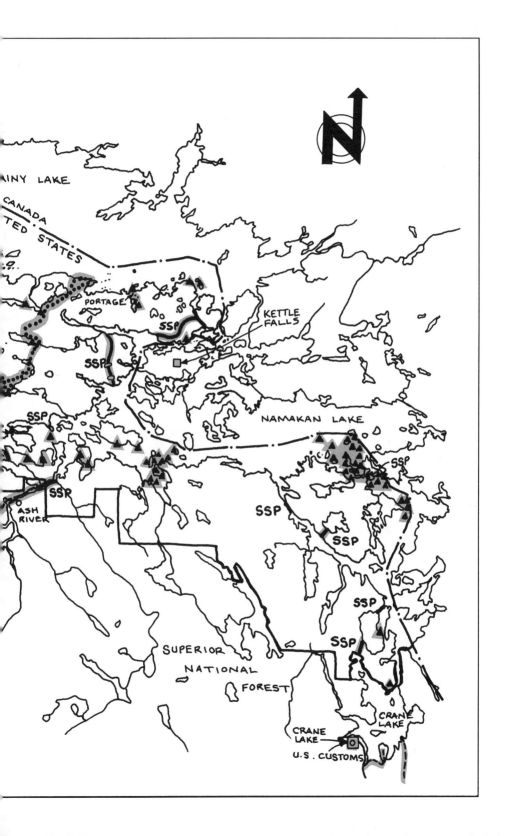

26-foot replica of the North Canoe, used by the voyageurs. Two National Park Service concession boats provide tours into the park from May through September. Reservations are advised for the North Canoe Voyage and the tour boat trips.

On Rainy Lake, the 49-passenger Pride of Rainy Lake tours the lake four times per week in summer. Highlights include naturalist-guided evening programs that range in topic from Ojibway tales to geology to wolves. Nighttime starwatch cruises (with a naturalist) are also popular. The other tour boat, the 19-passenger Sight-Sea-er, explores Kabetogama and Namakan lakes. The evening cruises travel through the islands of West Kabetogama Lake with a naturalist on board. Four days a week, the Sight-Sea-er journeys to the scenic and historic Kettle Falls Hotel, more than 20 miles from the nearest road. The Pride of Rainy Lake makes the trip to the isolated hotel each Saturday.

The Kettle Falls Hotel, a renovated 1913 inn on the Kabetogama Peninsula, can be reached only by boat. In its heyday, the hotel was frequented by commercial fishermen, gold miners, fancy ladies, loggers and bootleggers. Now it welcomes park visitors who come for lunch, dinner or an overnight stay. For hotel information or reservations, call 218-374-3511 in summer or 218-286-5685 during winter.

If you'd rather sleep under the stars than in a colorful hotel, you can choose from 120 primitive boat-in campsites scattered throughout the park. Most are on islands or near the lakeshores. Many have a bear-proof food storage locker. Motorboats can be packed with the same camping gear you take in a car.

Boating presents special challenges in the park. Because the lakes are large and topographic landmarks are few, you should know how to navigate with charts and be comfortable with using a compass. Weather can turn ugly in a hurry up here, so keep an eye on the clouds and head for a sheltered cove to wait out a storm if you have to.

Before going ashore in Canada and upon returning to the United States, you must report to customs offices. Canadian customs stations are located at Portage Bay on Sand Point Lake and at Sand Bay on Rainy Lake. When returning, you can clear U.S. Customs at the Crane Lake Public Landing or at the International Falls Bridge.

For visitor information about the area, contact the Greater

International Falls Chamber of Commerce (1-800-325-5766) or the commercial clubs and tourist information centers in Orr, Crane Lake and Ash River. Interpretive publications, topographic maps and navigational charts of Voyageurs National Park may be purchased by mail from the Lake States Interpretive Association, Box 600, Route 9, International Falls, MN 56649.

WILD RIVER STATE PARK

*Chisago County. 13 miles east of North Branch. From town,
drive about 10 miles east on Highway 95 to Almelund, then
turn north on County 12 for 3 miles to the park. Highway
map index: K-14.*

Wild River State Park wriggles like a noodle for 20 miles
along the banks of the St. Croix River. The park is named for
the St. Croix River, which Congress designated as one of the
original eight National Wild and Scenic Rivers in 1968.

The river is the park's focal point. Drive-in boat landings
at each end of the park provide easy fishing and canoeing
access. Anglers catch a variety of fish, including walleye,
northern, catfish and bass. The St. Croix River is most
famous for canoeing. Although stretches of the upper St.
Croix can pose a challenge for some canoeists, the river is
not classified as white water.

Besides being a National Scenic Riverway, the St. Croix is
a Minnesota State Canoe Route. You can rent canoes and
inner tubes from an outfitter in Sunrise (shuttle service is
available). Visitors can also rent canoes in the park (a
weekend shuttle service is available at the south boat
landing). The park maintains over a dozen primitive canoe
campsites along the river. Swimming is not allowed in the
park, but there are guarded swimming areas in nearby
Lindstrom and in St. Croix Falls, Wisconsin. Wild River State
Park is within easy driving distance of the Twin Cities and
draws large weekend crowds.

Water sports are only part of the attraction of Wild River,
however. More than 35 miles of wooded hiking trails
crisscross the length of the 7,000-acre park, including 20
miles of horse trails. Because of the varying trail difficulty at
Wild River, the park has been the site of the state
orienteering meet. The hills overlooking the river valley are
prime spots to observe hawks during their spring and fall
migrations. Sightings of bald eagles have increased over the
past decade. Wild River is also a good location to watch for
bluebirds.

Some of the park's horse trails begin at the Trail Center
and head north to the St. Croix River, following it up to
Goose Creek. Other loops wind through the park's

southeastern corner. There are 20 camping sites (100 capacity) for riders and their horses near the Trail Center.

The woodsy, 96-site (17 electric) semi-modern campground is usually busy on holidays and weekends, though it tends to be less crowded than its downriver neighbors, Interstate and William O'Brien state parks. Bicycle clubs sometimes make the trek from the Twin Cities to camp at Wild River (Highway 95 has a bike lane from St. Paul). Backpackers can hike in to one of seven primitive campsites in the park. Fall is the most pleasant season for backpacking because mosquitoes and ticks have declined. A 200-person primitive group camp may be reserved by contacting the park office.

The park's picnic area has both open and enclosed shelters. Some visitors pack a trail lunch and eat by the river at the old Nevers Dam site. At this spot, a large pile-driven wooden dam stood during the logging era. Only the ends of the dam are visible today. You can pause at the overlook to read the displays about the dam site and area logging history. A boat launch is on the Wisconsin side of the old dam.

Visitors can participate in an active interpretive program throughout the year at Wild River State Park. The impressive McElroy Interpretive Center has a wooden deck that overlooks the St. Croix River and the forested valley. Inside, exhibits of animals and artifacts catch the kids' attention, but not as much as the "feel boxes." Just put your hand inside one of these boxes (no peeking) and try to guess what you are touching.

An interesting side trip is the Rush Lake Island Scientific and Natural Area, in northwestern Chisago County. This 20-acre island contains one of the largest blue-heron rookeries in Minnesota. You're likely to see herons in Wild River State Park, too. Some photographers like to "shoot" the herons near Amiks Pond in the southeastern corner of the park.

Winter

No matter how much skiing experience you have, you'll find cross-country loops to suit your ability among Wild River's 35 miles of groomed trails. Most of these trails are for beginners, but there are some intermediate sections, and there's one advanced ski area in the hills south of the contact station.

Winter naturalist programs include basic ski instruction along with ski selection and waxing guidelines. Ski hikes are sometimes held at twilight or on moonlit nights. You can enjoy a break in the concession/warming house in the Trail Center at the winter trailhead parking lot.

Other organized outdoor activities include snowshoe hikes, winter astronomy, and animal tracking. The McElroy Interpretive Center is open on weekends and holidays. Visitors can view the displays, watch scheduled movies or slide shows, or observe winter birds munching at the Center's feeders. Winter camping demonstrations are also held at the Center. Ask at the office for details about setting up your own winter camp in the park.

Snowshoeing is another popular winter sport at Wild River. You can rent snowshoes (and cross-country skis) in the park. Although snowmobiling is not permitted on park land, more than 200 miles of snowmobile trails lace the surrounding area.

WILLARD MUNGER STATE TRAIL

St. Louis, Carlton, Pine, Chisago, Washington and Ramsey counties. From St. Paul to Duluth.

The Willard Munger State Trail is a web of interconnecting trails that (when completed) will link St. Paul to Duluth. The trail system is designed for all-season use by hikers, bicyclists, snowmobilers, cross-country skiers and horseback riders. The multiple-use corridors make it easy to sample the diverse historical and recreational attractions of this region of lakes, forests and rivers between two of Minnesota's major urban areas.

The eastern portion of the trail (formerly known as the Minnesota-Wisconsin Boundary State Trail) links St. Croix State Park with the St. Croix, Nemadji and Chengwatana state forests. Currently, snowmobilers can ride on more than 80 miles of marked and groomed trails in this section.

Besides the Willard Munger State Trail, each park and forest unit has its own system of designated trails for snowmobilers and cross-country skiers. An extensive network of local Grant-In-Aid trails branches off from the Munger, tying the park and forest segments together and providing additional spurs to explore.

As development of the eastern portion of the Willard Munger continues, Wild River, Interstate and William O'Brien state parks will also be connected by snowmobile trail. Eventually, the Gateway Segment (paved for bicyclists) will be completed, linking St. Paul to William O'Brien State Park in Washington County. Summer activity on the eastern portion of the trail includes hiking and horseback riding, though parts of it are too wet to use. Check with the manager at St. Croix State Park for details about what sections of the trail are passable during the summer.

The western portion of the Willard Munger State Trail currently includes over 50 miles of abandoned railroad grade. This allows snowmobilers to connect with Banning, Moose Lake and Jay Cooke state parks, as well as the General Andrews State Forest.

The western portion of the Willard Munger, sometimes

called the Fire Trail, is a tree- and shrub-lined bicycle route that passes through farm fields and some wooded areas between Hinckley and Barnum. You may see deer, beaver ponds, songbirds and wildflowers from the paved trail. Supplies, camping, parking and lodging are available in the main trail communities. You can also camp in Banning and Moose Lake state parks and in General Andrews and D.A.R. Memorial state forests (the latter is nearby, but off of the trail). An 11-mile horseback treadway parallels the bicycle trail from General Andrews State Forest to the Darson Road near Banning State Park. Check with local chambers of commerce or state park managers for details about camping, supplies and lodging.

The Fire Trail segment is named for the 1894 firestorm that swept through Hinckley, devouring the town and the surrounding forest. A train raced townspeople away from the blaze to the cooling waters of Skunk Lake, saving many lives. That train route is part of today's bicycle trail. If you'd like to learn more about the great fire, stop at the Hinckley Fire Museum. Victims of the Moose Lake-Cloquet Fire of 1918 were also carried to safety along this railroad grade.

The Carlton-West Duluth segment of the Willard Munger State Trail is a 14.5-mile paved bicycle route known for its scenic overlooks. The trail runs along a ridge from the town of Carlton, along the border of Jay Cooke State Park, through a forest of aspen, birch, maple and pine, to the west end of Duluth. Near Carlton, it passes over an old railroad bridge across the cascades of the St. Louis River.

From its height, the trail provides great views of the surrounding rolling forest and the Duluth harbor, with its distinctive aerial lift bridge. You can camp at Jay Cooke State Park (near Carlton) and at campgrounds near Cloquet and in Duluth. Motels are also located in each of these towns. It's possible to bicycle between the Carlton-West Duluth and the Hinckley-Barnum segments by following secondary roads. These bikeable roads are noted on the Willard Munger State Trail map. By the mid-1990s, however, these two segments will be linked by a paved path that will allow bicyclists to pedal between Hinckley and Duluth.

In an 1894 firestorm, a train saved many lives. The train route is now part of Willard Munger's network of bicycle trails.

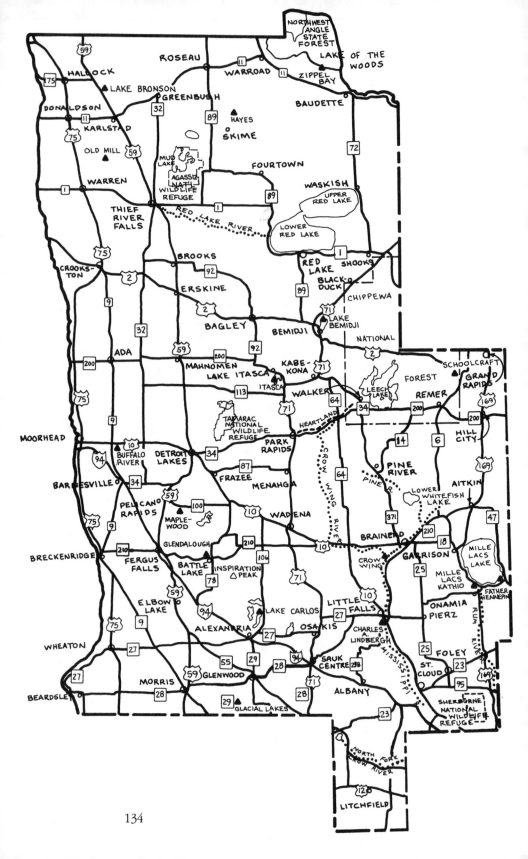

134

HEARTLAND/ VIKINGLAND REGION

Agassiz National Wildlife Refuge
Buffalo River State Park
Charles A. Lindbergh State Park
Chippewa National Forest
Crow River (North Fork) Canoe and Boating Route
Crow Wing River Canoe and Boating Route
Crow Wing State Park
Father Hennepin State Park
Glacial Lakes State Park
Glendalough State Park
Hayes Lake State Park
Heartland State Trail
Itasca State Park
Lake Bemidji State Park
Lake Bronson State Park
Lake Carlos State Park
Maplewood State Park
Mille Lacs Kathio State Park
Mississippi River Canoe and Boating Route
Northwest Angle State Forest
Old Mill State Park
Pine River Canoe and Boating Route
Red Lake River Canoe and Boating Route
Rum River Canoe and Boating Route
Schoolcraft State Park
Sherburne National Wildlife Refuge
Tamarac National Wildlife Refuge
Zippel Bay State Park

▲ ....STATE PARKS & RECREATION AREAS
△ ....WAYSIDES
■ ....NATIONAL MONUMENTS
— — — — ....STATE TRAIL
• • • • • ....CANOE & RIVER ROUTES

AGASSIZ NATIONAL WILDLIFE REFUGE

Marshall County. 61,052 acres. Headquarters is located 11 miles east of Holt on County 7. Highway map index: D-5.

Amidst the fertile farmland of northwestern Minnesota, Agassiz National Wildlife Refuge is a rich and protective oasis for a wide array of wildlife. The refuge provides excellent opportunities to observe and photograph wildlife in a peaceful setting.

It was not always so. During pre-settlement times, this area was a vast grassland scattered with hardwood groves, lakes and potholes. Waterfowl and other wildlife were plentiful. In 1909, an extensive, costly attempt was made to drain the area now occupied by the refuge. By 1933, the area had become so expensive to maintain (and so tax-delinquent) that the lands were purchased by the state. When the present-day U.S. Fish and Wildlife Service took over, the area was developed as a vital link in the chain of National Wildlife Refuges in the Mississippi Flyway.

Covering nearly 100 square miles, the refuge is spanned by the immense Agassiz Pool and 15 other broad, shallow ponds created by a system of dikes in the late 1930s. The pools are bordered by cattails, bulrushes and a wealth of other marsh vegetation. Other sections of the refuge include grassy uplands scattered with willows and various hardwoods, and about 4,000 acres of tamarack and spruce forest, managed as part of the National Wilderness Preservation System.

Agassiz is home to an estimated 274 bird species, including white pelicans, loons, five species of heron, eagles, hawks, an occasional rare peregrine falcon, and scores of songbirds and shorebirds. The refuge also hosts at least 49 mammal species. It is one of the best places in Minnesota to spot a moose in the wild. Agassiz is the only national wildlife refuge outside Alaska to host a resident pack of eastern gray wolves. The pack travels the entire refuge during the winter but is primarily restricted to the uplands of the east side during the rest of the year.

Itasca State Park, Minnesota's second-largest, is the birthplace of the Mississippi River.

Before exploring Agassiz, stop at refuge headquarters for tips on where to go and what to watch for. Brochures and species checklists are available. You can climb a 100-foot observation tower for an overview of the refuge (bring your binoculars). Self-guided walking and driving tours are mapped out and certain other roads may be accessible (check with refuge staff).

Two-hour guided bus tours (per-person charge) are conducted one evening a week out of the Thief River Falls Convention and Visitors Bureau. Call 218-681-3720 for tour dates and details.

BUFFALO RIVER STATE PARK

Clay County. 13 miles east of Moorhead on Highway 10. Highway map index: B-10.

The tall-grass prairie within Buffalo River State Park and the adjoining 1300-acre Bluestem Prairie Scientific and Natural Area combine to form one of the largest and best tracts of grassland left in Minnesota. The park's 12 miles of easy footpaths give hikers a chance to see some 250 species of wildflowers and grasses. The Buffalo River bisects the park, and is the center of most activity. A 44-site semi-modern campground (with 8 electric sites) can be busy during the summer, so reservations are a good idea. A large primitive group camp is located downriver, close to the park's entrance.

CHARLES A. LINDBERGH STATE PARK

Morrison County. Park entrance is off of Lindbergh Drive (County 52) on the south side of Little Falls. Highway map index: H-13.

History and recreation add up to family fun along the Mississippi River at Charles A. Lindbergh State Park. Visitors enjoy water and winter sports here, as well as camping and hiking. Associated with the park is the Charles A. Lindbergh House and a stylish history center administered by the Minnesota Historical Society.

CHIPPEWA NATIONAL FOREST

Cass, Beltrami and Itasca counties. 660,000 acres; forest headquarters is in Cass Lake. District offices are in Blackduck, Cass Lake, Deer River, Marcell and Walker.

The fortunes of the bald eagle in the Chippewa National Forest mirror those of the forest itself. Both have struggled to survive and now enjoy a degree of well-being.

The Chippewa National Forest is home to the largest breeding population of bald eagles in the lower 48 states. In 1963, when bald eagle population surveys were initiated in the forest, only 20 breeding pairs were known. A recent survey recorded over 160 breeding pairs. This is a tribute to conservation methods that protect and monitor nesting areas in an intensively managed forest.

The conservation picture in this area was not always so rosy. In 1908, the Chippewa was the first national forest established east of the Mississippi River. Originally known as the Minnesota National Forest, the name was changed in 1928 to honor the original inhabitants. Its creation was the climax of a long, bitter and treacherous struggle that began in 1899. Before this time, lumbering interests often stole timber from Indian lands in the present-day forest.

Today, the Forest boundary encompasses about 1.6 million acres, with about 660,000 acres managed by the U.S. Forest Service. The remaining lands are state, county, tribal and private. The Leech Lake Indian Reservation is within the forest boundary. The Chippewa is a "working" forest. You may encounter recreation developments, wildlife habitat projects, and timber harvesting. Timber and tourism are the major industries here.

The Chippewa National Forest lures visitors with over 1,300 lakes, 920 miles of streams, and 150,000 acres of wetlands. Fishing, canoeing, camping, water-skiing and swimming are popular activities. Twenty-six developed campgrounds (both semi-modern and rustic), located on 12 of the major lakes, offer places to relax or to fish for muskie, walleye, northern, bass or panfish. Primitive campsites are spread out in more remote areas. Numerous resorts are located throughout the forest. Ask at one of the district offices for details about camping and facilities in the area. To reserve a campsite in the national forest, call 1-800-283-CAMP.

You can explore the forest on over 160 miles of trails, where deer, ruffed grouse and waterfowl are common. Loon calls and northern lights add to the experience of the northwoods. The gray wolf, a threatened species, lives in the area but is rarely spotted. In season, you can pick berries, photograph the fall colors, or hunt. Winter means cross-country skiing, snowmobiling and ice fishing.

Canoeing is a peaceful way to appreciate the forest's beauty. The Chippewa National Forest features nine canoe routes, ranging from the Mississippi River and the unpredictable Leech Lake to the slow-paced Shingobee River and small creeks. These are not wilderness trips, though usage is relatively light. Chances are good that you'll spot bald eagles, loons and ospreys. Fishing is good on most of the routes. Use caution on the large lakes (Winnibigoshish, Leech and Cass). You can camp in primitive campsites along most of the rivers (water must be boiled or treated for drinking).

Two recreation areas in the forest are noteworthy. The Shingobee Recreation Area, 5 miles southwest of Walker off of Highway 34, is nestled along the rolling hills of the Shingobee River Valley. The Civilian Conservation Corps built the sliding and ski slopes, hiking trails and a toboggan slide in the 1930s. The ski area closed in 1984, but you can still slide and cross-country ski (intermediate to advanced loops). A warming chalet is open on weekends. A 68-mile segment of the North Country National Scenic Trail passes through Shingobee, and the Heartland and Paul Bunyan state trails are nearby.

Cut Foot Sioux is the other noteworthy recreation area in the forest (17 miles northwest of Deer River, on Highway 46). The area gets its name from the last battle between the Chippewa and Sioux Indians. In 1748, a Chippewa war party from Leech Lake defeated the Sioux. The Sioux retreated across Lake Winnibigoshish. The Chippewa Indians followed their rivals to a point where they found a dead Sioux with his feet either cut or frozen off. The Chippewa chief ordered the fighting to stop. The nearby lake then became known as Cut Foot Sioux Lake.

The Cut Foot Sioux Visitor Information Center provides information and displays on the natural resources of the area around Highway 46. The center has a bookstore and schedules films or presentations on a regular basis during the summer. Ask for details about the Cut Foot Sioux Trail (22 miles) and the Simpson Creek Trail (13 miles). Six developed campgrounds are within 5 miles of Cut Foot Sioux.

The Cut Foot Sioux Ranger Station is the oldest remaining ranger station building in the Forest Service's Eastern Region. It is listed on the National Register of Historic Places (tours can be arranged at the Cut Foot Sioux Visitor Information Center). Turtle Mound, also on the National Register of Historic Places, is a turtle effigy built in the 1700s by the Dakota (Sioux) and Ojibway (Chippewa) Indians. A half-mile self-guided hiking trail circles the area. Turtle Mound still has significance as a sacred spot for traditional Indian religion.

The Rabideau Lake CCC Camp, south of Blackduck, is one of the few remaining Civilian Conservation Corps camps in the United States with buildings still standing. It's also listed on the National Register of Historic Places. The CCC constructed the three-story log building that serves as the Chippewa National Forest headquarters in Cass Lake. This

CHIPPEWA NATIONAL FOREST

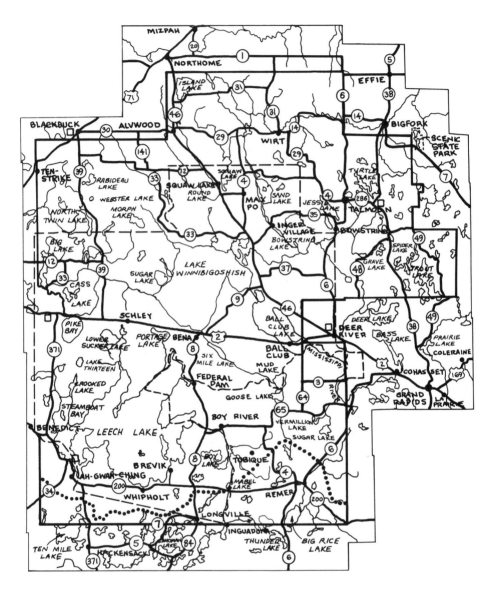

beautiful building was made from native red pine and built in Finnish log construction style under the supervision of Finnish craftsmen.

To cap off your Forest visit, go for a drive on one or more of the three designated National Forest Scenic Byways. The Avenue of Pines is a 39-mile stretch of Highway 46 that cuts diagonally across the center of the forest. You'll see Island, Round, Squaw, Cut Foot Sioux and Little Ball Club lakes, along with Lake Winnibigoshish (the state's fifth largest), along the highway's path.

The Northwoods Highway, in the Marcell District, winds through glacial hills covered with aspen and hardwoods. This is a picturesque drive in autumn. You can fish for trout in several of the nearby lakes and hike on the scenic Suomi Hills trail system. The Scenic Highway, in the Cass Lake and Blackduck Districts, passes near the Norway Beach Campground, a popular spot for swimming, fishing, boating and picnicking.

For interpretive information that covers the human history and natural features of the Chippewa National Forest, contact the Lake States Interpretive Association, Box 600, Route 9, International Falls, MN 56649.

CROW RIVER (North Fork) CANOE & BOATING ROUTE

Meeker, Wright and Hennepin Counties. 126 miles, from Lake Koronis to the Mississippi River near Dayton.

The North Fork of the Crow River is not a wild river. Its pastoral setting and quiet nature make it enjoyable for a family canoe outing. The North, Middle and South forks of the Crow are all part of the state-designated canoe and boating route, but the North Fork is generally considered to be the main stem and the best for canoeing.

Some canoeists put in at the access on the south shore of Lake Koronis, a hill-ringed lake popular for its year-round fishing. After portaging the dam to start downriver, you'll canoe through a channelized stretch for two miles. From Lake Koronis to Kingston, the river is shallow and generally clean with a mixture of hardwoods and prairie grasses along the banks. This upper section can be difficult for beginners because of snags. The rapids (rated Class I) are easy to navigate, but hidden snags and overhanging branches call for keen eyes. Fences across the river and sharp bends also contribute to tough going for novices. During low water, this stretch of the river is impassable, while high water means faster current and more problems with unseen snags.

Below Kingston, the river deepens and the valley widens. The few rapids present no problems for novices. Although families will find this section easy to canoe, snags are still common.

The South Fork joins the North Fork near Rockford, forming an even broader and deeper stream that flows northeast into the Mississippi River at Dayton. This stretch, close to the Twin Cities, is the best for family weekend or day trips. Two dams, both with mills next to them, must be portaged. The Hanover Dam should be portaged on the left; portage the Berning Mill Dam on the right.

There are eight county parks and two park reserves along the river, providing scenic breaks amidst the farmland. Most of the accesses, campsites and rest areas are in these units. Lake Maria and Sibley state parks, Sand Dunes State Forest, Sherburne National Wildlife Refuge and the Mississippi River Canoe & Boating Route are also within close range of the Crow River. For those who pack bicycles as well as canoes, the Luce Line State Trail runs west of the metropolitan area, south of the canoe route.

The Crow River got its name from the Ojibway Indians for the bird they called "the marauder of newly planted corn." The river once flowed through the Big Woods, a large hardwood forest that was a sacred hunting ground to the Indians. Many battles were fought between the Ojibway and Dakota Indians near the Crow River.

As European settlers flowed in, supplies were hauled upriver to Dayton by steamboat from St. Anthony Falls (Minneapolis) and transferred to smaller boats for the trip up the Crow River. Tempers grew hot between the growing numbers of settlers and the Dakota Indians, whose land was disappearing. In August 1862, the U.S.-Dakota Conflict broke out in Minnesota. Brief fighting took place in Manannah and Forest City, both on the upper North Fork. Today, a stone monument commemorates the battle in Manannah, and a historic site is being developed just south of Forest City.

CROW WING RIVER CANOE & BOATING ROUTE

Hubbard, Wadena, Todd, Cass and Morrison counties. 110 miles, from 10th Crow Wing Lake near Akely to the Mississippi River at Crow Wing State Park.

Rising in a chain of 10 lakes in southern Hubbard County, the Crow Wing flows through low marshy lands for its first 20 miles. The river broadens and the banks increase in height as it continues southward. Although there are many cottages and homes along the river, the tree cover is dense enough that you'll get a wilderness feeling as you paddle downstream. The vegetation varies from evergreens to maples, basswoods and cottonwoods, with grasslands and bogs scattered along the way.

The river forests shelter a rich variety of woodland animals. Canoeists are likely to see deer, beaver, turtles and various types of birds. Some black bear and bobcat are present but are hard to spot. The Crow Wing River Valley does not attract ducks and geese as much as other flyways that have more extensive backwaters and aquatic plants.

The local communities actively support water and land recreation trails. Canoeists will find information and outfitters in Akeley, Huntersville, Nimrod and several other places along the river. The Crow Wing Trails Association, Wadena County and the Minnesota DNR have cooperated in developing many of the primitive riverside campsites. Area saddle clubs help to maintain miles of horseback trails through the coniferous and hardwood forests flanking the river. Snowmobilers use these trails in winter.

Public forests are as thick as trees around the Crow Wing River Valley. The Chippewa National Forest and the Badura, Foot Hills and Huntersville state forests are close to the river's upper section. The Lyons and Pillsbury state forests are near the lower stretch. The Brainerd area, famous as a vacationland, is just northeast of the Crow Wing's junction with the Mississippi.

Also at the river junction is Crow Wing State Park. The park (and the river) is named for a wing-shaped island at the river's mouth. The Ojibway people called the river "ka-gi-wig-wan" ("raven's wing"). About the same time that the Ojibway began pushing the native Dakota Indians out of the forests (early 1700s), French fur traders filtered into the region. They established several trading posts, including one on the site of the park.

CROW WING STATE PARK

Crow Wing County. About 9 miles south of Brainerd on Highway 371. Park entrance is on County 27, 1 mile west of Highway 371. Highway map index: G-12.

Indian battles, voyageurs and a ghost town provide a colorful historical backdrop for today's explorers at Crow Wing State Park. Located at the confluence of the Crow Wing and Mississippi rivers, the park's name derives from the wing-shaped island that seems to guard the junction of the two rivers. The Indian name for the Crow Wing River was "ka-gi-wig-wan" ("raven's wing").

FATHER HENNEPIN STATE PARK

Mille Lacs County. 1 mile west of Isle off of Highway 27. Highway map index: J-12.

A visit to Father Hennepin State Park is a seasonal celebration of the senses. The park is named for the French Jesuit priest who was one of the first recorded European explorers in Minnesota. Dominated by grand Mille Lacs Lake, the park's moods reflect those of the great water, the largest natural lake in Minnesota. The 316-acre wooded peninsula park is popular by virtue of its extensive shoreline.

GLACIAL LAKES STATE PARK

Pope County. 5 miles south of Starbuck; park entrance is off of County 41. Highway map index: E-14.

Glacial Lakes State Park is not "on the way" to another destination, so the folks who bother to come here want to stay awhile. Visitors are rewarded by several spring-fed lakes surrounded by virgin prairie and a virgin oak forest. Mountain Lake, at 56 acres the park's largest, is tucked in a rectangular valley rimmed by high hills. The hills in the 1,900-acre park, like the lakes, ponds and marshes, were formed by the last glacier as it receded some 11,000 years ago.

GLENDALOUGH STATE PARK

Otter Tail County. About 4 miles north of Battle Lake off of Highway 78. Highway map index: D-12.

The new park with the musical name is bound to be as well-loved by the public as it was when it was a private corporate retreat. This 2,000-acre mix of elm and basswood forests, fields, hills, and a handful of unspoiled lakes has been managed as a natural wildlife preserve. When the park is opened to the public in the mid-1990s, land stewardship will continue to be a hallmark of Glendalough.

Park development will be in tune with the conservation practices that have been the trademark here since Glendalough was established as an 80-acre camping retreat in 1927. Wildlife preservation will still be a priority. The Department of Natural Resources will probably continue to plant some food plots for wildlife, which is not usually done in state parks.

Glendalough, named for a monastery and city in Ireland, was first owned by Fred E. Murphy, publisher of the Minneapolis *Tribune*. During the Depression, Murphy expanded the original acreage, establishing a turkey and game farm. When the Cowles family purchased the *Tribune* in 1941, Glendalough came with it. The family soon started vacationing here in a cluster of cabins known as the Glendalough Camp. Cowles Media also used Glendalough Camp for entertaining corporate guests and occasional VIPs (including Dwight D. Eisenhower and Richard M. Nixon). Visitors hunted waterfowl and walked the fields for upland game.

On April 22, 1990—the 20th anniversary of Earth Day—Cowles Media Company donated Glendalough to the Minnesota Chapter of The Nature Conservancy, a private, nonprofit conservation group. The Nature Conservancy then turned over the land (valued at $2.4 million) to the DNR, as it has done with more than 40,000 acres in its 30-year history.

The park will be kept as natural as possible. Some of Glendalough's twisting, narrow roads will become part of the hiking and cross-country ski trail system. Other roads will be upgraded and parking lots put in to accommodate visitors. Camping and day-use facilities (picnic grounds, etc.) will be developed and an existing building may be turned into a visitor center.

The jewels of Glendalough are its lakes. The park includes about 30,000 feet of lakeshore on five lakes, including two that are entirely within the property. Water-based recreation (swimming, fishing, canoeing, boating) will be emphasized.

Blanche Lake, whose southern shore forms the northwestern border of Glendalough, is the park's largest lake and a popular fishing destination. The park's lakeshore is a natural stretch of sand and wetland vegetation that merges into the lowland hardwood forest. Of the other four lakes in the park, only Annie Battle has seen any development (Glendalough Camp). The clear, uncluttered lakes (especially Annie Battle and Molly Stark) are precious because of their rarity.

A special way to see Glendalough and part of the surrounding area is by canoeing on a chain of lakes that begins south of the park on East or West Battle Lake. From there, you can paddle into Molly Stark Lake, on to Annie Battle Lake and Blanche Lake, and then continue north into Otter Tail Lake.

Wildlife will be abundant at Glendalough State Park. The previous waterfowl management practices have attracted large duck populations and over 4,000 migrating geese. Though eagles, moose and even a timber wolf have been spotted in the area, you're more likely to see deer, fox, otter and beaver.

HAYES LAKE
STATE PARK

Roseau County. 22 miles southeast of Roseau; park entrance is off of County 4, about 7 miles east of Highway 89. Highway map index: E-4.

Hayes Lakes State Park straddles opposite environments. To the east spread hundreds of square miles of wild lands in the Beltrami Island State Forest; to the west stretch vast flatlands that used to be grassland and savanna. The park's highlight is Hayes Lake, formed by a dam on the north fork of the Roseau River. Fishing on the lake and below the dam can be good for northern, walleye and crappie, but most people come to Hayes Lake to swim. There aren't many lakes in the area, so visitors like to make a day of picnicking, sunbathing and swimming at the beach.

HEARTLAND
STATE TRAIL

Hubbard and Cass counties. 49 miles, between Park Rapids and Cass Lake.

Paul Bunyan and Babe the Blue Ox, legendary giants of the northwoods, were created in the logging country that the Heartland State Trail traverses. The trail follows the route of a logging railroad, built in 1897, that hauled timber to area sawmills.

The trail is split into two segments. Bicyclists can enjoy a scenic, level ride on the paved 27-mile-long east-west segment, between Highway 34 in Park Rapids and Cass County Road 12 in Walker. The first leg of the trail, from Park Rapids to Nevis, passes by lakes, pastures, crop land and woods. The middle third, along a country highway between Nevis and Akeley, is a mixture of forest and farmland. The eastern third of the trail, from Akeley to Walker, cuts through the Chippewa National Forest.

The Chippewa National Forest section of the trail, with its lakes, jack pines, tamarack swamps, beaver ponds and nesting eagles, is a particularly interesting part of the trail. The bicycle route crosses the North Country National Scenic Trail on its way to Walker.

The north-south segment of the Heartland Trail runs north of Walker for 22 miles to Cass Lake. This portion is not paved. Both the east-west and north-south segments have a mowed path suitable for hiking, horseback riding and mountain biking. During the winter, the entire trail is groomed for snowmobiling.

Wildflowers and wildlife abound on the Heartland. Watch for forest animals and the ospreys, great blue herons and ducks that frequent the lakes and wetlands near the trail. The "bluebird trail," a string of 110 birdhouses spaced along the trail from Park Rapids to Akeley, has a 90 percent occupancy rate. Bluebirds nest in over 40 percent of the houses; wrens, swallows, red squirrels, and flying squirrels live in the others.

Watch also for the trail-side interpretive signs that depict aspects of logging and life in the lumber camps, railroad history and forest management practices. Most of the vast stands of tall timber that helped make Paul Bunyan famous were clear-cut by the 1920s. You can still see remnants of the large red- and white-pine forests that once covered this area, though jack pines, spruce, balsam, mixed hardwoods and aspens are more common now, especially on the north-south trail segment.

This region is also famous for its clear lakes. From the Heartland State Trail, you'll get a good view of 11th Crow Wing Lake near Akeley. Try your luck fishing for sunfish, crappies and northern from the trail bridge between Shallow Lake and Lake Belle Taine, or from the Nevis fishing pier. Swimming beaches are available in Walker, Nevis and Akeley.

The local area offers a variety of activities and attractions. Akeley claims to be Paul Bunyan's birthplace, and has the cradle to prove it. You can also sit in the palm of the "world's largest Paul Bunyan statue" in Akeley and visit the Paul Bunyan Historical Museum. Summer festivals in the towns along the trail include the Minnesota State Chili Cook-Off in Nevis, the annual Taste of Dorset, Logging Days in

Park Rapids and the Leech Lake Regatta in Walker. Nevis boasts the world's largest tiger muskie statue. Check with the local chambers of commerce for information on restaurants, resorts, motels, and bed and breakfast homes in the area.

Itasca State Park offers 31 miles of groomed ski trails, and a warming house where you can revive chilled limbs.

ITASCA STATE PARK

Clearwater, Hubbard, and Becker counties. 20 miles north of
Park Rapids on Highway 71. Highway map index: F-9

What would Tom Sawyer and Huck Finn think if they could see the birthplace of the mighty Mississippi? Like Mark Twain's characters, the Mississippi River in Itasca State Park is forever youthful.

The unsullied setting of the river's birth attracts over a half million visitors each year. The 32,000-acre park, Minnesota's second largest (behind St. Croix State Park), is the state's most developed park yet also one of its most pristine. The bulk of the development (cabins, campgrounds, gift shops, Douglas Lodge, interpretive center, food service, etc.) is concentrated along the eastern arm of Lake Itasca. The rest of the park is a spacious mix of virgin timber, secluded lakes, second-growth forest, and a 2,000-acre wilderness area.

You can reach the headwaters of the Mississippi by driving around the north end of Lake Itasca and following the signs. It's a short walk from the large parking lot, crossing over the young river on the way. At the lake's outlet, a marker notes the great river's first "steps" on its 2,552-mile-long journey to the Gulf of Mexico. It takes 60 days for the waters spilling out of Lake Itasca to reach their destination.

It took almost 300 years from the time the river was discovered in 1541 to find its source. The first white men to visit Lake Itasca were French fur traders who called it Lac La Biche (Elk Lake). They probably didn't know that the lake was the source of the Mississippi River. In the early 19th century, several explorers each claimed to be the discoverer of the river's true source. The confusion persisted because no one realized that the river flowed north from its source, not south. When Henry Rowe Schoolcraft and his expedition came to northern Minnesota (not yet a state) in 1832, they traveled directly to Lake Itasca only because their Ojibway Indian guide, Ozawindib, knew where the river started. Schoolcraft coined the name Itasca.

Even after Schoolcraft's discovery, a few other explorers claimed they had found the source in various tributaries of Lake Itasca. The controversy continued until 1889 when

Jacob V. Brower studied the topography of the Itasca basin. He concluded that several creeks do contribute to Lake Itasca, but only at the lake's outlet is a river formed. To learn more about this great North American river, stop at the interpretive center next to the parking lot before leaving. A souvenir shop is located in the same complex.

Brower struggled for years to preserve Itasca. In 1891, the legislature established Itasca State Park. It is Minnesota's first state park, and one of the oldest in the country. But Brower, appointed the first park commissioner, received no pay and no funds or support to make the park a reality. Logging companies muscled their way into the park and began to clear-cut the timber. It wasn't until 1919 that the major logging operations were completed. Today, however, there are still stands of virgin red and white pine in the park with some of the oldest and largest pine trees in Minnesota.

Access to Itasca's wild country, including the park's unique Wilderness Sanctuary, is from hiking trails and the 10-mile-long Wilderness Drive. The one-way drive, heading west from the headwaters, is also popular with bicyclists. A rustic cabin on the shore of Squaw Lake is open to visitors on a reservation basis. Farther south on the drive, across from the Wilderness Sanctuary, is a Forestry Demonstration Area where you can see the difference between a managed forest and a natural area.

The Wilderness Sanctuary is a 2,000-acre tract of undisturbed forest bordering the western arm of Lake Itasca. The area contains a major portion of plants and animals once common to Minnesota and has been designated a State Scientific and Natural Area and a Registered Natural Landmark by the National Park Service. Within the Sanctuary, the Bohall Wilderness Trail leads down a corridor of giant red and white pines to isolated Bohall Lake. The virgin pine stand here is 100 to 300 years old. On the way to the lake, you'll pass a small marsh on the left with a trail-side bench. Numerous mosses and orchids flourish in the Sanctuary, including bog adder's mouth, a relatively rare orchid in Minnesota.

Midway around the Wilderness Drive is the trailhead for the Two Spot Trail. This path, originally an old forest road, will take you to South and North Twin lakes on the park's western edge. The diversity of vegetation along the trail attracts birdwatchers.

Minnesota's largest white and red pine are visible from short paths just off the Wilderness Drive. The red pine (also called Norway pine) is a species especially adapted to withstand fire. Scars on this record red pine indicate that it has survived six forest fires in its 300 years. The white pine is 112 feet tall; the red pine is 120 feet.

The Bison Kill Site, near the Big Pine Trail, marks the location of campsites used by Indian hunters some 8,000 years ago. These nomadic Indians ambushed bison, deer and moose using flint-tipped spears. The site was discovered when the Nicollet Creek bridge was being built, and was excavated by archaeologists from the University of Minnesota. You can see other evidence of early people in Itasca at the Indian Mounds near the headwaters. These burial mounds, 500 to 900 years old, were built by Woodland Indians who lived here before the Dakota and Ojibway tribes.

Some long hiking trails head south from the Wilderness Drive through mixed forests of virgin pine and hardwoods. You can reach the backpack sites on Hernando De Soto Lake from these paths. Several connecting trails allow hikers to make shorter loops.

The remote lakes and deep forests of Itasca provide a fertile environment for the park's plant and animal life. Beaver dams are visible on Allen Lake, on Nicollet Creek (about half a mile south of the Wilderness Drive off the Nicollet Trail), and on the Mississippi River (just south of the north-entrance contact station). Bald eagles nest near Chambers Creek between Lake Itasca and Elk Lake. They usually build their large nests (which average 7 feet across and 9 feet deep, and weigh several hundred pounds) in tall red or white pines.

The trail to the Aiton Heights Observation Tower cuts through some impressive maple/basswood stands. In early October, the hardwoods are various shades of orange and yellow, forming a colorful canopy over the hilly trail. Some paths, like the Brower Trail, parallel the east shore of Lake Itasca, linking many of the attractions in the park's core. Preacher's Grove, named for a religious convention that once camped here, is a stand of fire-scarred red pines. Many couples marry each year under the 250-year-old pines. Peace Pipe Vista is a great spot to watch the sunset as loon calls echo across Lake Itasca.

Dr. Robert's Trail is a self-guiding nature loop. (A companion booklet is available at Douglas Lodge.) Park naturalists lead hikes and special outings such as canoe or car caravans. Interpretive programs cover park history, plants and animals, the Mississippi River and other topics. Slides, films and talks are presented in the Forest Inn, a massive log and stone structure built by the Civilian Conservation Corps in the 1930s. Schedules of events, including ecumenical church services, are posted throughout the park. Itasca has a small natural history museum in addition to the Headwaters Interpretive Center.

The 17-mile bicycle route may be the most enjoyable and peaceful way to experience Itasca. The air is fresh and the forest is more immediate when you pedal through the park under your own power. Most of the bicycle route is on the paved Wilderness Drive, which also has vehicle traffic. The other paved segment runs from the east-entrance contact station up to the Mississippi headwaters. This is a curving, rolling delight of a trail that is a treat for bicyclists and hikers.

Lake Itasca is the focal point of the park. You can launch a boat or canoe onto the lake to explore the shoreline or try the walleye, northern, bass or panfish action. Squaw, Elk and Mary lakes also have boat landings. Water-skiing is not permitted on park lakes and motors are restricted to 10 mph. Daily narrated commercial boat tours of Lake Itasca run throughout the summer. The tours board at the Douglas Lodge pier in the South Itasca Center. The park swimming beach, on Lake Itasca, is up the lakeshore from the boat landing.

Douglas Lodge is a historic log hotel and restaurant built in 1905. Rooms are available in the main lodge and in Nicollet Court, a motel-type unit. The Club House is a two-story log structure ideal for family gatherings and special groups. Cabins of various sizes can be rented near the lodge, in the Bear Paw campground and (one) on Squaw Lake.

Itasca's family campsites are split into two semi-modern campgrounds. Pine Ridge has 130 sites (65 electric) and Bear Paw has 80 sites (34 electric), including 11 cart-in sites less than 300 yards from the parking area. Backpackers can choose from 11 primitive campsites in the southern half of the park (a hike of 1 to 5 miles). The park also has two group facilities. The Elk Lake Group Center is a 50-person primitive camp with a small shelter and water supply. The Squaw Lake Group Center is a semi-modern camp (75 capacity) with staff cabin, dining hall and kitchen, sanitation building and tent area. You can reserve the group centers through the park headquarters up to one year in advance. The semi-modern campsites, cabins and all other park lodging can be reserved by calling 1-800-765-CAMP.

Winter

The snowmobile trails in Itasca State Park connect with local Grant-in-Aid routes and trails in the nearby Mississippi Headwaters, Paul Bunyan, and White Earth state forests. The 115-mile-long Park Rapids Trail is another popular snowmobile trail. This path connects with the Heartland State Trail and Paul Bunyan State Forest snowmobile trail.

Itasca's 31 miles of groomed cross-country ski trails are designed mostly for beginner and intermediate skiers. The park's Aiton Heights Trail is for advanced skiers. The Itascatour Ski Trail, south of the park, provides a longer advanced cross-country route plus a short beginner trail.

Snowshoers like to explore the Wilderness Sanctuary and the point of land between the arms of Lake Itasca. The chance to spear northerns attracts ice fishermen to Itasca's lakes. Winter campers can set up in the Pine Ridge campground, where water and electricity are available. The Forest Inn stays open as a winter warming house and as the center of the park's winter interpretive programs.

LAKE BEMIDJI STATE PARK

Beltrami County. On County 20, about 6 miles northeast of Bemidji via Old Highway 71. Highway map index: F-7.

Regardless of weather conditions, the interpretive center should be your first stop in this park. Upstairs is the contact station, where you can register for campsites and get information about events in Bemidji. The action takes place downstairs, where the naturalist plots fun and (don't tell the kids) educational activities for park visitors. Kids usually make a beeline toward the animal displays and the touch boxes. The boxes are wooden compartments with hand-holes that permit the kids to reach in, feel, and guess the contents.

Perhaps the best feature of the interpretive center is the overview of the park. Clear, colorful diagrams depict the major park environments (lake, bogs, hills). Another graphic depicts Lake Bemidji fish life and the lake's food web (anglers take note).

To supplement the naturalist activities, pick up a park map and select a trail for your own exploration. On a boardwalk hike through a conifer bog, for example, you can observe some unusual flora, such as pitcher plants, orchids and insect-eating sundews. Early morning hikers will be serenaded by rosebreasted grosbeaks and a host of other woodland songsters. When the lakeshore is quiet, especially at dusk or dawn, you might notice loons, black terns or even white pelicans. The twilight woods comes alive with a chorus of tree frogs, leopard frogs and spring peepers.

Disabled visitors can enjoy a lakeshore stroll on the paved Rocky Point Trail from the picnic ground to County 20. There is also a paved loop along the beach. Bicyclists use these paths, too, but should be aware that people in wheelchairs have the right of way. Rocky Point Trail is a popular one, with many overlooks of big Lake Bemidji (6,765 acres).

In fair weather, Lake Bemidji is a giant playground as sailboats, powerboats (some towing skiers) and canoes share the lake. Fishing for walleye, northern and perch is always popular with park visitors. If you don't have a boat, you can rent one in the park. Ask for details at the contact station.

The park's lakefront is its busiest spot. The large picnic grounds are shaded by some of the big trees that the park is noted for. The enclosed picnic shelter is ideal for family reunions or special group gatherings (check with the manager for reservations). The swimming beach and boat landing are also located along the shoreline.

The spacious semi-modern campground (100 sites; 43 electric) can fill quickly on summer weekends. The park has two group camping centers; one is primitive (near the lakeshore) and the other (at the end of the main campground) features a dining hall. The group centers can be reserved through the park office.

Some visitors plan camping vacations at Lake Bemidji State Park because of the many festivals and attractions in the Bemidji area. The Mississippi River Canoe Route passes through Lake Bemidji and you can drive (or canoe) upriver to the river's headwaters in Itasca State Park. Nymore Beach, on the south shore of Lake Bemidji, was the site of a lumber mill that operated during Minnesota's last logging rush. Scuba divers occasionally discover logging artifacts in the water near the beach.

Winter

Outdoor activity at Lake Bemidji State Park barely slows down when the snow falls. Cross-country skiers tour on 9 miles of groomed loops designed for all ability levels. Snowmobile trails (3 miles) cut across the hills and lowlands of the park, connecting it with the North Country Grant-in-Aid Trail. There's also winter camping and ice fishing. The Bemidji area is a center for curling (similar to shuffleboard, but played on ice). Interested participants/spectators can call the chamber of commerce for curling dates. If you'd like to learn more about winter outdoors, Lake Bemidji State Park offers interpretive programs designed to change your perspective on Minnesota's most complained-about season. To make sure you don't miss special programs like the full-moon snowshoe hike, the candlelight ski tours or the March maple sap harvest, contact the park office for a schedule of events.

LAKE BRONSON STATE PARK

Kittson County. 1 mile east of Lake Bronson on County 28. Highway map index: B-3.

Lake Bronson State Park is an island in an ocean of farmland. It is a popular stop for Americans driving north to Winnipeg (2 hours away) and for Canadians driving south (the border is 20 miles up the road). The park provides a fertile blend of prairie, oak savanna, aspen woodland, lake and stream that supports a wide variety of wildlife.

LAKE CARLOS STATE PARK

Douglas County. 10 miles north of Alexandria on Highway 29. Highway map index: E-13.

The lakes and rolling terrain of Lake Carlos State Park were born from the last glacier. The mammoth ice block that melted to form Lake Carlos left a deep, clean lake (150 feet deep in places) noted for its abundance of fish. The 1,250-acre park lies within the scenic Leaf Hills Region, a transition zone between the prairies to the southwest and the coniferous forests to the northeast. With more than 15 miles of hiking trails, you can hike through stands of hardwood trees one minute, then cross a grassy meadow to a woodland pond or marsh the next. It is this combination of grassland, wetland, and wooded ridge that makes the park a treat for hikers.

MAPLEWOOD STATE PARK

Ottertail County. 7 miles east of Pelican Rapids on Highway 108. Highway map index: D-11.

From the crest of Hallaway Hill in Maplewood State Park, the view sweeps over a green-blue world of lakes, fields and woods. Boats below on Lake Lida are like water spiders gliding swiftly across the water, leaving widening wakes behind them. It's peaceful and breezy up here, the kind of place that is tailor-made for relaxed trail lunches and lazy afternoons under blue sky and white puffy cloud.

Maplewood State Park (over 9,000 acres) is blessed with a peaceful natural beauty that encompasses more than 20 lakes interspersed among hilly woodlands, and an extensive trail system. Two of the lakes, Lida and Beers, have drive-in boat landings. Lake Lida also features a guarded swimming beach and a large picnic area that is spread out across a hilly peninsula.

The trail network might be Maplewood's best asset. Over 15 miles of horseback riding trails, laid out in loops, ramble through the park. A century or more fades away as you cross ridgelines and amble into valleys that have changed little since pre-settlement times. Some riders strap a rod on the saddle for fishing breaks at trail-side lakes. The trail center in the park is designed for horse campers, although there are currently no buildings or other facilities.

Hikers are also welcome on the riding paths and on the interpretive loops and connecting trails. One self-guiding trail leads visitors through a forest demonstration area where a variety of trees are identified.

Fishing is popular on many of the park's lakes. Anglers on Lake Lida try for walleyes and northerns, while several of the smaller lakes are favorites for panfish. Ironcially, Bass Lake attracts rainbow trout fishermen.

MILLE LACS KATHIO STATE PARK

Mille Lacs County. 5 miles northwest of Onamia on County 26. Highway map index: I-12.

Mille Lacs Kathio is an ideal state park for doers: challenging trails, water sports and all-season activities in a rugged forested setting. With over 10,000 acres, Minnesota's fourth-largest park has plenty of space to play in.

Although within eyesight of giant Mille Lacs Lake, Kathio has no direct access to its waters. The nearest public landing is 4 miles north of the park on Shah-Bush-Kung Bay (off of Highway 169). Cove Bay and many nearby resorts also have boat landings. Father Hennepin State Park, a small park about 15 miles east of Kathio, does have a beach and extensive frontage (with boat launches) on Mille Lacs Lake.

Anglers can choose between a couple of good spots in Mille Lacs Kathio. Some like the action below the dam on Ogechie Lake; others like to try for northern, bass or panfish on Shakopee Lake. Canoeists also have both lakes to explore as well as the Rum River Canoe & Boating Route. The Rum River begins in the park and connects Ogechie and Shakopee lakes before winding its way south for 146 miles to the Mississippi. Many canoeists start their river trip from the canoe landing between the lakes. The park rents canoes and boats at the landing, next to the primitive canoe campground. The picnic area, interpretive center and a man-made swimming pond (with a sand beach) are located on the southeast end of Ogechie Lake.

Mille Lacs Kathio's 70-site semi-modern campground is spread out in the woods on the east side of Ogechie Lake. Though the campground is full on most summer weekends, you can usually find open sites during the week. The primitive group camp (capacity 50) near the canoe landing can be reserved through the park office.

The interpretive center, next to the picnic grounds, highlights the extensive Indian history of the area. Much of the pottery, arrowheads and tools in the center came from some of the 19 archaeological sites in the park. Researchers have found evidence of civilizations that lived here long before the Dakota and Ojibway Indians.

For more than 4,000 years, people have been attracted by the abundance of this region. The park's rolling, wooded hills supported a rich variety of wildlife, and Ogechie Lake was noted for its lush growths of wild rice. The Dakota chose this area as the capital of their nation. Today, a historical marker stands at the site of the old Dakota village of Izatys, located at the source of the Rum River on Mille Lacs Lake. These people came to be known as the Mdewakanton, or those who live by the Water of the Great Spirit (Mille Lacs Lake).

The Ojibway brought their own rich cultural tradition with them from the east and settled along the shores of Mille Lacs (they still live in the area today). They, like the Dakota, depended on the natural bounty of wild rice, fish and other foods. You can learn more about Ojibway history and culture at the Mille Lacs Indian Museum (administered by the Minnesota Historical Society) north of the park on Highway 169. Because of the interwoven history of Dakota, Ojibway and European people in this area, Mille Lacs Kathio State Park is a designated National Historic Landmark.

Mille Lacs Kathio has 40 miles of hiking trails and 30 miles of horseback trails. Some people like to bicycle on the 4.5 miles of park roads. Horseback riders can park their trailers in the Trail Center parking lot. The trails twist and turn throughout the park, but my favorite section is in the undeveloped southwest corner of Kathio. This is a scenic area of hills and meadows where you might come across beaver lodges or spot a deer feeding at dusk. The north-end trails are pretty, too, including two short nature trail loops.

A special experience at Kathio is climbing to the top of the 100-foot-tall observation tower. The undulating carpet of forest sweeps away in three directions from the tower, while Mille Lacs Lake dominates the view in the other direction. On a clear day, you can see the north shore and spot the legions of boats on the lake. But at times fog, like a massive gray wall, blocks the great lake from view. The wind is cool and gusty off the lake, so bring a jacket for your climb.

Winter

Cold weather and snow doesn't stop the fun at Mille Lacs Kathio State Park. Snowmobilers can zip along on the 20 miles of park trails that connect to other regional trails. Ice fishing is big news on Shakopee Lake and, of course, on Mille Lacs Lake. You can snowshoe anywhere in the spacious park and have a front-row seat for winter wildlife photography if you wish. Winter camping is becoming more popular, too.

The 18-mile cross-country ski system is considered one of the best in Minnesota and provides a challenge for skiers of all abilities (ski rental is available). The modern Trail Center building is used as a warming house, complete with cut wood and a fireplace. During winter, the park naturalist leads snowshoe hikes and many other nature programs.

MISSISSIPPI RIVER CANOE & BOATING ROUTE

674 miles, from Lake Itasca (Clearwater County) to the Iowa border.

At its birth in Itasca State Park, the Father of Waters is a humble brook that bubbles over rocks and flows quietly between narrow, wooded banks. But as it winds through Minnesota for almost 700 miles in great serpentine curves, the growing river lives up to its name. From its wilderness origins, the Mississippi River is transformed into a broad, commercially busy river at the Twin Cities and below. Families and beginning canoeists can enjoy canoeing on the river, now substantially subdued by dams.

The first white man to see the river was Hernando De Soto, in 1541. Though many tried to find its source, it was not until 1832 that Henry Schoolcraft and his Ojibway guide, Ozawindib, discovered the headwaters of the Mississippi River at Lake Itasca. Most of the wildlife and scenery that Schoolcraft saw on his quest are still part of a canoeist's experience on the 60-mile stretch between Lake Itasca and Lake Bemidji. In this portion, marshes alternate with 60-foot banks cloaked with jack, red and white pines.

The first 15 miles are impassable at times because of shallow water and beaver dams. The intermittent rapids upstream from Lake Bemidji are not difficult to canoe, but windfalls, brushy areas, and sand bars make for rough passage in spots. You might see beavers, otters and a variety of waterfowl along the way. Black bear, deer and even timber wolves inhabit the Mississippi Headwaters State Forest, which lines the channel.

In the conifer bogs below Stumphges Rapids, look for wild orchids in the shade of tamarack and black-spruce trees. Insect-eating sundew and pitcher plants live in these bogs, too.

The stretch from Pine Point to Iron Bridge is characterized by swampy lowlands and rice beds where Ojibway Indians still harvest wild rice. Canoeing here is an exercise in patience, as the river meanders in a series of large oxbows, often doubling back to within yards of a bend you just paddled around.

As you near lakes Irving and Bemidji, the landscape changes from wilderness to agricultural to residential. Lake Bemidji State Park, at the northeast corner of the lake, has a semi-modern campground and naturalist programs. Accesses and campsites spaced along this 60-mile headwaters section mean that you can plan three- to five-day trips. Outfitters are located near Itasca State Park and Bemidji.

Below the hydroelectric dam several miles downriver from Lake Bemidji, the Mississippi enters a region of lakes. The marshes between the lakes provide breeding areas for mallards, blue-winged teal and other waterfowl. Fishing is good at times for walleyes, largemouth bass, muskies and northern.

The river flows through the Buena Vista and Bowstring state forests and the Chippewa National Forest on its way from Cass Lake to Lake Winnibigoshish. Dams require portages at the outlets of these lakes. Lake Winnibigoshish is too large to cross safely by canoe—sudden winds and waves can catch canoeists far from land—but you can follow its south shore, where a couple of primitive campsites offer shelter.

The Mississippi River again coils back and forth on itself in a convoluted maze from Ball Club Lake almost to Schoolcraft State Park. About 14 miles below the park is the first of two dams in the Grand Rapids area requiring portages.

Between Deer River and Libby, the upper Mississippi changes to banks of pine and hardwoods. Waterfowl are not as plentiful, but deer herds are large around the Golden Anniversary and Hill River state forests.

In Aitkin County, the Mississippi River flows through forested flatlands. Numerous oxbows that once were part of the main channel now form secluded backwaters. The largest of the steamboats that used to travel between Aitkin and Grand Rapids sometimes clipped the riverbanks while rounding the sharp bends in this area.

You'll pass by the Savanna State Forest and Big Sandy Lake before the river turns southwest toward Aitkin. The lake was the site of another Indian battle during the Ojibway campaign to force the Dakota out of the forests. Below Aitkin, the river becomes straighter and broader. White pines tower above the hardwoods in the Crow Wing State Forest as the river flows beneath low-lying hills. You'll have to portage around the Potlatch Dam in Brainerd, which is a major visitor center for the surrounding lake country. South of Brainerd, the river flows through a deciduous forest typical of central Minnesota. This stretch of river is popular with anglers for walleye and smallmouth bass.

Crow Wing State Park, at the confluence of the Crow Wing and Mississippi rivers, is the site of yet another Ojibway-Dakota battle. The park is also the site of Crow Wing, one of the state's oldest ghost towns. Several miles south is the Mississippi River Slough, a 2-mile stretch dotted with more than 45 islands.

By the time you reach Little Falls, the Mississippi River has lost its wilderness character. Four dams require portages from here to below St. Cloud. The riverscape consists of hardwood groves interspersed with houses, farms and cities. Below Little Falls, you'll pass Charles A. Lindbergh State Park. The summer home of the famous flier is preserved on the banks of the river he loved. (The home and interpretive center are administered by the Minnesota Historical Society.)

Just above St. Cloud, where the Sauk River joins the Mississippi, is a stretch of boulder-bed rapids that inexperienced canoeists should avoid, especially in high, cold water.

Numerous accesses and rest stops make the St. Cloud to Anoka stretch ideal for day trips. You'll find outfitters in St. Cloud and Elk River. Just below the St. Cloud dam are 30-odd Beaver Islands, which choke the river for 2 miles, forming a network of channels. Three power plants and increasing numbers of riverbank homes signal the approach to the Twin Cities.

Before reaching Minneapolis, you'll have to portage around the Coon Rapids dam. Fishing is good below the dam and old powerhouse. Though the river flows through downtown Minneapolis, many buildings are atop bluffs, and a strip of natural land survives along the stream, so wildlife can be observed even in this urban setting.

The growth of the Twin Cities has not helped river quality. The water is silty and, in places, contaminated with sewage and industrial chemicals. The Minnesota Department of Health has placed restrictions on consumption of fish caught in the river from here to below Wabasha.

Downstream from the Twin Cities, the river is interrupted by locks and dams. Canoeists can safely navigate the locks by following the attendant's instructions and steering clear of commercial barges. Motorboats and a deceptively swift current in the wide river require caution from canoeists.

Despite heavy industrial development below Fort Snelling, the Mississippi remains a ribbon of nature flanked by cottonwoods, willows and flowering shrubs. Bald eagles, ospreys, red-tailed hawks and falcons patrol the channel. Pig's Eye Lake supports populations of egrets and great blue herons amid the bustle of commerce.

The Mississippi National River and Recreation Area (MNRRA) has been created by the National Park Service. This is a 72-mile stretch of the river as it flows through the Minneapolis-St. Paul metro region. A master plan for MNRRA will be available in 1994, reflecting an effort to coordinate the complex uses of the Mississippi River as it flows through the metro area.

The fascinating river regains its natural character south of the Twin Cities. Below the confluence with the St. Croix River, the Mississippi forms the Minnesota-Wisconsin border and "runs between two chains of mountains," as Father Louis Hennepin wrote in 1683. The majestic wooded bluffs and sheer cliffs are the setting for Frontenac and O. L. Kipp state parks and the Richard J. Dorer Memorial Hardwood State Forest. Most of the bottomlands are part of the Upper Mississippi Wildlife and Fish Refuge.

NORTHWEST ANGLE STATE FOREST

Lake of the Woods County. Road access: take Highway 310 north from Roseau or Highway 313 north from Warroad to Canadian border. Follow Manitoba Highway 12 to Sprague, then north on 308 to 525. Follow 525 northeast to Angle Inlet, Minnesota. Angle Inlet is also accessible by boat or plane. Highway map index: F-1 and 2.

As you look at a map of Minnesota, the curious projection of territory at the top of the state that sticks up like a smokestack is the Northwest Angle. This chunk of America is cut off from the rest of the country by Buffalo Bay, the southwestern arm of Lake of the Woods. Logically, it seems, the Northwest Angle should belong to Canada, but due to a geographical blunder made over 200 years ago, it is a proud part of Minnesota.

Back when the present Great Lakes states were known as the Northwest Territory, and Britain owned Canada, the United States tried to define its northern boundary. At the treaty of 1783, it was agreed that the boundary would follow the water communication route west from Lake Superior to Lake of the Woods, run through that lake to its northwestern point, and then continue due west to the Mississippi River. No one knew then that you could go due west of Lake of the Woods forever and still not touch the Mississippi River.

In the early 1800s, around the time of the Louisiana Purchase, Americans realized the mistake and reopened boundary discussions with Britain. It wasn't until the Convention of 1818 that a simple solution was agreed upon. Because it was impossible to run a line straight west of Lake of the Woods to the Mississippi River, a new line would drop straight south from the northwest point of the lake to the 49th parallel. This parallel, extending westward, formed the northern border of the United States.

You can reach the Northwest Angle by way of Manitoba, by floatplane from Warroad or Baudette, or by boat. Lake of the Woods is big and unpredictable, so large private boats are recommended. There are no public campgrounds in the forest, and most of the Angle is part of the Red Lake Indian Reservation.

The town of Angle Inlet is the main destination for visitors who wish to stay in a private resort or sightsee on the lake. There are many resorts around the town and on a handful of islands in both U.S. and Canadian waters. Lake of the Woods is sprinkled with thousands of rocky wilderness islands and some fishermen prefer to hire guides who know the lake and the fishing hot spots.

Near the northeast tip of the Angle is Fort St. Charles, a small restored log fort on Magnussen Island. Built as a fur-trading post in 1732, it was abandoned in 1749 and left to the elements until rediscovered 150 years later. The fort, restored by the Minnesota Fourth Degree Knights of Columbus, provides a glimpse of life in the isolated island and forest wilderness of Lake of the Woods. For further information about the historical site and how to get there, ask at one of the resorts in Angle Inlet.

OLD MILL STATE PARK

Marshall County. Off County 4 between Argyle and Newfolden. Highway map index: B-5.

As you walk into the clearing, it's as though you've stepped back into another century. To the left is the old mill, a simple building that was the business and social center for pioneer farmers. A settler cabin faces the mill on the opposite side of the clearing. The gristmill is the pride of the park. It is operated on Labor Day weekend each summer to demonstrate flour grinding.

During Grinding Days, visitors can purchase a bagful of fresh stone-ground flour or bran and get an earful of pioneer tales and lore. Grinding Days usually draws a crowd, and the 26-site semi-modern campground can fill on those weekends. Special groups can reserve the primitive group camp and make arrangements for tours of the old mill.

Hiking trails are laid out in loops of various lengths that give a complete picture of the park. If you have time for only one loop, pick up a brochure at the office and enjoy the .7-mile Agassiz self-guided trail. You'll learn about the plant communities in Old Mill State Park and the wildlife that makes its home here. Although the surrounding area is heavily farmed, the river corridor is an animal highway where you can see beaver, deer, or even a moose.

PINE RIVER CANOE & BOATING ROUTE

Cass and Crow Wing counties. 52 miles, from Pine Mountain Lake (access in Backus) to the Mississippi River.

Minnesota's newest designated canoe route is a clear, scenic river that families and beginning canoeists can enjoy. The Pine River has occasional Class I rapids that may be impassable in low water.

The route could be regarded as three separate sections. Most river trips on the upper stretch run from the Cass County 118 bridge to the Whitefish chain of lakes. To reach the bridge, take Highway 84 north of the town of Pine River to County 118 and turn left. The river flows through an area of mixed hardwoods and conifers, mostly birch, elm, jack pine and red pine. Some farmland interrupts the forest along the riverbank.

The Pine River enters the Whitefish chain of lakes, continuing for 9 miles to the Army Corps of Engineers dam at the river's outlet at Cross Lake. The lakes in the chain are large and potentially dangerous for canoeists. If doubtful about the weather, stick close to shore for a fast escape.

Below Cross Lake, the Pine has remained more primitive where it flows through the Crow Wing State Forest. The dense tree cover is rarely broken by development. Rapids here, as elsewhere on the river, are dotted with boulders but are easy to canoe. Beyond Pine Lake, the river broadens into a marshy area characteristic of the rest of the route.

One of the Pine River's main attractions is the constant change of scenery along its route. Canoeists paddle from woods to farmland and from big lakes to marshes. Riverbanks vary from low wetlands to high sand-and-gravel banks. The river itself changes from mild rapids to meanders, pools, and lakes. The river's environment is fragile. Sand banks erode swiftly when people walk on them, and litter detracts from everybody's outdoor experience. Numerous unofficial landings and campsites compound these problems.

The Pine River passes by too much farmland and cottage development to be called a wilderness stream, but its easygoing nature and diverse backdrops add up to a pleasant northwoods outing within a 3-hour drive of the Twin Cities. Besides canoeing, tubing is popular on the lower Pine River (bring your own inner tube or rent one locally). Before leaving home, ask the state Department of Natural Resources about river conditions and whether there's enough water flow for canoeing.

The last take-out is on Crow Wing County 11, just above the confluence with the Mississippi River. Some canoeists continue their trip on the Mississippi River Canoe Route.

RED LAKE RIVER CANOE & BOATING ROUTE

*Clearwater, Pennington, Red Lake and Polk counties. 193
miles, from Lower Red Lake to the confluence of the Red River
of the North, in East Grand Forks.*

The upper Red Lake River is almost as isolated today as it
was when explorers and missionaries first saw it. The first 18
miles of the route flow through the marshy wildlands of the
Red Lake Indian Reservation. A variety of water plants,
including wild rice and cattails, flourish in the water and
along the banks. The marsh attracts blue herons, ducks and
gulls. There are no marked rest areas or campsites on this
stretch. A tribal permit is required to use the section of river
within the boundaries of the Red Lake Indian Reservation.

The river curves through a prairie to High Landing, where
cottonwoods, willows and elms stand in the midst of
cropland. Below High Landing, the river twists its way to
Thief River Falls, where it passes through residential areas.
The access points and campsites around Thief River Falls are
well used, as many canoeists purchase supplies and start
their trip from here.

From St. Hilaire to about 11 miles below Huot (45 miles),
the river is characterized by rapids, short pools and
intermittent boulders. This section is rated Class II, requiring
some maneuvering. The banks are heavily wooded and the
river drops 110 feet in 17 miles. Above Red Lake Falls, you'll
pass under high-banked eroded cliffs where entire hillsides
have torn loose from spring floods.

The Old Crossing Treaty State Wayside, near Huot, marks
the place where the Ojibway Indians ceded 10 million acres
of land in the Red River Valley in 1868. This spot was also
the site of an early settler post office, and a place where the
squeaky-wheeled ox carts could ford the river.

Below Old Crossing, the river widens, and gravel bars,
rocks and snags are common. Crookston is a popular stop
because of its convenient city park. Between Crookston and
East Grand Forks, there are no established campsites. The

river meanders through farmland. The banks are sometimes screened by trees, many of which slump into the river from erosion. The lower reaches of the Red River can be muddy and full of snag piles.

RUM RIVER CANOE & BOATING ROUTE

Mille Lacs, Sherburne, Isanti and Anoka counties. 145 miles, from Mille Lacs Lake to the Mississippi River at Anoka.

The Rum River is spirited in stretches. The series of rapids from Lake Onamia to Princeton is safe for canoeists with intermediate skills. During spring high water, the river spills and tumbles along a rocky obstacle course to Milaca. This section is usually not canoeable in late summer and fall. If you've never run these rapids, plan your route carefully. You may choose to portage your gear around the rapids, depending on the water levels.

Families and beginners can launch near the headwaters in Mille Lacs Kathio State Park and canoe to Shakopee Lake and Lake Onamia. Combine a headwaters canoe trip with a visit to the state park. There's a primitive campsite near the launch and plenty of scenic hiking trails.

Novice canoeists who would like a longer trip will enjoy the lazy pace of the lower Rum. The few rapids from Princeton to Anoka are easy, but be wary of underwater obstacles. The river below Milaca is generally high enough for canoeing throughout the season. Except for small stands of red and white pine along the southern course, hardwoods line most of the river route.

Pack a picnic and your fishing gear for a day on the Rum. Smallmouth bass lurk in the holes above and below the rapids on the upper river, but you might get lucky with walleyes or northerns, too.

The DNR's canoe route map shows access points, primitive campsites and private campgrounds. Obstacles, like rapids and dams, are also noted.

SCHOOLCRAFT STATE PARK

Cass County. About 15 miles west of Grand Rapids. Drive west on Highway 2, south on Highway 6, and turn west onto County 28, following the park signs. Highway map index: I-9.

On his way up the Mississippi River in search of its origin, Henry Rowe Schoolcraft camped near here with his party of explorers. He found the headwaters on July 13, 1832, in present-day Itasca State Park. The area bounded by Schoolcraft State Park remains virtually unchanged since the explorers paddled through. The park boasts many virgin white-pine trees in woods where songbirds seem louder than voices. Wild rice still thrives in the marshes, and deer still sip from the river at dawn. Schoolcraft State Park is open nine months of the year.

SHERBURNE NATIONAL WILDLIFE REFUGE

Sherburne County. Refuge headquarters is southwest of Princeton off of Highway 169. Highway map index: I-15.

Canoeing is a gentle experience on the Sherburne National Wildlife Refuge. Maybe it's because the St. Francis River doesn't seem to be in a hurry, twisting past high sandy banks and through lowland marsh. You could spend about three hours on the river if you were going to paddle the whole 12-mile route in the southeastern corner of the refuge. It'll take even longer if you fish.

Camera and binoculars come in handy here, no matter how you explore the refuge. Canoeists and boaters (no motors) may spot great blue heron, great egrets, white-tailed deer and many kinds of waterfowl. You can also get good views of wildlife from roads and trails. Many visitors take their time on the Wildlife Management Drive during spring and fall migrations. This 12-mile drive is open only on weekends and holidays during a two-month period both in spring and fall.

Sherburne's trails are used all year by hikers and cross-country skiers. The Mahnomen Trail, 2.5 miles long, features an observation tower, boardwalk and rest area. Pick up the leaflet for the Mounds Loop. The Blue Hill Trail is a 6.25-mile trail system that also has an interpretive loop.

Groups are welcome here. The Old School House, near the refuge headquarters, is an outdoors center with displays, a library and audio-visual equipment. School groups and other organizations begin their refuge visit here. Snowshoes are available for school group outings.

The 30,665-acre Sherburne National Wildlife Refuge encompasses much of the St. Francis River Valley. The shallow marshes and natural lakes that dot the landscape were formed from the last glacier. Human history dates back over 10,000 years, with Indian village sites discovered on the refuge from 1300 A.D. When white men arrived during the 1870s, the St. Francis River basin was considered one of the finest wildlife areas in Minnesota. The combination of marsh, wild rice, open water and tamarack swamps was a wildlife haven.

Settlers, scratching out a new life, logged the oak forests and drained the wetlands. The oak savannas, protected from fire, were invaded by woody vegetation. Wildlife declined. By the early 1940s, sportsmen and conservationists recognized the potential for preserving and restoring the St. Francis River Valley as a wildlife area. Their dream was realized with creation of the Sherburne National Wildlife Refuge in 1965. Sherburne is now an important link in a chain of refuges operated by the U.S. Fish and Wildlife Service along the Mississippi flyway.

Sherburne supports a diversity of wildlife within three main habitats: wetlands, woodlands, and grasslands and oak savannas. The refuge wetlands include over 20 pools and natural lakes that provide homes for many species of waterfowl, shorebirds, wading birds, mammals, frogs, turtles and salamanders. Although most of the wetlands are shallow and freeze out in the winter, some are capable of supporting populations of northerns, panfish and rough fish, which attract migrating ospreys and bald eagles. Not all of the pools are kept at the same depth. By controlling water levels, the refuge creates a variety of wildlife habitats.

The refuge is open for public use during daylight hours. Hunters may get a leaflet that outlines hunting regulations on the refuge. You can cross-country ski and snowshoe throughout the refuge, except for the Blue Hill and Mahnomen trails, which are for cross-country skiers only. There are no camping facilities at Sherburne, but ask at the office for information about nearby public and private campgrounds.

TAMARAC NATIONAL WILDLIFE REFUGE

Becker County. About 18 miles northeast of Detroit Lakes. Drive east of Detroit Lakes on Highway 34, then turn north through Rochert on County 29 to the refuge. Highway map index: D-9.

Deep forests and abundant wetlands form a picturesque setting for wildlife habitat in a part of the state already noted for its scenic lakes and woods. The bald eagles must think so. They nest in the pines beginning in April, producing between 15 and 17 eaglets each year, more than any other national wildlife refuge outside Alaska.

To the Dakota people, and the Ojibway who came later, these dark hills and blue waters were a prized hunting, fishing and ricing territory. Lumbermen prized the tall timber, clearing off most of the area's giant white and red pines. Settlers followed, trying to farm and homestead. Many left when they couldn't make a go of it in the forested bog country.

The abandoned, unproductive land eventually evolved into the Tamarac National Wildlife Refuge in 1938. The primary goal has always been to serve as a breeding ground and sanctuary for migratory birds and other wildlife. The refuge's 43,000 acres were purchased with funds from the sale of federal duck stamps. Early development such as roads, trails, buildings, and water control structures, was completed by the Civilian Conservation Corps (CCC) in the 1930s. In the late 1960s, a Job Corps Conservation Center was added to refuge development.

The refuge gets its name from the tamarack tree, the only conifer to lose its needles in fall. Much of Tamarac is open for the public to enjoy year-round, but the middle section is only open seasonally and the northwest corner of the refuge is a Wilderness Area.

There is a lot to enjoy here. You can fish, boat, hike or birdwatch (a list of over 200 species seen at the refuge is available at the visitor center). Some visitors return in-season for berry-picking and mushrooming. Each of these activities may be limited to certain parts of the refuge, so stop at the visitor center before starting out. Check the summer schedule for weekend hours and special programs between Memorial Day and Labor Day (interpretive programs can be arranged for organized groups). The visitor center also has an observation deck overlooking the refuge.

Pick up the information leaflets that outline hunting, fishing and other recreational activities on the refuge. You can hike on the Old Indian Historic Trail near Tamarac Lake and on the nature trail that begins near the visitor center. During winter, you can cross-country ski on 5 miles of trails near Pine Lake and Tamarac Lake. If you'd like to tour the refuge by car, ask for the Blackbird Auto Tour leaflet. This is a 45-minute self-guided tour on 10 miles of refuge roads, providing a closer look at the habitat types and scenic areas of Tamarac. Pack a lunch and take a break at one of the attractive picnic areas on Pine Lake or Chippewa Lake.

Tamarac National Wildlife Refuge is nearly one-third water, either lakes or bog, and the land is rich in wetland flora and fauna. More than 3,500 pairs of ducks and several hundred geese nest here. Peak duck numbers during fall migration have exceeded 40,000 in recent years. Since 1938, over 245 species of birds have been observed on the refuge, including the trumpeter swan, which is making a comeback at Tamarac.

ZIPPEL BAY STATE PARK

Lake of the Woods County. 10 miles northeast of Williams on Lake of the Woods. Park entrance is off of County 8. Highway map index: F-3.

If you time it right, the wild blueberries will be ripe when you visit Zippel Bay State Park. Add some to your breakfast pancakes for a savory memory of your stay here.

Take a walk along the 3-mile sand beach on Lake of the Woods. The scale of the lake is hard to imagine: 1,485 square miles of water, 65,000 miles of shoreline, and 14,000 islands. From the park beach, it's 80 miles to the northern tip of the lake. The lake is 55 miles wide at its widest and varies from 4 to 35 feet deep in the southern bays to over 150 feet deep in northern areas.

While hiking or horseback riding on the six-mile trail system at the 3,000-acre park, you might spot some ruffed or sharptail grouse. The rustic campsites at Zippel Bay are divided into four separate wooded loops. Although most campers come up here for Lake of the Woods fishing, the campground is rarely full. The primitive group camp is available for riding clubs and other special gatherings on a reservation basis.

Winter

When people talk about winter around Lake of the Woods, they usually mention ice fishing. You can rent an ice-fishing shanty at any nearby resort and even fly into your favorite spot to catch your limit of walleyes and northern. Each winter the Baudette VFW sponsors a fishing derby with prizes in several categories, including largest and smallest fish, and oldest fisherman.

Zippel Bay State Park has groomed snowmobile and beginner cross-country ski trails. Snowmobilers can extend their ride on local Grant-in-Aid trails. A growing number of hardy souls enjoy winter camping. They combine camping with skiing, ice fishing or snowmobiling. If you wish to try winter camping, ask the manager about water and where to camp when you register.

Visitors to Zippel Bay discover a three-mile sand beach on Lake of the Woods.

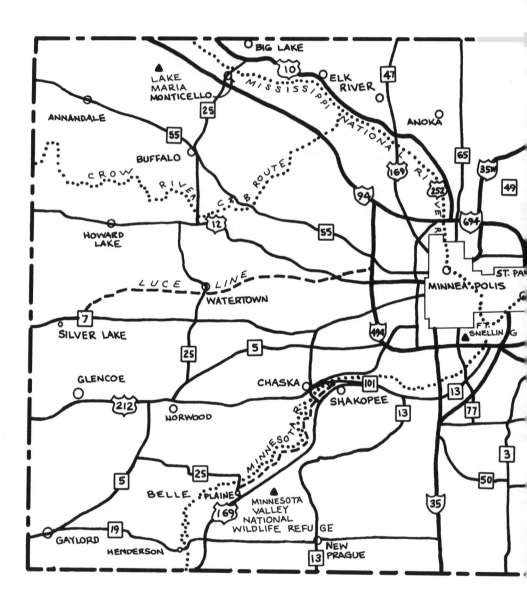

METROLAND REGION

Afton State Park
Fort Snelling State Park
Lake Maria State Park
Luce Line State Trail
Minnesota Valley National Wildlife Refuge
   Recreation Area and State Trail
Mississippi National River and Recreation Area
Willard Munger State Trail (Gateway Segment)
William O'Brien State Park

▲ ....STATE PARKS & RECREATION AREAS
△ ....WAYSIDES
■ ....NATIONAL MONUMENTS
— — — — ....STATE TRAIL
• • • • • ....CANOE & RIVER ROUTES

185

AFTON STATE PARK

Washington County. About 10 miles north of Hastings at junction of County highways 20 and 21. Highway map index: K-17.

Bring comfortable walking shoes when you visit Afton State Park because you'll have to hike in order to picnic, camp or swim here. Although only a 40-minute drive from the Twin Cities, Afton offers a solution for traffic snarls and freeway mania: motorless motion. Afton, one of the newer additions to Minnesota's state park system, is still being discovered by visitors.

Those who have already found the trails that plunge into deep ravines and climb up to ridgetops where you can overlook the St. Croix River Valley would prefer that Afton remain their secret, but the news is bound to get out.

If you feel out of touch with the natural world because of too much city, Afton State Park will help you mark the seasons. The St. Croix River Valley is one of the state's best birding areas. As the flocks fly overhead, you can hear the collective fluttering of their wings, like a wind urging them on their way. In spring, warblers and bluebirds return to the park, filling the woods with song. You'll also see many hawks during the migrations and might notice red-tailed hawks circling above the fields, hunting for rabbits or rodents. Eagles are often spotted soaring above the bluffs on their way through the park, but they don't nest here.

Afton's 18 miles of hiking trails (some of which are strenuous) begin from the parking lot near the interpretive center. To reach the backpack sites or the trails in the main body of park land, you'll have to drop into the ravine, cross Trout Brook near its mouth, and climb the bluffs on the other side of the stream. Some trails follow the 2-mile-long river shoreline in the park, while others twist through the hills and valleys farther inland. The quietest trails are in Afton's northern and western extremes.

A 5-mile-long bridle trail allows horseback riders to enjoy the park's hilly terrain. A recently developed bicycle trail parallels the park road and extends along the river, totaling some 4 miles of pedaling for cyclists. The paved trail may also become popular with disabled visitors.

Establishment of the Mississippi National River and Recreation Area should help ensure the mighty river's health in the Twin Cities area.

The 24 wooded and open sites in the backpack camping area are on an upland plateau. The secluded primitive sites, spaced along the forested edge of a former pasture, are attracting more backpackers as people hear about Afton. Water is available from a hand pump. A group camp will be developed in the southern corner of the park.

Most visitors stick close to the river at Afton. They hike down here to swim at the beach, picnic or fish. Anglers try for walleye, silver bass, smallmouth bass or sauger from the riverbank. The St. Croix River is a state-designated canoe and boating route (the park has one canoe campsite near the river). Since the river is heavily used by larger powerboats and houseboats in the summer, the park maintains an area for self-contained craft to anchor. A self-registration station is available at the mooring area for boat campers. Plans are under way to develop a new shelter near the river.

Be sure to stop at the visitor center adjacent to the parking lot, next to the park's other picnic area. Easy-to-understand displays describe points of interest and park resources. Park staff members encourage visitors to assist with interpretive programs and resource management. If you're interested in volunteering, contact the park manager.

Include a side trip to the historic village of Afton in your travel plans. Gaslights cast a warm glow over the restored 19th-century buildings that now house local businesses. The village is north of Afton State Park at the junction of Highway 95 and County 21.

Winter

The interpretive center stays open year-round and is used as a warming house by winter trail users. Weekends draw crowds from the Twin Cities metro area, mostly for the excellent cross-country skiing and for the winter sliding hill. The marked and groomed 18-mile trail system at Afton (including 7 miles of skate-skiing track) provides challenging skiing for expert and intermediate skiers.

Some people like to ski down to the St. Croix River to try ice fishing. Snowshoeing and hiking are permitted anywhere in the park (snowmobiling is not allowed), but it can be difficult to navigate in the slippery ravines. You can camp at Afton in the winter by hiking or skiing to the backpack camping area.

FORT SNELLING STATE PARK

Hennepin and Dakota counties. Junction of Highway 5 and Post Road. Take the Fort Snelling exits from Highway 5 or 55. Highway map index: J-17.

It's not every day that you can walk up to a stranger and ask him about the hardships at a frontier fort in the 1820s. But the costumed guides at historic Fort Snelling will be happy to answer your questions. Although the park offers much more for family day visits besides the historic site, the fort is the main attraction in a park that is full of surprises. Historically, Fort Snelling has been a gateway for soldiers, explorers and settlers into the upper Mississippi River Valley. Today this area is still a major gateway, as you'll discover when you hear the roar of jets from the nearby international airport and the rumble of traffic on Minneapolis-St. Paul freeways. Ignore the background noise as you walk through the front gate, and pretend you've just pulled off the dusty trail for a break.

Built on a strategic bluff above the confluence of the Mississippi and Minnesota rivers in the early 1820s, Fort Snelling was the last U.S. outpost in the northwestern wilderness. For over 30 years, the fort was a center of government policy-making and a place of safety for those who sought shelter within its stone walls.

Modern travelers are encouraged to participate in the fort's daily life. Visit the blacksmith, shoulder a musket, or bargain with the sutler over the price of tobacco. With more than half of Minnesota's population living in the seven-county metropolitan area, Fort Snelling State Park and the historic site (operated by the Minnesota Historical Society) attract large day-use crowds, especially on weekends. The interpretive program includes films, outdoor hikes, and special events. Headquarters for the park's naturalist programs is in the year-round interpretive center on Pike Island.

Picnic Island has shaded, pleasant riverside picnic areas with a shelter. Most visitors grab the table closest to their car, but it's worth the short walk to the tables along the river. A drive-in boat landing on Picnic Island provides access for anglers and sightseers to the Minnesota and Mississippi rivers.

The canoeing is easy on the rivers (both are designated canoe routes), but commercial barge traffic can be heavy. If you don't want to dodge boats and barges, try canoeing on Gun Club Lake (two bodies of water linked by a stream) or on Snelling Lake. Fishing and wildlife observation occupy canoeists who trace the shorelines of Gun Club Lake. Spring-fed Snelling Lake is popular for its fishing, swimming and canoeing. No motors are allowed on this lake.

The bottomlands, wet meadows and small lakes of the park are best explored by foot. On the 18-mile trail system, you'll pass below lofty, thick-trunked hardwoods as well as the towering Mendota Bridge. One big loop trail swings through the park's undeveloped land across the Minnesota River. The main access for this loop is off Highway 13 near Lone Oak Road. The best river valley overlooks are from Highway 13 and from the trail that leads to the Fort Snelling Historic Site. Don't be alarmed if, while hiking on Pike Island or elsewhere, you suddenly hear a loud boom that echoes above the usual noise. It's just the firing of the fort cannon, which still startles unsuspecting bystanders.

A paved bicycle trail starts at the park entrance and continues out of the park to Minnehaha Falls. This scenic route is also accessible to disabled visitors.

Fort Snelling State Park offers a nine-hole golf course (privately owned). Polo, baseball and other field games are played on the grounds across the road from the golf course. To reach this area, take the Historic Site exit off Highway 55.

The park does not have a campground, but Afton State Park, southeast of the Twin Cities, has 24 backpack sites. To see more waterfowl and wildlife in the Minnesota River Valley, drive downriver to the various units of the Minnesota Valley Trail State Park, extending from Fort Snelling to Le Sueur. The Minnesota Valley National Wildlife Refuge extends from Fort Snelling to Jordan, with a new visitor center and headquarters in Bloomington.

Winter

The 18 miles of cross-country ski trails in the 3,300-acre park (including 9 miles of skate-skiing track) are relatively level. Snowmobiling is not allowed, but snowshoers are free to wander throughout the park. Hikers and snowshoers will see many animal signs in the woods along the banks of the Mississippi and Minnesota rivers.

The Pike Island Interpretive Center is open for a variety of winter programs. The naturalist guides several snowshoe walks designed to help visitors identify animal tracks, find their way in a winter environment or learn about Indian snow games. Other programs focus on winter survival techniques, ice fishing or animal preparations for winter. Skiers, hikers and other visitors are welcome to warm up in the center and to participate in the indoor naturalist activities. Contact the interpretive center or the park office for details about winter activities.

LAKE MARIA STATE PARK

Wright County. About 23 miles south of St. Cloud. From I-94, take the Silver Creek/Hasty (Maple Lake) exit and follow the signs to the park. Highway map index: H-15.

Part of Lake Maria (pronounced "Mariah") State Park's appeal to some is that it doesn't appeal to everybody. The 1,580-acre park is one of the few state parks where backpacking is the only camping allowed. George H. Crosby-Manitou and Afton state parks are the others.

Lake Maria is on the northern edge of the Big Woods. This region, about 100 miles long from north to south and 40 miles wide at its southern end, was a dense hardwood forest. The trees were so thick in places that sunlight couldn't penetrate to the forest floor. Early French explorers called this forest the "Bois Grand"; settlers anglicized it to Big Woods.

Lake Maria's 15 backpack sites are spread throughout the park, but are primarily clustered near Bjorkland Lake and Putman Lake. Campers can park in the trail center lot and walk 1 or 2 miles to reach the primitive sites. Once you set up your camp, it's easy to plan day hikes in the park. Reservations are recommended for the backpack sites. Groups may make reservations for the primitive group camp in the north end of the park. An equestrian camping area is located near the trail center parking lot.

The picnic area on Maria Lake has facilities for disabled visitors. From the boat access next to the picnic ground, fishermen can get out on the lake to try for northern, walleye, bass or panfish. Bring your canoe and enjoy a lazy day exploring the shoreline or just drifting in the breeze.

Winter

Winter is a busy season at Lake Maria State Park, mostly because of the heavy cross-country ski usage. No snowmobiling is allowed. Although spring and fall are the busiest camping seasons here, winter camping has increased over 100 percent in the last few years. Talk with the manager before setting up winter camp; he will show you which site to use.

The 12 miles of cross-country ski trails (including 2 miles of skate-skiing track) are rated easy and more difficult. With the rolling, wooded terrain, the park is a scenic place to ski. The trails are well-marked and each junction has an orientation map. (Dogs are not allowed on cross-country ski trails.) Visitors also can enjoy the park's ice-skating rink and sliding hill. The trail center is open in the winter, kept cozy by a wood-burning stove.

LUCE LINE STATE TRAIL

Hennepin, Carver, McLeod and Meeker counties. 64 miles, from Plymouth to Cosmos.

When the Dakota Indians traveled the footworn prairie path that has evolved into part of the Luce Line State Trail, the grass was tall and the horizon was broken only by the rolling ridges of a broad-shouldered land. The route was later developed into a railroad by W. L. Luce, who wanted to build his line from Minneapolis to Brookings, South Dakota.

Luce had gotten as far as Gluek, Minnesota, when money problems halted construction. The Chicago North Western bought the railroad later, but abandoned the right of way in 1971. The idea of a recreation trail was conceived by the Luce Line Trail Association, which helped to convince the Minnesota legislature to authorize the trail in 1973.

Not all of the trail is prairie. In the east the influence is definitely woodland, a carry-over from the past when the large forest known as the Big Woods covered the region. From the trail, you can see rolling stands of sugar maple and basswood, along with many colorful forest-floor plants. East of Hutchinson, the Big Woods gives way to remnants of the tallgrass prairie, with some prairie plants still visible.

The Luce Line State Trail starts westward in the hardwood hills of suburban Plymouth and Wayzata and curves north of Lake Minnetonka. Visitors will pass by many smaller lakes on the eastern section of the trail. Currently, the 28-mile section from Vicksburg Lane (Plymouth) to Winsted is surfaced for bicyclists and hikers. A parallel treadway for horseback riders, hikers and cross-country skiers is completed along this stretch of the Luce Line. Snowmobilers are welcome on the trail, except for the section between Vicksburg Lane and Stubbs Bay Road.

West of Winsted, the trail has a natural surface that hikers, horseback riders, skiers, snowmobilers and mountain bikers can use. At some points, however, the trail has breaks that require detours. Tentative plans call for hard surfacing to be continued to Hutchinson and, later, to Cosmos.

Bicyclists can take advantage of the Luce Line's connections to adjoining roads and trails for some fun side trips: camping in Baker Park, swimming in Parker's Lake, pier fishing on Swan Lake or touring around Medicine Lake, to name a few. Snowmobilers have access to a large network of Grant-in-Aid trails that connect in Hennepin and Meeker counties.

MINNESOTA VALLEY NATIONAL WILDLIFE REFUGE, RECREATION AREA & STATE TRAIL

Hennepin, Dakota, Carver, Scott, Sibley and Le Sueur counties. About 75 miles, between Fort Snelling and Le Sueur.

The big reason that people are "discovering" the lower Minnesota River Valley is the network of national, state and local recreation lands that extends up the valley from Fort Snelling State Park to the city of Le Sueur. The Minnesota Valley National Wildlife Refuge, a 34-mile urban greenbelt from Fort Snelling to Jordan, and the Minnesota Valley State Trail form the bulk of this complex.

The Minnesota Valley State Trail, when completed, will link a series of national wildlife refuge units, local recreation areas, and state park units stretched along 75 miles of the lower Minnesota River. Only the portion of the trail system from Belle Plaine to Chaska and Shakopee (20 miles) is currently completed. Eventually 24,000 acres of flood-plain marsh, grassland and woodland will be included within the refuge, recreation area and state trail.

The refuge portion of the area is managed by the U.S. Fish and Wildlife Service with two main objectives: to provide habitat for a diversity of plants and animals, and to provide opportunities for people to observe and learn about the valley's wildlife. The recreation area is managed by local and county governments and by the Minnesota Department of Natural Resources. The Minnesota Valley State Trail is also managed by the state DNR.

The river valley was carved over 11,000 years ago by the torrential waters of Glacial River Warren. At the close of the ice age, the glacial river receded, leaving a broad valley and the much smaller, meandering Minnesota River. The lower portion of the river and valley contains seeps, springs and creeks. These emerge from the bluffs to be impounded by natural levees along the river channel, creating fertile marshes that have attracted wildlife and people for centuries.

Muskrat and beaver inhabit the valley lowlands, and thousands of songbirds and waterfowl rest here on their annual migrations. About 250 bird species have been sighted in the Minnesota River Valley. More than 150 species nest here, including owls and wood ducks, which live in the cavities woodpeckers have drilled out of dead trees. Warblers, common egrets, and double-crested cormorants are a few of the other birds you might observe.

The hillsides and bluffs support oak groves and prairie remnants. Trails that hug these hills provide hikers with sweeping views of the river valley. Other trails parallel the riverbanks, shaded by giant cottonwoods, basswoods, and silver maples. Beaver cuttings can be seen from the river trails, and soft-footed visitors might spot deer browsing in the bottomlands.

The Minnesota River is a state-designated canoe and boating route. Accesses and campsites abound between Le Sueur and Fort Snelling State Park, where the river meets the Mississippi. The safest and most interesting stretch of river to canoe is from Le Sueur to Shakopee (commercial barges navigate the river below Shakopee). Fishing is popular on the river, but anglers should consult Health Department guidelines before eating any of their catch. Although walleye, northern and smallmouth bass are sometimes taken, carp and other rough fish are more common.

From horseback riding to cross-country skiing, the outdoor fun in the Minnesota River valley lasts all year. The varied units of the Minnesota Valley National Wildlife Refuge, Recreation Area and State Trail feature multi-use trails and facilities, reflecting the changing nature of the river corridor. As you head upstream from Fort Snelling, the valley changes from urban to rural landscapes with the federal, state and local units interspersed between the river communities.

The seven management units that form the Minnesota Valley National Wildlife Refuge are spaced along the Minnesota River between Fort Snelling and Jordan. Make the distinctive visitor center your first stop (4101 E. 80th St. in Bloomington; follow the refuge signs off of Highway 494). Outside, walk to the end of the deck for a scenic view of Long Meadow Lake.

The Long Meadow Lake unit includes 2,200 acres of marshes, fields, hardwood forested bluffs, and bottomlands. Black Dog Lake is owned by the Northern States Power Company but is leased by the U.S. Fish and Wildlife Service. Cooperatively managed by NSP and the refuge, this area is a good place to observe migrating waterfowl and native prairie.

Bloomington Ferry was the site of one of the first Minnesota River crossings. This unit's 380 acres contain lush flood-plain forests and wetlands between the river and the nearby bluffs.

The newest unit of the wildlife refuge, Wilkie-Rice Lake, contains exceptional wetlands. Part of it is closed seasonally to protect a great blue heron nesting area.

Upgrala derives its name from Upper Grass Lake, one of two lakes in the unit. Upgrala's 2,400 acres of lake, marsh, fields and forested riverbanks lie below the Eden Prairie bluffs and can be seen from Highway 169.

Chaska Lake nestles in the flood plain between the river towns of Chaska and Carver. The 580-acre unit consists of an open-water, marsh-edged lake surrounded by farmland and flood-plain forest.

Louisville Swamp is a 2,400-acre mix of marsh, bottomland hardwoods and oak savannah with an 8-mile network of hiking and cross-country ski trails.

The Minnesota DNR also maintains seven management units in the Minnesota Valley. Fort Snelling State Park, located at the confluence of the Minnesota and Mississippi Rivers, maintains extensive recreational facilities (including a swimming beach on Snelling Lake), as well as interpretive programs at the park's Pike Island Interpretive Center. Pick up park maps at the contact station.

The Gifford and Nyssen Lakes units contain a bottomland forest, meadows, marshlands and shallow lakes. Trail access and parking is provided for hiking, horseback riding and snowmobiling. A trail crosses the Minnesota River on a historic railroad swing bridge. At Carver Rapids, you can see a prairie restoration project as well as bottomland forest and wetland areas. Water, shelter, picnic area and primitive campsites are provided. Trails connect with the neighboring Louisville Swamp Unit (U.S. Fish and Wildlife Service), passing historic sites such as the Jabs Farm. Thompson Ferry is a day-use area for picnicking and fishing. Visitors also have access to the river and the river trail.

Headquarters for the Minnesota Valley State Trail is in the Lawrence Unit, between Jordan and Belle Plaine on County 57, just north of Highway 169. Camping facilities include a secluded 25-site rustic campground (no showers or hookups), eight walk-in campsites, a canoe campsite, an equestrian campground and a primitive group camp (call headquarters for reservations). From the trail center, you can explore the river valley on 22 miles of marked trails for horseback riding, mountain biking, and hiking. The Lawrence Unit contains the only remaining building from the 1850s town of St. Lawrence. Try fishing at Beason Lake near the Quarry Campground or on the Minnesota River (public access is 2 miles north of Jordan on County 9).

The Rush River Unit is a favorite spot for family picnics and outings. This 300-acre wooded site with rolling hills next to the Rush River is one of the most scenic locations in the Minnesota Valley.

There is so much to see and do in the Minnesota Valley region that several seasons may pass before you've sampled most of its units and attractions. No rush, though. The Minnesota River keeps a slow, steady pace, and it will still be there for you when you return.

MISSISSIPPI NATIONAL RIVER & RECREATION AREA

Anoka, Dakota, Goodhue, Hennepin, Ramsey and Washington counties. 72 miles, from the Crow River confluence (near Dayton) to the Goodhue-Dakota county line, south of the St. Croix River confluence.

The Mississippi National River and Recreation Area is a new unit of the national park system. Created by Congress in 1988, the mission of the national river and recreation area is to "protect, preserve and enhance the significant waters and land of the Mississippi River corridor within the St. Paul-Minneapolis metropolitan area."

Because of the web of agencies that deal with the river's resources as it flows through the metro area, planning for the new unit will take several years. A representative planning commission began work in 1990 and will draft a management plan by late 1993. This plan will be a blueprint of actions to bring the Mississippi National River and Recreation Area to life. The public will have several chances to provide input as planning evolves.

As outlined in legislation, the national river and recreation area will encompass about 55,000 acres of public and private land on both sides of the river (except south of the St. Croix River confluence, where only the Minnesota side is within the boundaries). Four miles of the Minnesota River and adjacent lands upstream from its confluence with the Mississippi River are also included.

Many existing metropolitan public parks and trails already lure legions to the Mississippi River. Thousands of visitors enjoy picnicking, hiking, bicycling, cross-country skiing and fishing in these parks. On the Mississippi, boaters and canoeists may share the river with barges moving coal, sand or grain. More than 2 1/2 million people living in the Twin Cities metro area can travel to the river within an hour.

The appeal of the new national river and recreation area is that it is a coordinated effort to manage the complex resource that energized the growth of the Twin Cities in the first place: the Mississippi River. The river has always handled recreation and commerce on its journey through Minneapolis and St. Paul. Though the river corridor traverses urban landscapes, outdoors lovers in the metro region have known for a long time that the river also flows through many stretches of largely natural and undeveloped land.

Abused, ignored or taken for granted in the past, the Mississippi River is benefiting from a renewed concern for its welfare in the Minneapolis-St. Paul area. Establishment of the Mississippi National River and Recreation Area goes a long way toward ensuring the river's health and appeal for generations to come.

WILLARD MUNGER STATE TRAIL (Gateway Segment)

Ramsey and Washington counties. 18 miles, from St. Paul (east side of 35E a few blocks south of Wheelock Parkway) to Pine Point Park near Stillwater.

The Willard Munger State Trail is a multiple-use trail being developed from St. Paul to Duluth. It consists of a system of interconnecting trails offering hiking, bicycling, snowmobiling and horseback riding.

The Gateway Trail segment of the Willard Munger State Trail has often been referred to as the Soo Line Trail because of its location on an old Soo Line railroad bed. Initial trail development began in St. Paul, a few blocks south of Wheelock Parkway (east side of 35E). The trail traverses Phalen Park, heading northeast to the junction of highways 694 and 36.

The second half of the segment's 18 miles (developed in 1992) goes from the Highway 694/36 junction to Pine Point Park in Stillwater. This eastern portion of the trail includes a second treadway for horseback riders. Eventually, the trail may be continued farther north. Contact Washington County for details about county bicycle routes. To find out about the rest of the Willard Munger State Trail, turn to the Arrowhead section of this book.

WILLIAM O'BRIEN STATE PARK

Washington County. About 2 miles north of Marine-on-St. Croix on Highway 95. Highway map index: Z-23 (metro St. Paul-Minneapolis map on back of state map) or K-16.

William O'Brien State Park, only a short drive northeast of the Twin Cities, draws large numbers of campers and daytime visitors. People are attracted by the wooded, rolling land along the St. Croix River and the variety of ways they can unwind from city life.

Because of O'Brien's proximity to the Twin Cities, the campgrounds are usually full on weekends. If you don't have a reservation, get here early to register for a site. The park has two semi-modern campgrounds. The lower campground (near the riverfront) has 60 sites. Of these, 43 have electrical hookups and 4 are specifically designated for disabled campers. In the upper campground (65 sites, 19 electric), some sections are open and sunny, while others are deeply wooded.

The park has two group camping areas. There is also a primitive, canoeists-only campground along the St. Croix River (capacity 50). Contact the park office for reservation information about these camps.

The St. Croix River is a National Wild and Scenic River and also a state-designated canoe and boating route. The lower St. Croix (the section below Taylors Falls) offers easy canoeing in a pristine setting. You can rent canoes by the day or hour through private concessionaires in Taylors Falls. Shuttle service is available for cars and/or passengers.

You can also rent canoes in William O'Brien State Park (near the boat landing; shuttle service available) for an outing on the St. Croix River or on man-made Lake Alice. This 15-acre lake, fed by underground springs, is stocked with panfish. Fishing on the St. Croix River can be good for walleye, northern, bass and brown trout. Access to the river is from a drive-in boat landing in the park.

Boaters and canoeists can cross Pine Slough to Greenburg Island, donated to the state by David Greenburg in 1958.

The island, accessible only by water, is a secluded refuge for wildlife and vegetation. Great blue herons nest on the island, otter and beaver play here, and scarlet cardinal flowers bloom in August.

Swimming is not allowed in the river because of strong currents, but Lake Alice offers good swimming and a sandy beach. The lake is named for Alice O'Brien, who donated 180 acres of land in 1945 for the state park in memory of her father, a pioneer lumberman of the St. Croix River Valley.

The first residents of the valley were Dakota and Ojibway Indians. The Ojibway eventually pushed the Dakota out of the forests to the grasslands, only to face competition from European trappers for the valley's fur riches. In the mid 1800s, the lumberjacks who came to harvest white pine established the state's first logging settlement at nearby Marine-on-St. Croix. You'll find further information about the natural and human history of the park in the Sam Morgan Trail/Interpretive Center. Naturalists lead canoe floats, guided hikes and other programs during the summer.

The park's 9.5 miles of hiking trails include the two high points in Washington County. From one overlook, you can see Taylors Falls on a clear day. Though the park is heavily used, the trails are rarely crowded, inspiring a feeling of isolation in the wooded hills and grassy meadows. Other trails cut through scattered stands of red and white pines, a maple-basswood forest, and the bottomlands near the river. The sandstone outcrops in the park were formed by ancient inland seas. As subsequent glaciers melted, the torrent of water carved through this sandstone to form the St. Croix River Valley.

William O'Brien State Park features a paved bicycle and wheelchair path. It parallels Highway 95 the length of the park, ending in Marine-on-St. Croix. Some bicyclists pedal to the park from the metro area on a network of Washington County routes (contact the county for maps).

The St. Croix River Valley offers visitor attractions on both sides of the river. In Minnesota, you can drive upriver to Interstate State Park or downriver to historic Stillwater. Between William O'Brien Park and Stillwater is the St. Croix Islands Scenic Reserve, where canoeists are permitted to camp on some of the islands.

Winter

The hiking trails turn into cross-country ski trails during winter. Although the loops through upland fields and bottomlands are easy, the wooded hills and rolling meadows provide good skiing for intermediate and expert skiers. Whether on skis or on foot, you'll be able to see for miles over the snowy countryside from the park's high ridges. Winter campers can ski, hike or snowshoe into the upper campground. Snowmobiling is not allowed in the park.

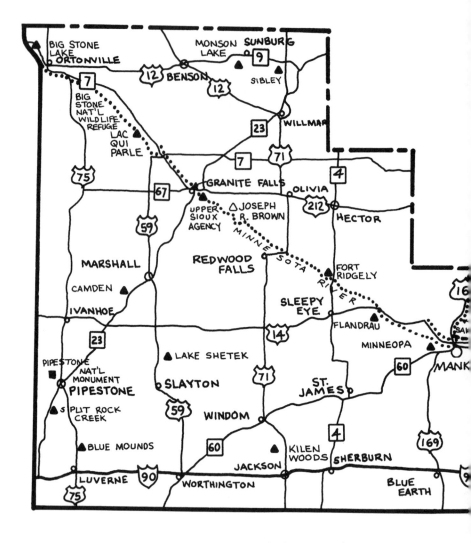

Beaver Creek Valley State Park
Big Stone Lake State Park
Big Stone National Wildlife Refuge
Blue Mounds State Park
Camden State Park
Cannon River Canoe and Boating Route
Cannon Valley Trail
Carley State Park
Des Moines River Canoe and Boating Route
Douglas State Trail

Flandrau State Park
Forestville State Park/Mystery Cave
Fort Ridgely State Park
Frontenac State Park
Kilen Woods State Park
Lac qui Parle State Park
Lake Louise State Park
Lake Shetek State Park
Minneopa State Park
Minnesota River Canoe and Boating Route

SOUTHERN REGION

▲ ....STATE PARKS & RECREATION AREAS
△ ....WAYSIDES
■ ....NATIONAL MONUMENTS
— — — — ....STATE TRAIL
•••••• ....CANOE & RIVER ROUTES

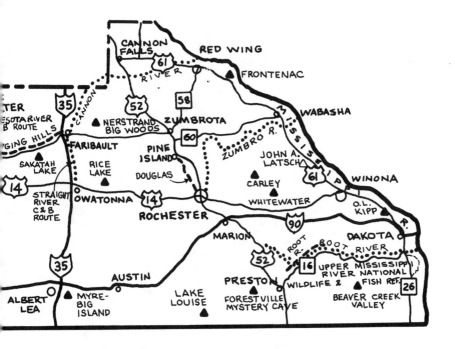

Monson Lake State Park
Myre-Big Island State Park
Nerstrand Big Woods State Park
O.L. Kipp State Park
Pipestone National Monument
Rice Lake State Park
Richard J. Dorer Memorial Hardwood
   State Forest
Root River Canoe and Boating Route
Root River State Trail

Sakatah Lake State Park
Sakatah Singing Hills State Trail
Sibley State Park
Split Rock Creek State Recreation Area
Straight River Canoe and Boating Route
Upper Mississippi River National Wildlife and Fish Refuge
Upper Sioux Agency State Park
Whitewater State Park
Zumbro River Canoe and Boating Route

BEAVER CREEK VALLEY STATE PARK

Houston County. 4 miles west of Caledonia on County 1 off of Highway 76. Highway map index: O-21.

Depending on priorities, Beaver Creek Valley State Park is a hiker's park or a trout angler's park. If you like to do both, you'll probably want to come back again. The creek bubbles out of an artesian spring and threads its way through a picturesque wooded valley beneath 300-foot bluffs. Brown trout can be found in the quiet pools below the sandstone and limestone bluffs. Experienced trout fishermen are sometimes spotted tiptoeing up to a stream because they know that the browns have an uncanny "feel."

There's a fishermen's parking lot on the park's northern edge where the creek widens into a long, skinny pool. The Schech Mill, built in 1876, is a historic site downstream from the parking lot. This two-story gristmill still uses water power and features the original millstones and New Process milling equipment. The mill (privately owned) is open to tours.

Whether you're after trout or photographs, you can hike along Beaver Creek on park trails. The creek flows for about 2 miles through the park and continues to the Root River (which empties into the Mississippi). The other trails in the 8-mile system, like Plateau Rock Trail, Switchback Trail and Hole-in-Rock Trail, offer bluff-top vistas if you're willing to make the uphill climb. Even these trails are not too strenuous if you take your time. Wildflowers add a fragile beauty to the rugged slopes.

From any of the overlooks (or at the park entrance), the countryside looks mostly level. But between you and the farm in the distance could be another hidden valley that drops swiftly from the plateau into a wooded ravine like the one at Beaver Creek Valley. The water that formed these valleys by eroding sandstone and limestone also can form caves by eroding similar rock formations underground. Southeastern Minnesota has caves of all sizes. Some of the biggest caves are popular attractions, like Mystery Cave (in Forestville State Park) and Niagara Cave; others are "wild"

Minneopa State Park is the park where "water falls twice."

caves that experienced spelunkers like to explore. Contact the Minnesota Speleological Survey for more information (P. O. Box 13436, Dinkytown Station, Minneapolis, MN 55414).

The park's main development lies along Beaver Creek near the central parking lot. The picnic area and shelter are on the other side of the swinging bridge that spans Beaver Creek. Trailheads and the kids' wading pool are also nearby.

The 42-site semi-modern campground at Beaver Creek Valley State Park is popular on summer weekends (16 electric sites available). The park also features six walk-in sites and a large primitive group camp that can be reserved by special organizations.

Winter

Although Beaver Creek Valley State Park is known for its hilly terrain, the 3 miles of beginner cross-country ski trails stick mostly to the bottomlands. Snowmobiling is not allowed in the park, but there are extensive trails nearby.

Hiking and snowshoeing are part of the winter fun in the park's hilly terrain. Some people hike into the campground to try snow camping for a weekend. Ask the manager about water. All winter visitors can warm up in the enclosed shelter.

BIG STONE LAKE STATE PARK

Big Stone County. About 6 miles northwest of Ortonville on Highway 7. Highway map index: B-15.

According to legend, Paul Bunyan's 110-ton granite anchor was found at the bottom of Big Stone Lake. Although some doubt the veracity of Bunyan's exploits, there is no doubt that the 30-mile-long Big Stone Lake (Minnesota's 10th largest) is almost spacious enough for Paul to have taken a bath.

Most visitors who come to use the lake put in from the drive-in access in Big Stone Lake State Park. Anglers are attracted by the lake's walleyes, perch and panfish. Because Big Stone Lake is a border water, the fishing season opens two weeks earlier than inland waters. Water-skiers and sailboaters enjoy lots of elbow room on Big Stone, though winds can become powerful as they storm down the length of the narrow lake. Canoeists usually paddle close to shore unless the water is calm. Boats can be rented in the park (details at the contact station).

The park is split into two parcels. The northern section, called Bonanza, is a peaceful, quiet, day-use area. You can hike on self-guided nature trails or relax on a sandy beach.

The main campground (42 sites, 10 with electric hookups) is in the Meadowbrook area of Big Stone Lake State Park. Normally you'll have no difficulty finding a vacant site here, but holidays and weekends are usually busy. The campground is on the lakeshore, next to the picnic area and boat launch. Reservations are needed for the primitive group camp in the Bonanza section of the park.

The Meadowbrook hiking trails pass by small patches of native prairie and some bluebird boxes. Deer, pheasant and Hungarian partridge may be spotted in the main-use areas of the park and in the wildlife sanctuary to the east of the fish rearing pond. The lake and sanctuary are excellent birdwatching areas where some observers have seen pelicans (rare in Minnesota).

BIG STONE NATIONAL WILDLIFE REFUGE

Big Stone and Lac Qui Parle counties. About 2 miles southeast of Ortonville on Highway 75. Highway map index: B-15.

The upper Minnesota River Valley has always been a haven for wildlife and a magnet for those attracted by the region's abundance. Early native tribes depended on the river and the variety of game that thrived on the surrounding prairies and in the valley. More recently, the Dakota people lived along the riverbanks when the first European settlers migrated to western Minnesota.

Today, the river valley lures those who enjoy its wildlife-oriented recreation. Visitors can hike, canoe, fish, hunt, ski or snowshoe in the 11,000-acre refuge. You don't even have to leave your vehicle to experience part of Big Stone National Wildlife Refuge. A 4-mile auto-tour route highlights the various habitats here: wetlands, lowland woods, native prairie, crop and grasslands, and granite rock formations. Pick up the auto-tour interpretive leaflet at Stop No. 1.

Wildlife observation is easy here and provides a fun outing for the whole family. During spring and fall migrations, 17 species of ducks can be spotted around the refuge, including mallards, blue-winged teal, pintail, redhead and northern shoveler. You might also see Canada and snow geese. Many species become summer residents. Western grebes, uncommon in Minnesota, rear their young in the refuge.

White-tailed deer, gray partridge, muskrats, beaver and woodchucks are other natural residents to watch for. The best times for wildlife observation are morning or evening, when animals are most active. Be sure to pick up copies of the bird and animal checklists before you start exploring.

If you have a little time, walk the trail that starts at the rest area near the interpretive shelter. The hike takes about an hour and offers a close-up view of prairie plants, granite rock outcrops, the meandering river, and some of the refuge's wildlife. The granite formations support unusual species of cactus and other plants and provide excellent vistas of the refuge. You can pick up a foot-trail leaflet at the trailhead.

The favorite fishing spots in the refuge are along the banks of the reservoir or along the Minnesota and the Yellowbank rivers. Hunting is permitted during season for gray partridge, pheasant, small game and deer. Winter visitors can cross-country ski or snowshoe throughout the refuge.

Restrooms are provided, but there are no picnic, camping or swimming facilities at Big Stone National Wildlife Refuge. Bring your own drinking water. Ortonville is the nearest town for lodging and other services. You can camp at private campgrounds in the area or at Big Stone Lake State Park north of Ortonville and at Lac qui Parle State Park, just downriver from the refuge. The 27,000-acre Lac qui Parle Wildlife Management Area, which lies between Big Stone National Wildlife Refuge and Lac qui Parle State Park, is the center of a string of public lands that preserve the natural character of the upper Minnesota River Valley.

BLUE MOUNDS
STATE PARK

*Rock County. 4 miles north of Luverne on Highway 75 to
park entrance road. Highway map index: C-21.*

Daytime thunderstorms rumble eastward from South
Dakota in sinister blue-black formations that darken the sky
for miles. At sunset, the mile-long, 100-foot-tall cliff looks
blue, which inspired the westbound pioneers to name the
prairie landmark Blue Mounds.

The best sky-watching is from the hiking trails on the
mound. Of the park's 13-mile trail system, these trails are the
longest and least crowded. The interpretive center, formerly
the home of Frederick Manfred (a historical novelist), has
been remodeled to assist visitors in understanding the native
prairie and the culture of the Plains Indians. Schedules of
activities like hikes, films and discussions are posted daily.
On one of the guided hikes, you'll pass a 1,250-foot-long
stone wall, aligned exactly east and west, that may have
helped prehistoric people mark the seasons. The naturalist
also will discuss birdwatching in the park, where more than
200 species have been sighted.

It's a two-mile hike from the interpretive center past the
buffalo pasture to the park office. Or you can drive to the
main park use area by following the signs from the
interpretive center. On this end, trails wrap around two small
lakes connected by a stream, then lead to the campground.
The 73-site semi-modern campground (with 40 electric sites)
is popular during the peak summer season. A 100-person
primitive group camp is available by reservation.

CAMDEN
STATE PARK

*Lyon County. About 10 miles southwest of Marshall on
Highway 23. Highway map index: D-19.*

The Redwood River Valley in present-day Camden State
Park traditionally provided refuge for Indians, settlers and
travelers. The narrow, steep valley is blanketed with dense
woods and blessed with free-flowing spring water. The
powerful prairie winds that occasionally blast across the
open land tend to barrel up and over the river valley.

The park has three historic sites relating to its early
history. The first one is the site of an American Fur Company
trading post. One fur trader, Joseph La Framboise, was the
first white settler in this area. He left his trading post when
George Catlin, an artist known for his paintings of American
Indians, asked him to be a guide and interpreter on a
journey to the famous Indian pipestone quarries. The
quarries, sacred to the Indians, are now preserved at
Pipestone National Monument in southwestern Minnesota.

The second historic site at Camden is the Sioux Lookout,
where the Indians had a commanding view of the river
valley. The third site marks the location of the Jones Mill.

Camden's upper and lower semi-modern campgrounds are
located at opposite ends of the park (93 total sites, 29
electric). The primitive horse camp is down in the valley at
the south end of the park. The group camp, near the south
picnic area, may be reserved by calling the park office.

Winter

The 4 miles of groomed cross-country ski trails at Camden
are worth a return visit in winter. There's a fun mixture of
beginner trails in the valley and some challenging
intermediate loops through the hillside forest. While the ski
trails are concentrated in the park's southern end, the 10
miles of snowmobile trails take you up and down the valley
from the open prairie to the wooded slopes and the frozen
river.

CANNON RIVER CANOE & BOATING ROUTE

Le Sueur, Rice, Dakota and Goodhue counties. 80 miles, from the Highway 13 bridge west of Sakatah Lake to the Mississippi River north of Red Wing.

The Cannon is an ideal river for families or novices because the few rapids are light and easy to navigate. Snags are scattered, but downed trees are a hazard in high water. You'll have to portage each of the river's seven dams, most of which have no developed portage trail. When the Lake Byllesby dam begins to produce hydroelectric power, it will affect canoeing downstream by altering the water level.

Highest water is usually in early April, although heavy rains can cause flooding at other times. The river's water level is generally high enough for canoeing throughout the season, depending on rainfall. During late summer dry spells, some stretches are too shallow for a successful run.

The upper Cannon, bordered by gently swelling hills, rambles through the woods and farmland of southern Minnesota. From Cannon Falls to the Mississippi, the river enters a broad gorge flanked by 300-foot-high bluffs. As you weave through the maze of backwaters and sloughs at the Cannon's mouth, watch for bald eagles, wood ducks and mallards, and beavers. Reservoirs and slow stretches are the hot spots for fishing on the Cannon. The most common catches are northern and panfish, but as you paddle downstream, you might land a walleye, smallmouth bass or channel catfish.

It would be easy to plan a canoeing, hiking and camping vacation on the Cannon. Sakatah Lake State Park, where most canoeists start out, features a dense hardwood forest known for its variety of woodland flowers. Besides the park trails, the 39-mile Sakatah Singing Hills State Trail roughly parallels the river to Faribault.

The Cannon River Wilderness Area, midway between Faribault and Northfield, has a canoe access and three primitive camping areas in a hardwood forest that straddles the river. If you like to photograph wildflowers, come here during spring when trillium and lady's slippers are in bloom. Or aim your camera at the graceful blue heron as it soars over the trees. Just downstream from the wilderness area are the limestone ruins of the Archbold Mill at Dundas. This old mill was one of 15 flour mills on the Cannon between Faribault and Northfield.

The Cannon is a good day-trip river, but there are a number of campsites available (mostly in the upper portions of the route) if you'd like to plan an overnight adventure. Consult the DNR's canoe route map for locations of canoe landings, rest areas, public and private campsites, and outfitters.

CANNON VALLEY TRAIL

Goodhue County. 20 miles, from Cannon Falls to Red Wing.

The surfaced hiking and biking trail (cross-country skiing, too) follows the former Chicago Great Western Railroad Line. The route is relatively level, and cyclists of all ages and abilities can enjoy an outing on the trail.

The Cannon Valley Trail connects Cannon Falls, Welch and Red Wing. Maps posted along the route pinpoint your location. Welch Station is about mid-point along the 20-mile trail. Just up the road, within sight of the trail, is the tiny village of Welch, where you can buy refreshments.

The Cannon Falls trail access and parking lot are downtown along the river, right on Highway 19. You can rent bicycles at a sports shop next to the parking area. The Red Wing trail access is at Old Main St. and Bench St. Both cities offer a variety of accommodations: motels, an historic inn, and bed and breakfast inns in 19th-century homes. Near Welch, the privately owned Hidden Valley campground has shady sites along the river.

The Cannon Valley Trail is a local project, unlike other Minnesota bicycle trails developed on railroad beds by the Department of Natural Resources. With the help of some state and federal grants, the trail was developed by area residents and is managed by a joint board with representatives from Red Wing, Cannon Falls and Goodhue County.

To help fund trail improvements, such as rest areas, a Wheel Pass is required for all trail users over age 16 (this includes skateboards, bicycles, roller blades, etc.). Visitors in wheelchairs and hikers do not need a pass. Wheel Passes are available from some local merchants, at designated stations on the trail, and from the trail office. The trail is groomed for two-way cross country ski travel in the winter (the Great Minnesota Ski Pass is required).

If you would like to buy a Wheel Pass, get further information about the trail, or join the Friends of the Trail organization, contact the Cannon Valley Trail Office, City Hall, 306 W. Mill St., Cannon Falls MN 55009 (507-263-3954).

CARLEY STATE PARK

*Wabasha County. 4 miles south of Plainview on County 4.
Highway map index: M-19.*

The hardwood/softwood forest at Carley State Park provides good cover for ruffed grouse and a variety of birds and wildlife. Beaver lodges can be spotted from hiking trails that follow the North Branch Whitewater River, one of southeastern Minnesota's famous trout streams.

The small park's five-mile trail system is woodsy and quiet, especially on weekdays. You can explore the bottomlands and the steep-sloped river valley, and one trail leads through a grove of white pines, unusual this far south.

The picnic area is the main family gathering spot in the park. Many people who camp at Carley tried unsuccessfully to get sites at nearby Whitewater State Park, which has a swimming area, naturalist area, and higher visibility. These people now choose to camp in Carley's wooded sites and drive the short distance to Whitewater for swimming or activities. Carley's 20 rustic campsites are separated by trees, adding to the park's intimate appeal. The campground usually has sites available, but it's best to register early on peak weekends. The primitive group camp (capacity 75) also fosters a feeling of being out in the woods.

Winter

Carley State Park offers snow fun for the family. You can cross-country ski on six miles of intermediate to advanced trails. Beginners like to stick to the flatter bottomlands. Kids gravitate to the park road near the campground (unplowed in winter), where they inner-tube or slide down the hill. Snowmobiling is not allowed in the park, but local Grant-in-Aid trails weave through the Richard J. Dorer State Forest.

DES MOINES RIVER CANOE & BOATING ROUTE

Cottonwood and Jackson counties. 70 miles, from Talcot Lake (near Dundee) to the Iowa border.

The Des Moines River, the only state canoe route in the southwestern corner of Minnesota, has become a favorite of families and beginners because of its easygoing nature and variety of wildlife.

The route begins below the Talcot Lake Dam, where you can launch from accesses on either side of the river. Some canoeists put in above the dam and paddle along the lake's north shore to the Talcot Lake Wildlife Area to photograph the waterfowl. County Highway 7 cuts across the eastern edge of this refuge and also crosses the river near the accesses.

From the Talcot Lake Dam to Windom is about a 30-mile trip through a broad, flat farm valley with few trees. The dam in Windom must be portaged; most river travelers start below the dam and canoe to the Jackson Dam. This 24-mile stretch is the most popular on the Des Moines because of its scenery. Between Windom and Kilen Woods State Park, the river valley narrows, and willows and ash line the gently sloped banks. As the river approaches the state park, the banks become steeper and more wooded. From Kilen Woods to Jackson, you'll pass below 100- to 200-foot bluffs and cut through flood-plain forests that swell to the water's edge. The Windom to Jackson segment also features almost all of the accesses, rest areas and campsites along the route.

Jackson also has an outfitter, two accesses and a rest area. The dam must be portaged to continue downstream, though one of the accesses is below the dam for those who wish to start there. From Jackson the Des Moines River flows through farm country to the Iowa border, where it continues on to the Mississippi River.

DOUGLAS STATE TRAIL

Olmsted and Goodhue counties. 13 miles, from Rochester to Pine Island.

The Douglas State Trail is ideal for a leisurely family bicycle ride. The level trail, developed on an abandoned railroad grade, rambles through a scenic mix of forest and the rolling fields and pastures of some of the richest agricultural land in Minnesota.

Wildlife watchers may spot some of the partridge and pheasant that live in the woods or some of the geese that become more abundant near Rochester. But even if all you spot is a herd of cows, an afternoon spent under your own power on the Douglas State Trail is bound to energize your senses and inspire a feeling of well-being.

The trail is split into two treadways. One treadway is surfaced for bicyclists, hikers and snowmobilers, while horseback riders and skiers use the other.

Rest areas and parking lots are in Rochester (County 4, about a mile northwest of the city), Douglas (County 14), and Pine Island (County 11 in the city park). Some bicyclists plan a circular route on some of the quiet county roads between Douglas and Pine Island.

FLANDRAU STATE PARK

Brown County. Adjacent to and partially within New Ulm city limits. The park is several blocks south of highways 15 and 68, 2 miles south of Highway 14. Highway map index: G-19.

Flandrau State Park retains its natural character even though it's just a short walk or bike ride from residential areas in New Ulm. The park is bounded by steep wooded slopes that seem to guide the Cottonwood River on its curvy course. The river wanders through bottomland forest and grassy openings, past oxbow lakes and marshes where it used to flow.

The Oxbow Trail is a loop that leads you into the lowland world of the Cottonwood River. This is a one-mile self-guided interpretive trail where you can learn about some of the natural features of the park.

Flandrau is a heavy day-use park. The guarded swimming beach draws sun worshippers for long afternoons of sunbathing while kids entertain themselves building sand castles and splashing in the water. The swimming pool was rebuilt in 1987 to include filtration and water treatment.

The campground has about 60 semi-modern (35 electric) and 30 rustic sites. They can fill up fast on holiday weekends, but midweek is not as busy. (Incidentally, some of the handsome park buildings in the campground, beach and office areas were constructed of native stone.) Flandrau has two group camps. One, near the main campground, is primitive. The other, on the south side of the river, has barracks, a mess hall and swimming area (organizations must furnish their own lifeguards).

Flandrau, known originally as Cottonwood State Park, was named for a prominent lawyer and Indian agent of the Minnesota River country during the 1860s. During the U.S.-Dakota Conflict of 1862, he organized a company of volunteers that helped to repel Indian attacks on the frontier town of New Ulm.

Winter

Cross-country skiing is the most popular winter activity at Flandrau. Though the park grooms about 8 miles of trails, some skiers and snowshoers prefer to forge their own paths through the river bottomlands.

FORESTVILLE STATE PARK/MYSTERY CAVE

Fillmore County. From Highway 16, turn south onto County 5 (about halfway between Spring Valley and Preston) for 4 miles, then turn east onto County 12 for 2 miles to the park entrance. Highway map index: M-21.

Forestville/Mystery Cave is a park for the passionate. The park's unique combination of resources lures visitors who are passionate about trout fishing, horseback riding, hiking, history and exploring caves.

The park is named for Forestville, a once-bustling village established on this site in 1853. The town thrived as a trade center initially, with about a dozen businesses and two stagecoach lines that passed through. Forestville began to fade when the railroad bypassed the town in 1868. The only remaining buildings are the Meighen Dry-Goods Store (built in 1856), the Meighen home and farm, and the brick house built by Robert Foster in 1867. The sites of other buildings have been marked and are within walking distance.

"Historic Forestville," administered by the Minnesota Historical Society, is a new renovation that represents the village center of Forestville in 1899. Costumed townspeople provide a living history interpretation of Forestville at that time, which had evolved into a company agricultural town (with less than half of its late 1850s population of 100), owned primarily by Thomas Meighen. The current renovation includes the Meighen home, stores and farm, and the Forestville post office. Future additions will be the Luedkte-Meighen Roller Mill and some of the farm buildings.

Though it's fun to experience living history at Forestville/Mystery Cave, the essence of the park is the natural environment. Forestville features over 14 miles of horseback riding trails that climb forested ridges, drop into steep creek and river valleys, and connect to trails in the Richard J. Dorer Memorial Hardwood State Forest. A large equestrian campground provides hitching rails and rustic campsites. The park records the highest horseback use of any state park in Minnesota. Although autumn rides through the colorful woods are especially scenic, riding is popular here throughout the summer due to the relative lack of insect pests. Hiking is allowed on all horseback trails and on paths designated only for foot travel.

Forestville is noted for its variety of birds (over 170 species) and wildflowers. You may spot wild turkeys during the day and hear the hoot of a barred owl at night. In late April and early May, the woods are filled with spring wildflowers, such as Virginia bluebells and mayflowers. Visitors have seen migrating warblers, eagles and osprey as well as nesting great blue herons, indigo buntings and eastern bluebirds.

Trout anglers, usually tight-lipped about favorite fishing spots, like to return to Forestville's three clear, spring-fed streams inhabited by brown and brook trout (Canfield and Forestville creeks and the South Branch of the Root River). Two parking lots provide easy stream access. Both Canfield and Forestville creeks, which join the South Branch of the Root River in the park, emerge from caves several miles upstream.

The park has 73 semi-modern campsites (23 electric) split into several camping loops. A large primitive group camp is available by reservation. Visitors can hike from the park into the Richard J. Dorer Memorial Hardwood State Forest.

Winter

The hilly terrain and scenic woods at Forestville provide exciting touring for both snowmobilers and cross-country skiers. The 9 miles of snowmobile trails are concentrated on the west side of the South Branch of the Root River, with connections to trails in the neighboring state forest. The 6.5 miles of cross-country loops are on the east side of the river. They are designed mostly for beginner and intermediate skiers, with some steep sections. All trails are marked and groomed.

Mystery Cave

There was always a mystery surrounding the South Branch of the Root River where it flows through the rolling hills of western Fillmore County. At a particular bend in the river, in the shadow of a steep limestone bluff, part of the Root vanishes into a hole in the ground. In 1937, a local farmer, puzzled by the disappearance of part of the river, discovered the entrance to what is now known as Mystery Cave.

Mystery Cave, the largest in Minnesota (36th largest in the country), is an intricate maze of more than 12 miles of interconnecting passageways. The water that disappears from the river channel flows through the cave in a complex network of stream passages and reappears above ground at springs along the river about 1.5 miles away. Though thousands of visitors enter the cave each year, its system of passages hasn't been fully explored.

You can experience the cave firsthand by participating in an hour-long tour guided by naturalists from nearby Forestville State Park. Park personnel have been managing Mystery Cave since it was purchased by the state in 1988. Tours are operated daily from Memorial Day through Labor Day (call ahead for tour times and information about group tours).

Two separate tours are offered at Mystery Cave. The Historic Entrance, where the commercial tours started before the state took over the cave, has been restored recently to its original topography. New lighting and increased accessibility make this tour popular for a wide range of visitors. The Minnesota Caverns tour is more rustic, requiring visitors to use hand-held lanterns.

The cave remains a constant 47 degrees year-round, so bring along a jacket and gloves. Sturdy walking shoes will provide the most comfort on both tours. In addition to the state park sticker needed for entry to the park, an admission fee is charged for the tours. A picnic area and restrooms are located near the ticket buildings.

On the tours, you'll get a glimpse of a surrealistic underground world. The caverns and formations have colorful names, such as the Garden of the Gods, the Dome Room, Diamond Caverns, Carrot Sticks, Hills of Rome, and Blue Lake. The cave's passageways wind through formations of ancient limestone. The guides will point out the collections of stalactites, stalagmites, flow stone and other unique and delicate formations.

With trout fishing, history, and nearby Mystery Cave, Forestville is a park for the passionate.

If you'd like to explore more of Minnesota's limestone cave country, Niagara Cave (south of Harmony off of Highway 139 on Niagara Cave Road) is the only other cave open to the public. This cave features a 60-foot waterfall.

Ask the Mystery Cave guide for more information. To find
out about exploring, studying and conserving caves, contact
the Minnesota Speleological Survey (P.O. Box 13436,
Dinkytown Station, Minneapolis MN 55414).

FORT RIDGELY STATE PARK

Nicollet and Renville counties. 6 miles south of Fairfax along Highway 4; park entrance is off County 29. Highway map index: G-18.

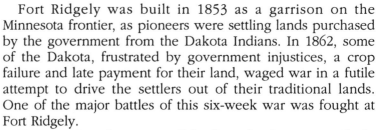

Fort Ridgely was built in 1853 as a garrison on the Minnesota frontier, as pioneers were settling lands purchased by the government from the Dakota Indians. In 1862, some of the Dakota, frustrated by government injustices, a crop failure and late payment for their land, waged war in a futile attempt to drive the settlers out of their traditional lands. One of the major battles of this six-week war was fought at Fort Ridgely.

You can trace the events of the fierce battle at Fort Ridgely by following a self-guided trail that connects the exposed foundations of the original garrison buildings. In the restored commissary, a scale model shows how the fort looked in 1862, and a video explains the causes and effects of the U.S.-Dakota Conflict. Both the interpretive center (in the commissary) and the trail are administered by the Minnesota Historical Society.

Though the historic site is an important part of the park, most visitors linger because it's fun to be outdoors here. Fort Ridgely has a good mix of scenery: prairie bluffs, forested ravines, and small snatches of native prairie. Prairie and oak savanna restoration is under way in some sections of the park. Hikers can meander through the prairie and wooded slopes on more than 11 miles of trails. Horseback riders explore the park on a 7-mile trail network. Hikers who climb to the crest of Airplane Hill will be rewarded with a view of Fort Ridgely Creek and the Minnesota River Valley. There is no direct access to the Minnesota River in the park, and therefore no fishing or water sports.

Despite the lack of water recreation, the campgrounds can be busy on weekends and holidays. The park maintains two drive-in camping areas (39 total sites; 8 electric), a primitive group camp, four backpack sites and a horse camp. The shady picnic grounds next to the fort site feature horseshoe courts, a volleyball court and a playground. The Chalet Picnic Area surrounds an enclosed, heated shelter building that may be reserved for private groups throughout the year. If you'd like more solitude, enjoy a picnic next to peaceful Fort Ridgely Creek, across from the campground.

Fort Ridgely has the distinction of being the only Minnesota state park that operates its own golf course. The 9-hole course (artificial grass greens) begins by the chalet in a scenic valley near Fort Ridgely Creek. Most of the holes are on the open land surrounding the old fort site. Golf club and cart rental is available.

The annual Fort Ridgely Historical Festival and Rendezvous, held the last weekend in June, is a memorable occasion to visit the park. The festival includes music and dance, foods, folk art demonstrations, wagon rides, and much more. At the same time, costumed "fur traders" from around the state gather for the rendezvous, where you can see them in their 1840s-style encampment, living in tipis and cooking over open fires.

Winter

The park grooms about 7 miles of snowmobile trails and about 3 miles of beginner and intermediate loops for cross-country skiers. Most of these trails twist through the golf course, but it's also fun to take in the view from the snowy hillside woods across Fort Ridgely Creek.

FRONTENAC STATE PARK

Goodhue County. 10 miles southeast of Red Wing on Highway 61. Turn east onto County 2 in Frontenac Station and drive 1 mile to park entrance.

Frontenac State Park has a story that's as old as the ice age. The sandstone and limestone formations that are today's bluffs were once sediments that hardened into rock at the bottom of shallow seas. Then, raging glacial rivers carved the broad river valley that we see today. The lake was created by a natural dam formed from material deposited by the Chippewa River as it emptied into the Mississippi.

Frontenac, the scenic river town that the park is named for, was established in the 1850s. Its growth was slowed by the Civil War, but one of its founders, Israel Garrard, returned afterward with southern craftsmen to continue developing the town. By the late 1870s, Frontenac had blossomed into a prosperous community. Because of the town's charm and the natural beauty of the bluffs and river, Frontenac became a fashionable summer resort for wealthy families from New Orleans, St. Louis and St. Paul who arrived by steamboat to vacation on the shores of Lake Pepin. When the railroads came, Frontenac, like other river towns, declined.

Frontenac State Park's 15 miles of hiking trails are a combination of open prairie and forest paths. Most of the overlooks are concentrated on top of the lakefront ridges. Some trails drop down the steep, forested slope with serpentine switchbacks to a bottomland path paralleling the lake. One trail leads behind the campground to In-Yan-Teopa Rock, a giant boulder perched on the edge of a bluff above Lake Pepin.

From the picnic area you can see down Lake Pepin to Lake City and beyond. The picnic area attracts many daytime visitors from the Twin Cities who enjoy eating outdoors with a view. There's an enclosed shelter with electricity. Daytime observers up here will usually see a flotilla of sailboats and pleasure craft on Lake Pepin.

The park's 58-site (19 electric) semi-modern campground is on a ridgetop with easy access to hiking trails. The primitive group camp is just to the west of the main campground. If you'd like to "rough it," you can hike a short distance to the six walk-in campsites near the park entrance. The park is close to the Twin Cities metro area, so it's a good idea to arrive early on holiday weekends and during the prime weekends for fall colors.

Winter

Come back to the river country during winter for some cross-country skiing, snowmobiling or hiking. Six miles of beginner to intermediate ski-touring trails start from the trail center parking lot and branch off through the bottomlands to Sand Point or climb up to the picnic area.

The eight miles of snowmobile trails also start at the trail center parking lot, then wind through the bottomlands and up to the ridgetop above Lake Pepin. The trail center serves as a warming house for skiers and snowmobilers.

KILEN WOODS STATE PARK

Jackson County. 9 miles northeast of Lakefield. The park entrance is 5 miles east of Highway 86 on County 24. Highway map index: F-21.

Kilen Woods State Park is attractive to families because of its day-use activities. Picnics are always popular in the green, shaded picnic area. Kids like the field by the parking lot for ball games. Another favorite with children (and their curious parents) is the small interpretive center in the enclosed picnic shelter building. Looking, touching and questioning are encouraged here, where you can feel the texture of beaver and fox pelts or examine the skulls of deer, wolf and cougar. The room is stuffed full of antlers, fish, duck wings, native prairie grasses and more.

The Rock Creek Trail follows the Des Moines River for most of its route through the park. To get a good view of the river, climb up to the Dinosaur Ridge Overlook. These bluffs are about 150 feet high and continue to flank the river to Jackson. You can also get a broad view of the river valley from the lookout tower near the picnic area.

From the Sioux Trail, you can see how the creeks have cut U-shaped valleys into the prairie and savanna to reach the river. To the west and south of the park is the "coteau des prairies" (slope of the prairies) that influences the flow of water. Water on the eastern slope, like the Des Moines River, flows into the Mississippi River, while water on the western side flows into the Missouri River.

The park's semi-modern campground is small (33 sites; 11 electric) but rarely crowded. Just downhill from the campground are four wooded walk-in sites that are about 100 yards from a hilltop parking area. The amphitheater and the picnic shelter are gathering spots for the park's interpretive programs.

Although this region is full of pioneer lore, it also has a rich Indian heritage. Near Jeffers, north of Windom (Cottonwood County), are the Jeffers Petroglyphs, a collection of ancient Indian rock carvings surrounded by native prairie. An interpretive center, administered by the Minnesota Historical Society, focuses on the carvings and the prairie landscape.

Winter

Cross-country skiers can glide from the parking lot into the valley and along the river on a 1.5-mile trail (ski rental is available). Snowmobilers also start from the parking lot, traversing the prairie and descending to the river bottom on a 3.5-mile trail network. Snow-tubing on the sliding hill and hiking are other popular winter activities at Kilen Woods State Park.

LAC QUI PARLE
STATE PARK

*Lac qui Parle County, 10 miles northwest of Montevideo.
Access from Chippewa County 13 or Lac qui Parle County 33.
Highway map index: D-16.*

French explorers living with the Indians along the upper Minnesota River gave Lac qui Parle Lake its musical name based on Dakota Indian legend. Lac qui Parle, or the "lake that talks," really does seem to talk when you listen to the collected voices of thousands of geese during spring and fall migrations.

The 530-acre state park at the foot of the lake lies next to the 27,000-acre Lac qui Parle Wildlife Management Area, which stretches to the northwest. When the Big Stone National Wildlife Refuge (an upriver extension of the Lac qui Parle Wildlife Management Area) was created, it transformed the upper Minnesota River Valley into a vast game preserve that harbors deer, geese, prairie chickens, pheasants and other game.

Watching the seasonal waterfowl migrations is a favorite visitor activity at Lac qui Parle. Spring migrations last from early March to the end of April, while fall flights begin in September and continue until December. During some years, more than 200,000 geese have noisily assembled here for their flight south, making this one of the biggest goose management areas in the country. The Canada geese are banded at Lac qui Parle to determine where they spend each season.

The native prairie, upland grasslands and farm fields form one of the best pheasant areas in the state. In some years, over 600 deer are harvested, confirming Lac qui Parle's reputation as a prime hunting ground in Minnesota.

The wetlands of this region are rich in food for waterfowl. Grasses, sedges and trees like willow and cottonwood provide food and shelter for water-loving birds. Ducks, pelicans, cormorants and herons thrive in the low, marshy areas of the upper Minnesota River. Special restrictions apply to human use of the Lac qui Parle Wildlife Management Area in order to preserve it as a refuge. The lake is closed to boating in the fall and 7,000 acres are closed to all hunting. Contact the wildlife area manager or the park manager for detailed dates and regulations.

Fish thrive in Lac qui Parle. At times, the action is good for walleye, northern, perch or panfish. The lake level fluctuates during the open season because of the U.S. Corps of Engineers' flood control efforts at Lac qui Parle Dam. At lower water levels, submerged reefs, floating logs and other debris make boating hazardous. Check boating conditions before going on the lake or river. You can launch directly into the lake from one of the two recreation area landings or from a landing (also in the recreation area) on the Lac qui Parle River.

Because of the water recreation and network of hiking/horseback riding trails at Lac qui Parle, the park is a popular day-use destination. Families like to come here because there's enough to do to satisfy everybody. You can spread out a noontime feast at a lakeshore picnic table, go for a swim at the beach, or do some canoeing or fishing on the lake. Easy hiking and horseback riding trails link the lakeshore to the dense woods that line the convoluted Lac qui Parle River.

Scout troops use the park as a day camp. Other groups can reserve the primitive camping area near an oxbow (U-shaped) lake. The main campground is split into two loops that have a total of 56 semi-modern sites (22 electric). These can fill on weekends, although you'll usually have no difficulty in getting a site at other times. Hunters like to set up camp in the park during autumn. The park's walk-in campsites are available on a first come-first served basis.

Two nearby historic sites across the river are worth a visit. Fort Renville was a fur-trading post built by Joseph Renville in the 1820s. Born in 1779 in Kaposia, an Indian village below present-day St. Paul, Renville grew up with Dakota Indian children and became one of the Northwest's most influential people. He served as a captain in the British army during the War of 1812 and later became a "coureur de bois" (independent fur trader) among the Dakota Indians along the upper Minnesota River.

In 1835, Renville invited Protestant missionary and physician Thomas S. Williamson to found a school and church near the trading post. For the next 20 years, missionaries worked at this remote settlement, attempting to convert the Dakota and to teach them the white man's ways. The missionaries translated the Gospel and several hymns into the Dakota language and completed the first grammar and dictionary of the language.

The Lac qui Parle Mission was the first church in the state. Today, visitors can see a replica of the original adobe chapel at the mission site (owned by the Minnesota Historical Society but operated by the Chippewa County Historical Society). To reach the Lac qui Parle Mission and Fort Renville, cross the Minnesota River from the state park and turn left (north) onto Chippewa County 32.

Winter

The park grooms 5 miles of cross-country ski trails (there are no snowmobiling trails). The flat terrain gives novice skiers a chance for an easy outing while observing winter wildlife such as bald eagles and deer. Winter camping, though not common, is possible in the park (water is available in the campground). Besides the late fall waterfowl migrations, ice fishing attracts the most cold-weather visitors to Lac qui Parle.

LAKE LOUISE STATE PARK

Mower County. 1.5 miles north of LeRoy on County 14. Highway map index: L-21.

As Minnesota's southernmost state park, Lake Louise is an attractive introduction to the recreational pleasures of the state. Families will find a peaceful lake setting for picnicking, swimming or hiking.

Weekends draw the most people to the park, but you can lose the crowds by exploring the 11 miles of foot trails. Horseback riders can wander through the park on 10 miles of trails (equestrian campsites are available). When you return to the picnic area, take time to visit the Hambrecht Historical Cottage and Museum.

The museum used to be the summer cottage of the Hambrecht family, which donated the land that later became Lake Louise State Park (named for a family member). When the Hambrechts homesteaded near here, the land supported a mixture of hardwood timber and lush prairie. A gristmill was built next to the present dam, and the town of LeRoy prospered nearby. The town relocated 2 miles south when the railroad came through.

Originally known as Wildwood Park, Lake Louise benefits from active community support. Old Wildwood Days are still celebrated early in June, and the Lake Louise State Park Association was formed to preserve and improve the park.

A small bridge just beyond the lakefront provides access to most of the park's trail system. This is also a shortcut to the campground. The semi-modern campground has 22 campsites (11 electric).

Winter

Lake Louise State Park's 2 miles of beginner cross-country ski trails are a good place for your family to learn how to ski. Snowmobilers can tour the park on a 9-mile trail system. Lake Louise is also a prime spot for winter solitude and wildlife photography. The park has become a traditional wintering area for white-tailed deer.

LAKE SHETEK
STATE PARK

Murray County. 14 miles northeast of Slayton and about 33 miles southeast of Marshall. Park access is off of County 38, north of Currie. Highway map index: D-19.

Loon Island is a bird sanctuary connected to this park by a causeway. Ducks, owls, woodpeckers and many other birds live here. Some nest in the dead elm trees that were stricken with Dutch elm disease and now resemble a stark winter woods in the midst of summer. You'll probably hear lots of bird and animal sounds on the island: the rat-tat-tat of a redheaded woodpecker, the scolding of a squirrel or the slap of a beaver's tail hitting the water by the shoreline.

Lake Shetek (translated as "pelican" in the Dakota Indian language) is southwestern Minnesota's largest lake and is the headwaters of the Des Moines River. The 3,600-acre lake is famous among visitors from Iowa, South Dakota and Minnesota who come to catch walleyes, northerns, bullheads and crappies off Loon Island and along the causeway. Kosak's Bay, up the shoreline from the park, is a good spot, too. The park has a drive-in boat access near the causeway.

Make the contact station your first stop in the park. You can rent boats and canoes here and purchase snacks and limited supplies. There is also a small gift shop. The semi-modern campground is spacious, and it's popular on holidays and summer weekends. About 85 percent of the sites have electrical hookups. There are 10 walk-in sites along the lakeshore, a short distance from the campground, and a separate, smaller rustic campground. The park also has three group camps. Two are primitive while the other has bunk cabins and a mess hall (available by reservation only). A new campground and more trails are part of the tentative development plan for the park.

Just north of the campground is a swimming beach and a pleasant lakeshore picnic area. In the interpretive center, visitors can see animal displays, an arrowhead collection and many "touch and see" artifacts. Check the daily naturalist schedule during the summer for special events.

The park has two historical sites. One is the pioneer Koch cabin (across the road from the campground); the other is the Shetek Monument (just off the entrance road), relating to the U.S-Dakota Conflict of 1862.

Winter

Trails are groomed and marked for snowmobilers (5 miles) and cross-country skiers (3 miles). A few visitors enjoy snowshoeing, but it is not common in the park. Ice fishing has grown in popularity each year since the state installed an aeration system in Lake Shetek in the mid-1970s. This has raised the winter oxygen levels and eliminated winterkill.

MINNEOPA STATE PARK

*Blue Earth County. 3 miles west of Mankato on Highway 68.
Highway map index: H-19.*

The trademark of Minneopa State Park is a lovely set of two waterfalls that plunge a total of 45 feet in the rocky gorge of Minneopa Creek. The park's other landmark is the graceful Seppman Windmill, built of pasture stone and wood from surrounding groves.

The word Minneopa means "water falling twice" in the Dakota Indian language. The double waterfalls were formed as Minneopa Creek cut into and eroded layers of sandstone at different rates.

For a good view of both falls, take the trail that starts from the large picnic area and crosses the creek between the falls on a footbridge. A short distance down from the bridge, an opening in the trees reveals a vista of the 15-foot upper falls and the 30-foot lower falls. The trail then drops into the deep gorge until it reaches stream level. You may either continue following the creek or cross over another bridge and circle back up to the picnic ground. There are many steps on this circular route, however, and the climb may be too strenuous for some.

The main body of Minneopa State Park is across Highway 68 from the waterfalls area. This is a large prairie area that the Dakota people called "Tinta-inya-ota" (prairie with many rocks). The big boulders (known as glacial erratics) were transported from a hundred miles away and deposited here by glaciers some 15,000 years ago. Some of these boulders, scattered around the park's grassland, are split in two, possibly from seasonal cycles of freeze and thaw. The land surrounding the campground is being restored to native prairie by periodic controlled burning and replanting. Before becoming a state park, the prairie was used as a sheep pasture, which destroyed the natural grasses.

Since Minneopa State Park is primarily a day-use center, visitors usually will have no difficulty in selecting a campsite. The Red Fox campground offers over 60 semi-modern campsites spread over a mixture of open and wooded land. The park also has a primitive group camp.

You can hike 2.5 miles on gravel road through oak savanna to Seppman's Windmill. The handsome structure, built in the European style by Louis Seppman and a neighbor in 1864, was one of Minnesota's first gristmills. Farmers hauled their grist as far as 20 miles by wagon and sometimes stayed overnight in the granary (which is still standing) until their grain could be milled. After lightning struck in 1873, the two arms (sailstock) were replaced. But when a tornado destroyed them again in 1880, it was no longer profitable to operate windmills, and the arms were not replaced. Today, you can walk up to each of the windmill's three levels. Preserved mill pieces and interpretive signs are on the ground level (a flashlight will be handy).

Winter

Birdwatchers visit Minneopa State Park in the winter to observe the year-round residents as they hunt for food in the river valley. Beginning cross-country skiers can practice on 4 miles of easy valley trails.

MINNESOTA RIVER CANOE & BOATING ROUTE

Headwaters in Big Stone County, then southeast to Nicollet and Blue Earth counties, and northeast to the Mississippi River in Hennepin and Dakota counties. 330 miles, from Ortonville to the Mississippi River.

This canoe route begins below Ortonville, although the river's headwaters are near Browns Valley on the Minnesota-South Dakota border. The river enters Big Stone Lake (also on the border), where fishing attracts many boaters. The lake is large, though, and windy days make for rough canoeing. For those who'd like to stay for sailing or boating on the lake, there is a campground at Big Stone Lake State Park, northwest of Ortonville.

About 4 miles below Ortonville and Big Stone Lake, the Minnesota River widens into the reservoir that forms part of the Big Stone National Wildlife Refuge. The refuge and its two downriver neighbors, the Lac qui Parle Wildlife Management Area and Lac qui Parle State Park, form a string of public lands that stretches for more than 40 miles along the upper Minnesota River.

Marsh Lake and Lac qui Parle Lake, the two lakes that the Minnesota River flows through in the wildlife management area, are shallow and weedy. The swamps and marshes surrounding the lakes are on a major flyway for migrating birds. Wetland birds such as ducks and herons make their home here, while the Canada goose is a seasonal transient. To protect the waterfowl, part of the Lac qui Parle Wildlife Management Area (including the canoe route from the Highway 40 bridge to the dam at river mile 285) is closed to the public from September 20 to December 20.

For canoeists on a flexible schedule, Lac qui Parle State Park (at the lake's lower end) is worth a stay. The Lac qui Parle River joins the Minnesota River in the park, forming miles of twisting channels that fishermen and birdwatchers love to poke into. You'll need a state park vehicle permit to stay in the park's campground.

Below Lac qui Parle Dam, the river widens into a broad flood plain. Exposed granite formations between Granite Falls and North Redwood are some of the continent's oldest rocks, dating back more than 3 billion years. Cedar and oak-covered granite domes, interspersed with prime agricultural land, border the river in this section. The bottomlands are forested with maple, elm, cottonwood and willow.

The only rapids of note on the otherwise easy river is Patterson's Rapids (River Mile 225.9), below Granite Falls. This is a short stretch of white water that rushes over a bed of glacial drift boulders. At low to moderate water levels, the rapids are rated Class I.

Below Highway 4, the Minnesota River meanders so much that it appears confused about which way to turn. The low riverbanks are covered with willow, ash, basswood and other hardwoods while the valley slopes are covered by oak, cedar and maple. The banks are sandy and eroded below Le Sueur, with gravel bars and snags choking the river in low water.

The Minnesota meets the Mississippi (also a canoe route) at Pike Island in Fort Snelling State Park. Zebulon Pike, a young army lieutenant and explorer, bought Pike Island and the surrounding land from the Dakota Indians in 1805.

Canoeists have a close-up view of the great diversity of wildlife in the woods, prairies, farmland and marshes of the Minnesota River Valley. Deer, beaver and muskrats feed along the riverbanks, while pheasants and Hungarian partridge find thick cover for nesting in the bottomlands. In addition to various water birds, you might see hawks and songbirds overhead. The river also supports a large fish population. Many walleyes, northerns and smallmouth bass are caught in the pools below the rapids and dams on the upper river. Carp and other rough fish are common throughout the route. When canoeing or fishing on the lower Minnesota River, watch out for commercial barge traffic.

MONSON LAKE STATE PARK

Swift County. 4 miles southwest of Sunburg. Access is off Highway 104, via County 18. Highway map index: E-15.

Off the main road and on the Glacial Ridge Trail, peaceful Monson Lake State Park has a lot to offer in a small space. Spring attracts the most visitors to Monson Lake. Early-season angling and birdwatching are common activities.

Fishing is good all year, but spring and late fall are favorite times to try for walleyes, northerns, bass or sunfish. The anvil-shaped peninsula in the park is a good shoreline spot for walleyes or bass. On the right shore of the anvil is a beaver lodge, where fall hikers may spot some activity. On cool autumn evenings, dozens of glowing lights dotting the lake are a pretty sight. Lantern fishing is popular among the warmly dressed fishermen who hope to be rewarded with a big northern or walleye.

Canoeists can explore Monson Lake's shoreline and then portage across the narrow isthmus to West Sunburg Lake. There's a boat ramp to the left of the campground as you enter the park.

A historic site in the park commemorates a skirmish in which warriors killed a pioneer family during the U.S.-Dakota Conflict of 1862. Anna Stina Broberg Peterson, then 16 years old, was the only survivor of the raid on the Anders P. Broberg homestead. The park was set aside in 1923 as a memorial to her family. The conflict, brought on by Dakota feelings of discouragement with reservation life and anger over broken promises and land swindles, affected much of this part of the state.

Winter

Fishing is popular all year on Monson Lake. Its 22-foot depth is deep compared to most other southwestern Minnesota lakes, allowing enough oxygen under the ice so fish are still hungry for your bait. You can also try skiing, though the mostly flat trail is not groomed. You'll need a sharp eye to spot rabbits and other forest dwellers, but it's easy to see their snowy tracks.

MYRE-BIG ISLAND STATE PARK

Freeborn County. 3 miles southeast of Albert Lea on County 38. Park exits are marked on both 1-35 and l-90, though Exit 11 on l-35 is the easier approach. Highway map index: J-21.

Because of its varied terrain, this park is one of southern Minnesota's prime birding spots. Hiking the Great Marsh Trail in the park's southwestern corner during spring and fall migrations, you'll see white pelicans, Canada geese and a variety of ducks. Shorebirds and waterfowl are common in the park during summer, as well as hawks hunting rodents in the grassy meadows. The park also boasts more than 450 kinds of wildflowers.

The Esker Trail, in the northern end of the park, features part of the area's glacial history. An esker is a long, narrow ridge of coarse gravel deposited by a stream flowing through a tunnel under stagnant ice. As the ice melted, the sinuous stream bed remained. The retreating glacier also left ice blocks that formed shallow lakes and marshes as they melted in basins. Albert Lea Lake is one such lake, with an average depth of 3 feet. At one time, the lake was clear and had a sandy bottom. Today it is rich in dissolved nutrients that have reduced the lake's oxygen level, favoring plant life over animal life. The lake still attracts summertime anglers, though, who go after panfish, carp and bullheads. The park has no guarded swimming beach, but there is a municipal pool in Albert Lea.

Participating in the naturalist programs is the easiest way to become familiar with the park's natural and cultural features. The Owen Johnson Interpretive Center, named for an area resident who campaigned for a state park here, is headquarters for naturalist activities. Nestled on the forest edge on Big Island, the year-round center has one of the country's largest collections of Indian artifacts. A picnic area with enclosed shelter is adjacent to the center.

Myre-Big Island State Park offers a wide range of camping facilities. A large semi-modern campground and a primitive group camp are located on Big Island. New York Point, on an arrow-tip peninsula of the mainland, is a full-facility group center with a dining hall, kitchen and crafts building. This camp is available for church groups, scout troops or any organization at a nominal fee. Contact the park manager for reservations.

The park maintains another semi-modern campground on the mainland, though it is more open than the one on Big Island (100 total sites, 32 electric, in both campgrounds). If you'd like a private camping experience, backpack to one of the park's four primitive sites, strung along the shoreline of a large peninsula just off one of the hiking trails.

Winter

Winter means action at Myre-Big Island State Park. The interpretive center, open weekends during winter, offers one-hour programs that cover such topics as attracting winter birds to your backyard, viewing evening stars and waxing cross-country skis. The naturalist also leads winter hikes, with tips on animal signs and tree identification. Snowshoe hikes and moonlight cross-country ski outings are other scheduled events.

Fifteen miles of trails are marked and groomed for winter use—8 for cross-country skiers and 7 for snowmobilers. The snowmobile trail connects with over 250 additional miles of Freeborn County Grant-in-Aid trails and with side trails to Albert Lea and onto the lake. A warming house, with picnic tables and a fireplace, is open for all winter visitors.

NERSTRAND BIG WOODS STATE PARK

Rice County. About 11 miles southeast of Northfield on Highway 246 (follow the signs to the park). Highway map index: K-19.

The mature, dense hardwood forest at Nerstrand has always been a place of refuge. Dakota Indians lived and hunted here, and settlers depended on the trees for fuel and building material. Today, people come to the same forest for a different type of refuge. Nerstrand is the last sizable glimpse of the Big Woods, a deciduous forest that once spread over all south-central Minnesota. Growing towns and farms have nibbled at the woods so much that only scattered parcels remain.

The park's 13 miles of hiking trails are popular on weekends, especially when the trees ignite in the reds, oranges and yellows of fall. The busiest trails lead into the hills and valleys behind the picnic/campground area. If you prefer more solitary walking, come back in midweek or explore the less-used trails across County 40.

The hike down to Hidden Falls on Prairie Creek is a treat for the senses. Stop to smell the earthy aroma of moist vegetation. Feel the sponginess of the trail, blocked from the sun by the tall trees. As you descend into the valley, campground and picnic area noise melts into the sound of wind rustling through the leaves. Soon, what you thought was the wind turns into the rushing voice of the waterfall. As you cross the hickory footbridge behind the falls, notice how pitch and tone shift with your position. Close your eyes and let the soothing hypnotic music of the falls pour over you. The air feels warmer as you climb up the valley trail, and the sounds merge from waterfall to wind and back to picnic area.

The park's 56-site semi-modern campground (28 electric) can be busy during summer, especially on weekends. Reservations are a good idea. Groups that want to reserve the primitive group camp should contact the park office. Nerstrand Big Woods also maintains 13 rustic walk-in campsites.

Winter

Winter camping at Nerstrand Big Woods becomes more popular each year. Check with the manager regarding water supplies and other details. The park's thick forest provides a scenic backdrop for winter hikers, who enjoy tromping through snowy valleys and up the steep hillside. Snowmobilers like the woodsy winter scenery, too, and can explore the park's south side on more than 6 miles of trails, some connecting with local branches.

O.L. KIPP
STATE PARK

Winona County. At the junction of U.S. 61 and I-90. Take the County 12 exit (north) from I-90 to County 3 (County 12 ends on the north side of I-90). Follow County 3 (Apple Blossom Drive) to the park entrance. Highway map index: O-20.

There is something about gazing down at life floating by on the Mississippi River that makes people linger at the overlooks in O.L. Kipp State Park. The young park (opened in 1976) boasts eight designated overlooks, but you'll discover other broad vistas of the legendary river from the park roads and trails.

From O.L. Kipp's overlooks, you'll see barges and a variety of pleasure craft, including canoes, cabin cruisers and houseboats. The maze of sloughs and backwaters on the Mississippi attracts legions of anglers and explorers. O.L. Kipp State Park does not currently have direct access to the river, but there are many landings in the La Crescent/La Crosse area.

The park's nine-mile trail system (including the King's Bluff interpretive trail) leads hikers through the varied environments of the park's highlands. From riverfront overlooks, you can see a grand succession of noble 500-foot, rock-faced bluffs on both sides of the valley. Although the bluffs resemble each other, you'll notice that their plant cover can be different. This is because each bluff has its own microclimate, which can favor different vegetation.

O.L. Kipp State Park is part of southeastern Minnesota's "driftless" area. "Drift" is the name given to the boulders, gravel and soil that the glaciers deposited. The driftless region, which wasn't covered by this glacial debris, includes parts of Winona and Houston counties, pieces of Iowa and Illinois, and most of southwestern Wisconsin. The glaciers influenced this area, however, even without touching it. Meltwater from the glaciers poured into the Mississippi River, increasing the river's erosive power. The torrent scraped and carved through hundreds of feet of sandstone and limestone to help form the park's topography. When the Indians first came, the land looked similar to what we see today: half-dome bluffs with sheer cliffs, steep valleys and rolling uplands on both sides of a wide river valley.

O.L. Kipp boasts two unique features. One is a bicycle campground, located on Highway 14-61 (known as the Great River Road Bicycle Route). This campground is the first of its kind in the state park system. Drinking water and fire rings are available in this self-registering campground.

The other unique feature is the Henslow's sparrow. The park hosts the only established nesting territory in Minnesota for this rare species. Birders have been aware of the Henslow's sparrow in O.L. Kipp for years, traveling from Florida, California and New York just to spot the elusive little birds.

Currently, the park offers a picnic area, a 31-site semi-modern campground and a primitive group camp. Future plans call for an interpretive center, naturalist programs and an additional campground.

Winter

Most of the park's nine miles of cross-country ski trails are designed for beginners and intermediates, but there are a couple of steep drops for advanced skiers. You can ski on easy bluff-top trails to many overlooks of the wintry Mississippi River Valley.

PIPESTONE NATIONAL MONUMENT

Pipestone County. Just north of the city of Pipestone. Follow the signs from Highways 75, 23 or 30. Highway map index: B-20.

For centuries, Indians from tribes all over the Midwest came to quarry the soft stone, traveling as much as a thousand miles by foot. Even tribes at war with each other met as friends at the pipestone quarry.

The soft stone quarried there was ideal for carving and shaping into pipes, even with primitive flint instruments. The pipes were then used in sacred ceremonies to seal treaties, strengthen alliances, and show intentions of war or peace. Each tribe had its own legend about how the Great Spirit blessed the quarry and how the first pipe came to its people, but all believed that the grounds were sacred.

George Catlin, who traveled among and painted the American Indians from 1829 to 1838, visited the quarries in 1836. Although not the first white man to visit the area, he was the first person to describe the quarries in print, and his pipestone sample was the first to be studied. Today, pipestone is called catlinite in his honor.

The quarry was designated a national monument by Congress in 1937. Visitors today can see Indians fashioning ornate pipes using the same methods used centuries ago. Other Indian crafts, such as quillwork, beadwork, and leatherwork, are kept alive at the Upper Midwest Indian Cultural Center located at the Pipestone National Monument, with demonstrations by Native Americans.

Pipe carvings are appreciated today as artworks as well as for ceremonial use. Quarrying here has always been accomplished with respect for the earth and for what it yields. The Dakota traditionally leave an offering of food and tobacco beside the group of boulders known as the Three Maidens in return for this land's gift of stone.

The bed of pipestone in the park slopes to the east, so as the Indians continue to dig the stone, they have to dig deeper and deeper to reach it. In some areas, nearly 12 feet of quartzite must be removed. Heavy equipment and explosives are not allowed in the quarry operations, for they would shatter the soft, brittle pipestone.

The national monument is open daily except Christmas and New Year's days. Visiting hours are 8 a.m. to 5 p.m. (hours are extended in summer). Begin your tour at the visitor center for an overview of the area's history and cultural significance from the slide program and exhibits. Then pick up an interpretive brochure for the three-quarter-mile scenic trail.

This paved loop winds through a small section of virgin prairie, parallels the quartzite ledge and returns to the visitor center after passing the quarry exhibit. Take your time. Read how the Indians used various plants for medicine, food and other needs. Pause by Pipestone Creek and Winnewissa Falls to let the sound of rushing water work its calming magic.

You can camp nearby at Split Rock Creek and Blue Mounds state parks. Private campgrounds and other services are found in the Pipestone area. The city of Pipestone boasts beautiful buildings built from Sioux quartzite, the harder stone formations that sandwich the thinner layers of pipestone.

RICE LAKE STATE PARK

Steele County. 7 miles east of Owatonna on County 19. Highway map index: K-20.

Rice Lake State Park, a popular day-use area, is known by local residents as a good place to see wildlife. The mix of marsh, lake, meadow and woods attracts large numbers of birds, especially during the spring and fall migrations. Because Rice Lake is the only lake of any size in the vicinity, geese, swans and ducks stop here to feed and nest. A remodeled interpretive center offers more information about the park's plants and wildlife and features an interesting arrowhead collection.

The spacious picnic area, on a peninsula jutting into Rice Lake, is shaded by tall hardwoods. The cross-breeze refreshes while keeping insects at bay. A small swimming area and a drive-in boat access are on the west side of the peninsula. You can rent canoes in the park for an outing on the lake or to paddle across Rice Lake to one of the five canoe campsites.

The campground is also shaded by hardwoods that screen the 42 (16 electric) semi-modern sites from each other. A primitive group camp, available by reservation, is connected to the main campground by road and trail.

Rice Lake is named for the wild rice that generations of Indians gathered here. The lake is one of the Zumbro River's sources, forming the South Branch of the Middle Fork. The village of Rice Lake, which once flourished north of the park, is marked today only by the Rice Lake Church, built in 1857 and located along Dodge County Highway 20.

Winter

The park has about 2.5 miles of snowmobile trails. Four miles of beginner cross-country ski trails trace the lakeshore and loop inland. Snowshoeing and winter camping, though allowed, are not popular here.

RICHARD J. DORER MEMORIAL HARDWOOD STATE FOREST

Dakota, Goodhue, Dodge, Olmsted, Wabasha, Winona, Fillmore and Houston counties. Access includes 10 recreation and management units: Brightsdale, Bronk, Hay Creek, Isinours, Kruger, Oak Ridge, Reno, Snake Creek, Trout Valley and Zumbro Bottoms.

The Richard J. Dorer Memorial Hardwood State Forest covers most of southeastern Minnesota's driftless area—a region untouched by the last glaciers Though the forest has large statutory boundaries (of which about 40,000 acres are actually managed by the state Department of Natural Resources), visitors will best experience the variety of this region by concentrating on the 10 recreation units described below. Other management units may be developed and mapped in the future.

Brightsdale

The Brightsdale Unit, site of the Southeast Minnesota Forest Resource Center, is located about 5 miles north and west of Lanesboro. You can reach it by driving on a township road that runs west off of Highway 250 about 2 miles north of Lanesboro.

The 900-acre unit lures hikers and cross-country skiers to the area with a 5.7-mile marked and groomed trail system. The trails are arranged in two loops with portions that provide fun and challenges to both beginner and experienced cross-country skiers. Lands in the unit, except those that are posted, are open to hunting and trapping during established seasons. The Forest Resource Center is a nonprofit corporation that provides forest research and education. Visitors are welcome.

The Brightsdale Unit is named after an old hydroelectric plant located on the site, along the north branch of the Root River. This site may be developed into a campground and canoe access in the future. There is a canoe campsite in the unit along the Root River Canoe Route.

Bronk

The Bronk unit is located in Winona County, near Stockton, Minnesota City and Winona. Take Highway 14 west from Winona to County 23; go north for about 2 miles to Hillsdale Township Road No. 6, then east on No. 6 to the lower parking lot. The 761-acre unit straddles the ridge between Stockton Valley and the Mississippi River. The slopes of the ridge rise to 500 feet above the surrounding valleys, providing many vistas of southeastern Minnesota's bluff country.

The Plowline Trail (6.5 miles) is a hilly, scenic path for hikers, horseback riders and mountain bikers in the summer and cross-country skiers in the winter. The trailhead is near the upper parking lot, about two-thirds of a mile up the hill from the lower parking lot.

The trail's north and south loops generally follow the edge of the woods, or the plowline, as they go around the ridge. Two trail spurs off of the north loop go out to overlooks of Stockton Valley and the Mississippi River Valley. Hunting and trapping in season is allowed, except on leased and posted land.

Hay Creek

You can reach this unit by driving about 2 miles south of Red Wing on Highway 58. Scenic bluffs, a twisting trout stream, and a well-marked trail system are the main attractions of the 1500-acre unit.

The Hay Creek Valley was one of the first blocks of forested land to be purchased in Goodhue County following establishment of the Dorer State Forest in 1961. The hilly country surrounding Hay Creek is forested in oaks, with elm, birch, basswood and black cherry mixed in. Black walnut and pine plantations are scattered throughout the area.

The 8-mile-long trail system features several connected loops, covering a variety of terrain from creek-bottom to bluff-top overlooks. The marked and groomed trail system is used by hikers and horseback riders in the summer and snowmobilers and cross-country skiers in the winter. A picnic area and parking lot are located at the extreme south end of the trail. Other trail access points have been developed near the north and east entrances. There are no designated camp sites in the Hay Creek unit, though you can camp in nearby Frontenac State Park.

Isinours

The Isinours unit is located about 3 miles north of Preston near the South Branch of the Root River. Take County 17 north from Preston to the Root River State Trail. The parking area is on the north side of the trail and west of County 17.

The 188-acre unit includes over 3 miles of hiking/cross-country ski trails and two walk-in campsites. The trails are split into four loops and range from easy on some portions to most difficult on the steep slopes. The scenic vista along the central trail overlooks the Watson Creek watershed and the Root River Valley.

Kruger

Kruger is located about 5 miles west of Wabasha, just off of Highway 60 on County 81. You can also reach the unit by taking County 81 from Kellogg. There are sweeping views of the steep-sloped Zumbro River Valley from the campground and from some of the trails. Access to the Zumbro River, a designated state canoe route, is nearby.

In addition to the 19 campsites (water is available), Kruger has a day-use section with picnic tables and two shelters. Three marked trails begin near the day-use and camping areas. The Easy Wheeling Nature Trail is a three-quarter-mile, hard-packed loop that is accessible for disabled visitors (some assistance may be necessary). A 2-mile hiking and ski-touring trail extends from the nature trail. The third trail (about 5 miles long) is open to all users except motorized vehicles and crosses the bluffs and valleys along the Zumbro River.

Oak Ridge

Oak Ridge (1,565 acres) is about 5 miles west of Houston on County 13. Mixed hardwoods on steep ridges are common sights from the two trails and four campsites.

A 2.2-mile-long portion of the Houston County Grant-In-Aid snowmobile trail crosses the northern part of the unit. The Wet Bark Trail (8.8 miles) is used by hikers, horseback riders, cross-country skiers and snowshoers. This trail has several loops of varying difficulty, with some loops rising and falling as much as 300 feet in elevation.

The parking area and campsites are about 5 miles west of Houston on County 13. You'll have to walk a short distance to reach the campsites from the parking lot. Drinking water is available from a hand pump.

Reno

Reno (3,681 acres) is in southeastern Houston County, about 15 miles south of La Crescent. Much of the unit is located on the bluffs overlooking the Mississippi River and the village of Reno.

The Reno Trail and the day-use area are the major recreation facilities in the unit. The 9.5-mile Reno Trail provides sweeping views of the Mississippi River and challenging hiking through the rugged ridges and valleys of the mixed hardwood forest. Hikers and horseback riders use the trail during summer, and snowmobilers take it over during winter. The trail connects with the Houston County Grant-In-Aid trail system.

The campground and day-use area can be reached by turning off of Highway 26 in Reno and following the gravel road for a quarter-mile. Backpackers can hike to several remote campsites along the trail that starts in the parking area. You can get water from the hand pump at the parking lot. Hell's Hollow Natural Area lies at the end of a trail spur overlooking the Mississippi River.

Snake Creek

The Snake Creek Unit (2,600 acres) is located 4 miles south of Kellogg; follow the access signs from Highway 61. Of the two trails here, the remote North Valley Trail is used by hikers, horseback riders and cross-country skiers. There is a short loop of 1.5 miles and a long loop of 3.5 miles. Logs have been left here and there on the trail to discourage motorized vehicles.

The South Valley Trail (8 miles) is open to all users except four-wheel-drive vehicles. Parking lots for both trails are accessible from Highway 42 and are plowed in winter.

The terrain around Snake Creek is steep and rough, as in other sections of the forest. The creek is well-known for its trout fishing. There are no designated campsites here, but privately owned campgrounds are located nearby on Indian Creek and on Sand Prairie. In addition, you can camp at the Kruger Management Unit and at Carley and Whitewater state parks. Hunting and trapping are permitted during established seasons.

Trout Valley

To reach Trout Valley (2,375 acres), take Highway 61 north from Winona or south from Wabasha to County 29. Follow 29 southwest for 1.75 miles to the Trout Valley Demonstration Woodland. This area is a showcase for various forest management practices.

The 7-mile-long Trout Valley Trail is used by hikers, horseback riders and snowmobilers. This marked trail connects the stream-bottom with bluff-top vistas of Trout Valley, Whitewater Valley and the Mississippi River Valley. Trout Creek is a spring-fed trout stream flanked by steep, wooded ridges covered with oak and hickory.

Zumbro Bottoms

The Zumbro Bottoms unit is located in Wabasha County, 2 miles south of Dumfries off of Highway 60. An abandoned township road bisects the unit, crossing the easterly-flowing Zumbro River on an old steel trestle bridge. The single-lane bridge, dating from 1893, crosses the river at Funk's Ford, named after one of the early settlers of the area. Most of the roads near here are located in the flood plain and can be damaged during wet periods. Gates have been erected to restrict traffic during such times.

Zumbro Bottoms' extensive trail system includes numerous connecting loops that allow you to experience different portions of the unit without doubling back. The trails are marked with brown signs that show appropriate uses. While the majority of the trails are designed for horseback riders, you're welcome on the path wherever the signs show your activity. The Wabasha County Grant-In-Aid snowmobile trail enters the unit at three areas and is blazed with orange signs.

A canoe access (to the Zumbro River Canoe Route) and two picnic areas are located near the western end of the unit. Another canoe access as well as a picnic area and campground are just downriver from Zumbro Bottoms in the Kruger Recreation Area.

ROOT RIVER CANOE & BOATING ROUTE

Fillmore and Houston counties. 90 miles from Chatfield to the Mississippi River south of La Crescent.

The Root River gets a lot of return business. Canoeists come back to paddle in the shadow of forest-carpeted bluffs, and anglers try their luck again for smallmouth bass, channel catfish, rock bass or panfish. Some cast for brown trout in the clearer and colder spring-fed streams as well as at the western end of the South Branch.

If you don't fish, bring your camera and catch a shot of the wildlife along the river. The sandstone and limestone bluffs and the hardwood forests that flank the river are home to over 40 species of birds and a variety of river-bottom and woodland animals.

Formed of two branches in the west, the North and the Middle, the Root River winds past towering bluffs topped with oak and hickory. Joined above Whalan by the South Branch, a tributary that flows from Mystery Cave, the river continues its way past bluffs and outcrops to Rushford. There the river straightens in a broad valley. The scenery settles into a gentle plain of pastureland and mixed cottonwood and maple with wooded, rolling hills visible in the distance.

Novice canoeists can easily navigate the Root River at normal water levels, though fluctuations will cause changes in canoeing conditions. Low water levels in late summer can make passage difficult on the North and South branches. Heavy rains can cause flash floods on the river, requiring campers to place canoe and gear high on the riverbank. Check the Department of Natural Resources canoe route map for other cautions: the old dam at River Mile 62, a submerged dam above Rushford, and dredging operations on the lower river.

Family canoe day-trips are popular on the Root River. Those more adventurous can take advantage of the canoe campsites for overnight trips. Drinking water is not provided at the DNR campsites. Several towns along the Root River offer services and hospitality to river users.

ROOT RIVER STATE TRAIL

Fillmore and Houston counties. 35 miles; between Fountain and the Money Creek Unit of the Richard J. Dorer State Forest (east of Rushford).

Time was when the trains rushed and roared through the valley of the Root River. Now, hikers and bicyclists enjoy the songbirds and scenery along this former southeastern Minnesota right of way.

The 35-mile Root River State Trail passes through Fountain, Lanesboro, Whalan, Peterson and Rushford. You can find services in these towns, as well as in nearby Chatfield, Preston and Houston. Some of these communities, like Lanesboro, are noted for their historical buildings, antique and craft shops, bed and breakfast inns, and other attractions.

Lanesboro and Rushford have trail centers with restrooms. An interpretive center is being planned at the Lanesboro site. Wayside rests, picnic areas, parking lots and camping facilities are being developed along the trail. Camping facilities are located in Lanesboro, Houston and Preston and at nearby Forestville/Mystery Cave and Beaver Creek Valley state parks. Call the local chambers of commerce or the Minnesota Office of Tourism for details about camping and lodging in the trail towns and the surrounding area.

The Root River State Trail is known for its outstanding scenery, with wooded hillsides and soaring limestone outcroppings. Winding through a small valley, the trail follows the Root River (a state canoe route) for much of the way. The trail passes by a small dam, along pastures, over 48 bridges (up to 500 feet long) and through a rock wall blasted away for the railroad. The section between Lanesboro and Whalen is a scenic favorite of many bicyclists. Trail extensions east to Houston and also on the western end may be developed by the mid- to late-1990s.

Though summer and fall are the busiest trail-use seasons, winter attracts growing numbers of cross-country skiers and hikers. The Houston County Grant-in-Aid trail also provides miles of groomed snowmobile trails.

SAKATAH LAKE STATE PARK

Rice County. 1 mile east of Waterville on Highway 60. Highway map index: J-19.

To some people, it's good news that Sakatah Lake State Park is en route rather than a destination. Cars zip by on Highway 60, bicyclists pedal through on the Sakatah Singing Hills State Trail, and canoeists paddle past on the Cannon River Canoe Route. When travelers do pause here, they are surprised at the beauty, diversity, and seclusion offered by this small park (842 acres).

Sakatah Lake Park is a blend of rolling woods and prairie stretched along the southern shore of Sakatah Lake. The hardwood forest is a remnant of the Big Woods that once carpeted east-central Minnesota and the Mississippi River valley. A five-mile trail system cuts through this woods comprised of oak, elm and walnut trees.

Sakatah Lake, a natural widening of the Cannon River, is the scene of most park activity. An elongated picnic area overlooks the lake and a swimming beach. The Cannon River Canoe Route begins at the western end of Sakatah Lake at the Highway 13 bridge and continues for 80 miles to the Mississippi River. This is an easy canoe trip for families. Canoeists can launch from the park's boat ramp to head downriver or to spend the day on the lake. Most of the fishing on Sakatah Lake is for crappies, sunfish and bullheads.

The park's semi-modern campground is one of the best in southern Minnesota. The spacious wooded campground (63 sites, 14 electric) can be busy on weekends, but midweek visitors might have to walk a bit to find some neighbors. Besides the main campground, bicyclists can camp in the park's four-site bicycle campground along the Sakatah Singing Hills State Trail. The park also has two primitive group camps (available by reservation); one is just east of the boat ramp near the bicycle campground and the other is near Lower Sakatah Lake on the park's east side.

The park's interpretive center/trail center is a short trail walk from the main campground. There is a parking lot for the center along the campground road. Check at the contact station for details about naturalist-guided hikes and other programs.

Winter

Five miles of cross-country ski trails in the park swoop down through the woods, parallel the lake and climb back uphill, providing a challenge for intermediate skiers. Snowmobilers and hikers cross through the park on the Sakatah Singing Hills State Trail.

SAKATAH SINGING HILLS STATE TRAIL

Blue Earth, Le Seur and Rice counties. 39 miles, from Mankato to Faribault.

Serious cyclists can easily breeze along the Sakatah Singing Hills State Trail in half a day or less, but if you prefer a slower pace, there are enough distractions along the route for a relaxing weekend mini-vacation, among them the numerous lakes along the way and Sakatah Lake State Park.

The trail, developed along an old railroad bed, is on the edge of two bygone plant communities. The Big Woods to the north was once a great hardwood forest; the prairie to the south and west was an immense sea of rolling grassland. Today, though most of the land is cultivated, trail users can still see patches of the former vegetation.

Sakatah Singing Hills State Trail is split by a half-mile break in Waterville, just west of the state park. To connect with the other segment, follow the city streets in Waterville. Many cyclists start in town and head east toward Faribault for an easy afternoon ride. The whole trail is currently surfaced for bicyclists, hikers and snowmobilers; another treadway will be developed for horseback riders and cross-country skiers. There is a trailhead parking lot on Lime Valley Road near Mankato on the west end of the trail.

SIBLEY STATE PARK

*Kandiyohi County. 15 miles north of Willmar on Highway
71. Highway map index: F-15.*

From Mount Tom, in Sibley State Park, the view sweeps in
a grand circle over miles of forest, farmland and lakes.
Fragments of stone pipes found here suggest that, like most
high places, Mount Tom held spiritual significance to the
Dakota Indians.

French and Indian fur traders used Mount Tom as a
lookout when they traveled the Red River Trail with fur-
laden oxcarts. Each spring, they ventured into the prairie
wilderness from Pembina, North Dakota, on their way to St.
Paul to sell their furs.

The countryside around Mount Tom is more wooded now
than when the Dakota scouted the horizon. Hardwood trees
took over former grassland after the settlers came and prairie
fires were brought under control. Within the park, you can
see remnants of the once-vast grassy sea on the knolls that
were never plowed. These knolls, like Mount Tom, were
born of the boulders, sand and gravel deposited by the last
glacier. As you explore the park, you'll see several lakes, like
Lake Andrew, which were left behind as the glacier
retreated.

Hikers and horseback riders will see (and climb) moraine
hills made of "drift" (rock and soil debris) that was bulldozed
into place by the massive glacier. Sibley features an
extensive 23-mile trail system that includes nine miles of
horseback trails. Whether riding or hiking, you'll come
across many overlooks that offer vistas of the woods, ridges
and wetlands.

For bicyclists, there is a designated trail that winds from
the interpretive center parking lot down to Lake Andrew and
along the lakeshore. The shoreline is a favorite spot for
photographers. Visitors in wheelchairs are also welcome to
enjoy this 5-mile paved trail.

During summer, Lake Andrew is where you'll find most of
the park action. A large picnic area with a handsome granite
shelter on the shoreline overlooks the lake. This shelter, and
other granite park buildings, were built by the Conservation

Corps in the late 1930s. The sandy swimming beach draws flocks of sunbathers and kids, while the nearby pier is a fishing hot spot.

Sibley offers a choice of 138 semi-modern campsites (52 electric) in two separate campgrounds. Reservations are a good idea since the campgrounds are usually busy during the summer. Some visitors prefer camping here in autumn when the campgrounds are less crowded and the hardwoods change color. Call the park office for information about family campsites, the primitive group camp, the equestrian center or the modern group center.

The interpretive program at Sibley is tailor-made for the curious. Throughout the year, the park's resources come alive through guided hikes, films and discussions. Hiking with the naturalist is a good way to find out where the wildlife hangs out or to learn more about Sibley's unique mixture of hardwood forest, grassland and aquatic habitats. The modern interpretive center also features seasonal exhibits.

Sibley State Park is named for Minnesota's first governor, Henry H. Sibley, who used to hunt near here. Mount Tom, Lake Andrew and the surrounding land became a state park with the help of Peter Broberg, who was the only member of the Daniel Broberg family to survive the U.S.-Dakota Conflict of 1862.

Winter

The interpretive program is active all year and lures more folks outside each winter with imaginative activities. Sibley's cross-country ski trails are rated easy through most difficult and are long enough to give you a good workout. The snowmobile trails link up with county Grant-in-Aid trails. All of the park's winter trails are popular on weekends, so it pays to get an early start if you want to beat the rush. Just outside the interpretive center is an action-packed inner-tube hill for those who enjoy sliding downhill at considerable speeds.

SPLIT ROCK CREEK STATE RECREATION AREA

*Pipestone County. 6 miles south of Pipestone on Highway 23.
Park access is off of County 20. Highway map index: B-20.*

Split Rock Lake, formed in 1938 by a dam on Split Rock
Creek, is the only lake in the county. It attracts visitors from
Iowa, South Dakota and southwestern Minnesota because of
the water sports and park facilities. You can rent boats,
canoes and paddleboats. Some anglers like the action from
the fishing pier near the dam on the lake's south end. As
Pipestone County's largest body of water, the lake attracts
aquatic birds, too. During spring and fall migrations, you'll
have a chance to observe almost every species of waterfowl
found in the Midwest.

The two-mile trail system in the 400-acre recreation area
stretches along the lake's western shoreline, linking the
beach and picnic ground with the campground and other
park facilities. One trail climbs a hilly slope that remains
native prairie. An interpretive center on the hillside features
exhibits relating to the prairie and other park resources.

Split Rock Creek's semi-modern campground (28 sites; 14
electric) can be busy during the summer, though midweek
visitors may be able to find a site without a reservation. The
primitive group camp is available by reservation through the
recreation area office.

Winter

The lake dominates winter fun at this park. Ice-skating is
popular, though you may have to clear a path after a
snowfall. Fishing huts dot the ice, and snowmobiles—not
allowed on park trails—zigzag between them. Cross-country
skiers take over the park's hiking trails, stopping at the
interpretive center/warming house for breaks.

STRAIGHT RIVER CANOE & BOATING ROUTE

*Steele and Rice Counties. 30 miles from U.S. highway 14
south of Owatonna to Cannon River at Faribault.*

Twisting like a mountain highway, the Straight River seems to be misnamed. It probably derived from the Dakota Indian word "owatonna," meaning upright or truthful.

The river flows north from Owatonna to Faribault through the fertile farm country of southeastern Minnesota. There are only a couple of small agricultural towns along the route between the two cities. The Straight River offers an easygoing pace for families and beginning canoeists. You'll drift past banks lined with willow, maple and other hardwoods that form a green canopy over parts of the narrow stream. These trees play host to the throngs of songbirds and waterfowl that stop during the spring and fall migrations. You can stop for a picnic in Medford's Municipal Park. Owatonna and Faribault also have pleasant city parks.

The only rapids along the short route is at Clinton Falls. Although usually mild, it is more difficult during spring. There's a dam in Owatonna and another just upstream from Faribault, near the River Bend Nature Center. The DNR's canoe route map indicates the rest areas and access points.

Like many other rivers, the best time for canoeing is during spring and early summer; after that, the water level can decrease enough to make the route impassable for canoes. The Straight River varies in depth from 1 to 4 feet, depending on whether it's a wet or dry year. Fishing is usually good on the river, even when canoeing is not. Common catches include carp and crappies, but there are hungry smallmouth bass and northern in the river, too.

The Straight River empties into the Cannon River near Faribault. The Cannon is also a designated canoe route, so you can continue your trip all the way to the Mississippi River if you wish.

UPPER MISSISSIPPI RIVER NATIONAL WILDLIFE & FISH REFUGE

284 miles, from Wabasha, Minnesota, to Rock Island, Illinois. Minnesota counties: Wabasha, Winona and Houston. Refuge headquarters is in Winona, Minnesota; the visitor contact station is in McGregor, Iowa.

It seems fitting that the grand valley of the Father of Waters is home to a National Wildlife Refuge that has the longest boundaries of any in the lower 48 states. The scale of the Upper Mississippi River National Wildlife and Fish Refuge (about 200,000 acres through four states) is exceeded only by the vast river itself.

The refuge contains a variety of life zones and climatic conditions. Habitats include wooded bottomlands, extensive marshes, sloughs, ponds, wet meadows and sand prairie. For most of the refuge corridor, towering cliffs and steep, forested slopes line the river valley. Many species of plants and animals normally associated with more southern or northern geography extend their ranges along the Mississippi River Valley. Some 270 species of birds, 57 species of mammals, 45 species of amphibians and reptiles, and 113 species of fish are found here.

Eleven dams and locks within the refuge form a series of pools that vary from 10 to 30 miles long. The dams have raised water levels, creating a maze of channels, sloughs, marshlands and open lakes over the bottomlands. Excellent stands of aquatic plants have developed, establishing habitat for waterfowl and other wildlife.

The abundance and diversity of wildlife in the refuge belie the changes that have occurred since the French missionaries and traders explored the valley. Cities and towns now occupy the sites of historic Indian villages and trading posts. Modern highways have replaced ancient trails along the riverbanks. Legions of small watercraft, yachts and massive barges travel the waterways. The lock and dam system maintains a nine-foot navigation channel. Yet, even considering all of man's changes, the Upper Mississippi Valley retains some of the wilderness beauty that the Indians and explorers knew. You can see this for yourself by scrambling to the top of a river bluff.

The refuge, established in 1924, is primarily managed for wildlife, yet attracts about 3 million recreationists each year. The most popular activities include wildlife observation, environmental education, boating, fishing, hunting, bird study and sightseeing. Tracing the history of the river valley is also fun. Signs and markers point out the sites of old Indian battlegrounds, villages, forts, trading posts and the routes of early explorers. Evidence of ancient mound-building tribes is found along the bluffs and bottomlands.

Fishing is popular year-round on the Upper Mississippi. Walleye, northern, sauger, bass, perch, crappies, sunfish and catfish are caught below the dams, in sloughs and in channels between islands. A state fishing license is required and state laws apply. Excursion trips and boat rentals are available at marinas, landings or municipal boatyards along the river. The navigation locks will pass your boat through the dams to the next pool. Some visitors choose to experience the river by houseboat (they can be rented from several places along the river). The pace is easy and you can fish and camp where you wish among the channels and islands.

Much of the refuge is open to hunting during state seasons, though 14 areas (more than 41,000 acres) are closed for the protection of migratory waterfowl. After duck season, these areas are open to trapping and to upland and big game hunting according to state and federal seasons. All state and refuge licensing and regulations apply.

UPPER SIOUX AGENCY STATE PARK

Yellow Medicine County. 8 miles southeast of Granite Falls on Highway 67. Highway map index: E-17.

Tempers were as hot as an August afternoon when the Dakota Indians destroyed the Upper Sioux Agency, in the summer of 1862. On another hot August afternoon, I wandered past the foundations of the vanished agency buildings and circled the only structure in the present-day park to survive the U.S.-Dakota Conflict. The restored brick employee duplex is now a historic site administered by the Minnesota Historical Society.

It's hard to visualize the tragic violence of that long-ago summer while strolling on the park lawn, reading historical markers. But by piecing together facts from the markers, some causes of the uprising emerge. In 1851, as pressure to open up the Dakota homeland to white settlement grew, the government engineered the Treaty of Traverse des Sioux. This treaty removed the Dakota from Iowa and Minnesota to a 20-mile-wide reservation along the upper Minnesota River.

One marker stands by the site of the Manual Labor School, where ill-trained teachers tried to transform the Dakota from hunters and trappers into farmers and carpenters. The Sisseton and Wahpeton bands who were relocated to this shoestring reservation were forced to rely on government handouts to survive. The Indians walked to the agency warehouse to collect their food on some of the same park paths we hike today. But as the marker by the warehouse foundation explains, annuity payments were often late, and food supplies were scarce. The famished Indians, already angered at the loss of their homeland and frustrated with government policy, exploded into a futile but bloody war that lasted into September of 1862. (When the agency was attacked, non-warring Dakota led many of the whites to safety.)

The countryside surrounding Upper Sioux Agency State Park has become more wooded since the days of the conflict. Murals in the interpretive center show what the land used to look like—grassy bluffs with few trees, buffalo on the prairie, a man plowing behind four oxen. The interpretive center is a useful first stop for your visit. In one room, instructive displays describe park ecosystems; in another, changing exhibits arouse the sensual curiosity of everyone. You'll find many touch-and-see objects here. My favorite was the series of smell boxes. Their olfactory challenge is successfully met by only a few.

Behind the interpretive center, a short trail drops off the prairie plateau into a hillside forest, passes under a great octopus-armed oak, and climbs back to the top. Other trails venture up and down through scenic bluffs that rise over both the Minnesota and Yellow Medicine rivers. The interpretive center, historic sites, campground and other main park facilities are spread along an open ridge between the two rivers. From the parking lots on the ridge, paths lead down the bluffs to the river-bottoms. The rugged scenery of wooded slopes, open prairie knolls and undeveloped riverbanks makes Upper Sioux Agency a popular park for trail users. Hikers and horseback riders currently explore the park on about 20 miles of marked trails.

Wildlife can be observed from the trails and from vantage points atop the bluffs. The Dakota scrambled up these same prairie knolls to spot bison herds during spring and summer. One of the best overlooks is at the end of the main park road. This is a peaceful place with a commanding view of the Minnesota River Valley.

Most fishing is done from the banks of the Minnesota River, where you might land walleyes, northern, catfish or bullheads. The Minnesota is also a designated canoe route and is an easy stream for novices. The swifter Yellow Medicine River holds scrappy smallmouth bass. It is only canoeable after heavy rains with large runoff.

Upper Sioux Agency is primarily a day-use park, popular for picnics, hiking, fishing and canoeing. Space and activities abound. A ball field is just across the road from the picnic ground, and the trails and historic sites are intriguing enough to hold even a child's attention. The campground on the ridge is not heavily used, though the primitive riverside canoe campsites are favorite overnight stops for canoeists. Future plans include a semi-modern vehicle campground, some walk-in sites and larger picnic areas.

The Minnesota Historical Society administers other sites within relatively close driving range of Upper Sioux Agency. Several of these, including the Birch Coulee Battlefield, Lower Sioux Agency and Fort Ridgely, deal with U.S.-Dakota Conflict events.

Winter

Kids flock to Upper Sioux Agency State Park for its famous snow-tubing hill. During winter, the park's paths become multi-use trails for both snowmobilers and cross-country skiers. Snowshoers can roam at will. Winter campers should set up in the picnic area and can get water in the all-season interpretive center/warming house.

WHITEWATER STATE PARK

Winona County. About 8 miles north of St. Charles on Highway 74. Highway map index: M-20.

Whitewater is southern Minnesota's busiest state park and has a pair of semi-modern campgrounds with about 120 sites to handle the crowds. There are six walk-in sites off one of the loops in the main campground. Organizations can reserve a group camp that's primitive or one that has cabins and a dining hall. Contact the manager for details.

People are attracted to Whitewater because of the natural beauty of its deep ravines, limestone formations, and hilly hardwood forest (remnant stands of white pine are relics of the cooler glacial era).

Although camping is popular (the campground fills on many weekends and holidays), day use in the park can also be heavy. The two spacious picnic areas may be crowded, but you can usually find a vacant table. There is an open picnic shelter (with electricity) in one area and an adjacent game field.

The park offers water sports for the whole family. The swimming pond, with a guarded beach, is usually the first destination for the kids. Parents like to relax in the sun on the big beach. The absence of much warm, standing water means that mosquitoes don't have a chance to breed. Trout fishing is good in stretches of the park's two streams. Brown trout are the dominant game fish here, but brookies and rainbows are caught in some sections. Channel catfish, northern and walleye inhabit the lower Whitewater River, below the park.

Before hiking the park's 10-mile trail system, stop at the Chimney Rock Geological Center and the new Whitewater Valley Visitor Center to gain some background on the area's human and natural history. The visitor center (also a trail center, interpretive center and park contact station) features engaging displays and hands-on activities. Naturalist programs, including nature games, guided hikes and slide shows, are held in the interpretive center and outdoor amphitheater.

The trails vary from easy river-valley walks to scenic ridge-top hikes that involve steep climbs. The Meadow is a self-guiding nature trail through an area of big bluestem grass that hikers of all abilities enjoy. Whitewater State Park features several trails that wind upward through dense woods and culminate in broad vistas. Chimney Rock, Ice Cave Point and Coyote Point are nearest the park's core. Sound carries uphill so well that from the Chimney Rock Trail you'll easily hear swimmers. As you hike toward Inspiration Point, however, the background roar of Trout Run Creek replaces the sound of human voices. Other trails overlook the Whitewater River Valley. Parents should realize that there are many steep cliffs in the park and should monitor their children closely at all overlooks.

Winter

Though Whitewater State Park has less than four miles of beginner cross-country ski trails, the entire 2,800-acre park is open for winter exploration. Visitors like to see the ice cave (an ice flow emerging from a small rock opening) and the large beaver pond. Open, spring-fed water in the park attracts deer, turkeys and bald eagles.

On many winter weekends, the park offers naturalist programs that focus on winter survival, animal-tracks identification and wildlife observation. Interpretive programs, ski rental and warming house are all in the Whitewater Valley Visitor Center. Contact the manager or naturalist for schedule information or to arrange special group programs.

Besides participating in the winter naturalist programs, visitors enjoy hiking and snowshoeing. Snowmobiling is not allowed in the park, but there are many nearby Grant-in-Aid trails.

ZUMBRO RIVER CANOE & BOATING ROUTE

Olmsted, Goodhue and Wabasha counties.
North Fork: 70 miles, from Zumbrota to the Mississippi River;
Middle Fork: 72 miles, from Oronoco to the Mississippi River;
South Fork: 80 miles, from Rochester to the Mississippi River.

The frisky Zumbro River has a history of catching canoeists off guard. Frustrated French voyageurs called it "Riviere des Embarras" (river of difficulties). The river's energetic pace and numerous snags can still surprise and hinder the unwary.

Snags, caused by bank erosion, are common on each of the Zumbro's three forks. The only rapids is a mild stretch near Hammond that is rocky during low water. Dams are few: one at Mazeppa on the North Fork, one at Oronoco on the Middle Fork, a power dam at mile 60 that forms Zumbro Lake, and a handful in Rochester on the South Fork.

The Zumbro forks are normally shallow and muddy, so modern explorers usually start out below the power dam. If you begin on the Middle or South forks, you'll canoe on linear Zumbro Lake and portage the dam before continuing downstream.

Below Zumbro Lake, the river's level fluctuates with the flow at the power dam. Water is generally released on weekends so the river is canoeable downstream. Be aware that the Zumbro can be dangerous after heavy rainstorms. Within about four hours of a storm, the water level may rise rapidly and cause flash floods.

The South Fork is the largest and most commonly paddled branch of the Zumbro. Many canoeists start their trip north of Rochester at the power dam or at Zumbro Falls. The river winds through a deep, narrow valley flanked by rugged limestone and sandstone bluffs most of the way to Theilman. Below Theilman, the valley broadens into wide, flat farmland. The riverbanks are lined with hardwoods and marshes, where you'll see anglers casting for smallmouth bass, catfish and suckers.

Most of the Zumbro's route wanders through the Richard J. Dorer Memorial Hardwood State Forest. The state Department of Natural Resources canoe route map indicates access points, rest areas, outfitters, public campsites, and private campgrounds.

ADDRESSES

ALL REGIONS

Minnesota Department of Natural Resources (DNR) Information Center, 500 Lafayette Road, St. Paul, MN 55155-4040. Twin Cities, 651-296-6157; toll free in Minnesota, 1-888-MINNDNR; TDD for hearing impaired, 651-296-5484 or 1-800-657-3929. **www.dnr.state.mn.us**

Minnesota Travel Information Center, 500 Metro Square, 121 7th Place East, St. Paul, MN 55101. Twin Cities, 651-296-5029; toll free in continental U.S. and Canada, 1-800-657-3700.

STATE TRAILS and STATE CANOE & BOATING ROUTES

No individual addresses. Contact Minnesota Department of Natural Resources, Trails and Waterways Unit, Information Center, 500 Lafayette Road, St. Paul, MN 55155-4040. 651-296-6157; toll free in Minnesota, 1-800-766-6000.

STATE FORESTS

For information and maps about camping, trails, etc. in any of the state forests, contact: Minnesota Department of Natural Resources, Division of Forestry, Information Center, 500 Lafayette Road, St. Paul, MN 55155-4040. 651-296-6157; toll free in Minnesota, 1-800-766-6000.

STATE PARKS

Addresses are listed individually by region in the section below. For general information or specific park maps, contact the DNR Information Center (listed above).

ALL OTHER STATE AND NATIONAL RECREATION UNITS

ARROWHEAD (Northeastern)

Banning State Park, Sandstone, 55072; 320-245-2668
Bear Head Lake State Park, Ely, 55731; 218-365-7229
Boundary Waters Canoe Area: see listing below for Superior National Forest

Cascade River State Park, Lutsen, 55612-9535; 218-387-3053

Franz Jevne State Park, Birchdale, 56629; call the DNR
    Information Center at 1-888-646-6367

George H. Crosby-Manitou State Park, Silver Bay, 55614;
    call Tettegouche State Park at 218-226-6365

Gooseberry Falls State Park, Two Harbors, 55616; 218-834-3855

Grand Portage National Monument, Grand Marais, 55604;
    218-387-2788

Grand Portage State Park, Grand Portage, 55605-3000;
    218-475-2360

Hill Annex Mine State Park, Calumet, 55716; 218-247-7215

Interstate State Park, Taylors Falls, 55084; 651-465-5711

Jay Cooke State Park, Carlton, 55718; 218-384-4610

Judge C.R. Magney State Park, Grand Marais, 55604-2150;
    218-387-3039

McCarthy Beach State Park, Side Lake, 55781; 218-254-2411

Moose Lake State Park, Moose Lake, 55767; 218-485-5420

Rice Lake National Wildlife Refuge, McGregor, 55760;
    218-768-2402

St. Croix National Scenic Riverway, St. Croix Falls, WI, 54024;
    715-483-3284

St. Croix State Park, Hinckley, 55037; 320-384-6591

Savanna Portage State Park, McGregor, 55760; 218-426-3271

Scenic State Park, Bigfork, 56628; 218-743-3362

Soudan Underground Mine State Park, Soudan, 55782;
    218-753-2245

Split Rock Lighthouse State Park, Two Harbors, 55616;
    218-226-6377

Superior Hiking Trail, The Superior Hiking Trail Association,
    Two Harbors, 55616; 218-834-2700

Superior National Forest and the Boundary Waters Canoe Area,
    Forest Supervisor, P.O. Box 338, Duluth, 55801;
    218-720-5324; for BWCA reservations only, call
    218-720-5440

Temperance River State Park, Schroeder, 55613; 218-663-7476

Tettegouche State Park, Silver Bay, 55614; 218-226-6365

Voyageurs National Park, International Falls, 56649-8904;
    218-283-9821

Wild River State Park, Center City, 55012; 651-583-2125

HEARTLAND/VIKINGLAND (Northcentral/West)

Agassiz National Wildlife Refuge, Middle River, 56737;
     218-449-4115
Buffalo River State Park, Glyndon, 56547; 218-498-2124
Charles A. Lindbergh State Park, Little Falls, 56345; 320-632-9050
Chippewa National Forest, Cass Lake, 56633; 218-335-2283
Crow Wing State Park, Brainerd, 56401; 218-829-8022
Father Hennepin State Park, Isle, 56342; 320-676-8763
Glacial Lakes State Park, Starbuck, 56381; 320-239-2860
Glendalough State Park, Battle Lake, 56515; 218-864-0110
Hayes Lake State Park, Roseau, 56751; 218-425-7504
Itasca State Park, Lake Itasca, 56460-9701;
     218-266-2114 (summer), 218-266-2100 (winter)
Lake Bemidji State Park, Bemidji, 56601; 218-755-3843
Lake Bronson State Park, Lake Bronson, 56734; 218-754-2200
Lake Carlos State Park, Carlos, 56319; 320-852-7200
Maplewood State Park, Pelican Rapids, 56572; 218-863-8383
Mille Lacs Kathio State Park, Onamia, 56359-9534; 320-532-3523
Old Mill State Park, Argyle, 56713; 218-437-8174
Schoolcraft State Park, Deer River, 56636; 218-247-7215
Sherburne National Wildlife Refuge, Zimmerman, 55398;
     612-389-3323
Tamarac National Wildlife Refuge, Rochert, 56578; 218-847-2641
Zippel Bay State Park, Williams, 56686; 218-783-6252

METROLAND

Afton State Park, Hastings, 55033; 651-436-5391
Fort Snelling State Park, St. Paul, 55111; 651-725-2389
Lake Maria State Park, Monticello, 55362; 612-878-2325
Minnesota Valley National Wildlife Refuge, Recreation Area &
     State Trail, Jordan, 55352; 612-492-6400
Mississippi National River and Recreation Area; 175 E. Fifth St.,
     Suite 418, St. Paul, 55101; 651-290-4160
William O'Brien State Park, Marine-on-St. Croix, 55047;
     651-433-0500